PIONEER DIES

March 23, 1943 source unknown

Lorenzo D. Walters, early day resident of Arizona and author of "Tombstone's Yesterdays," died yesterday at his home here following a three-weeks' illness.

L. D. WALTERS, PIONEER, DEAD

Veteran Peace Officer, Writer, Succumbs At His Home Here

March 23, 1943

Loren... author, died yesterday at his home, 325 North Second avenue, following an illness of three weeks. He was 74 years old.

Deeply interested in the southwest, Mr. Walters published a book, "Tombstone's Yesterdays," in 1928, and at the time of his death had several books in manuscript form. He possessed an extensive library of autographed first editions of western literature.

Special Officer

Since his retirement, nine years ago, from the Tucson police force, Mr. Walters had been a special officer assigned to night duty at the senior high school and at Roskruge school. He made his last rounds Friday, February 26.

Born November 8, 1869, at Millage Ville, Ia., he spent his boyhood in Minnesota and Kansas. Enlisting in the Sixth Cavalry in 1891, he served four years with that army regiment. After his discharge he settled in New Mexico, where he became a store manager for the Bar Cross Cattle Company.

Mr. Walters was married in 1905 to Rosella Morris at San Marcial, N. M.

Policeman 10 Years

He embarked on a career as a peace officer in 1908 when he was employed by the Santa Fe railroad as a special agent. Joining the Tucson force in 1924, under Dallas Ford, then police chief, he served as a patrolman until 1934, when he retired.

In the past few years Mr. Walters spent his time working on his hobby of wood craftsmanship and serving as chaplain of the Regular Veterans' Association. He attended the First Christian church.

Surviving is the widow, Mrs. Rosella M. Walters, of Tucson. Funeral arrangements, in charge of the Arizona Mortuary, have not been decided yet.

FORTY YEARS LATE.

'Tombstone's Yesterday' Reprinted By Publisher Of Rare Southwestern Americana.

If all the books about Tombstone were laid end to end, it might be a good thing—and there certainly would be a lot of them. Some are good, some are indifferent and some are downright bad. But, good, bad or indifferent, Tombstone today thrives on its notoriety of yesterday; it is, in its own time, a living legend—a town, a community, linked by millions of words to a vivid and even romantic past— a chapter, as it were, in the legend of yesterday's America.

The story of the town itself has been told and retold so many times, in such a variety of ways and by so many people that, in a sense, it has become a historic cliche. But this is not so of the story of the men who made Tombstone what it was in 1880. It took an ex-railroad detective

WHO WAS A BOY

when Tombstone was young to run down and record all the loose odds and ends about the bad men of Tombstone, and to relate their story with some effort at correct chronology (at least). This man was Lorenzo Walters, a citizen of Arizona most of his life, and of Tucson in his latter years. Walters was born in Milledgeville, Iowa, Nov. 8, 1869, and died in Tucson March 22, 1943. He wrote this book in the years prior to 1928, and it was published in Tucson in December, 1928, in an edition probably limited to 1,000 copies. Strangely enough, The Tombstone Epitaph carried advertising for the book, but never reviewed it or even remarked on its existence. Reviews and notices from the Tucson papers of the time are reprinted in this edition on the end-sheets (as well as this review itself), which seems to us to be something of an interesting innovation in book publishing.

Be that as it may, the reader interested in Western Americana generally, in Arizoniana especially, and/or in Tombstoniana specifically will find this volume interesting,.

EVEN FASCINATING.

It is, indeed, a "social register" of both the bad men and good men of Cochise county and adjoining country in the last days of the legendary frontier. Judging by the enormous (new) index, the author must have mentioned every last name he ever encountered in his research. The publishers of this edition have told us it took better than 100 hours to put together this alphabetized "social register"; from our own experience, we can attest this must have been a wearisome task, to say the least.

But more or less as the recorder of deeds large and small today in Tombstone, we are happy to take note that this rare book has now found its way back into print. For those who like the

SENSE OF HUMOR

that brought guffaws and bellylaughs in 1928, this volume is a veritable treasure. From to-day's viewpoint, the humor is heavy, pedestrian, even labored, but in itself this has a certain charm which makes an old book often better reading than a new one. We liked it, anyway, and we think you will like it, too.

As for the authenticity of the book's information—well, as the publishers say, take it with some salt. The author was not much of a writer, but he was a good story teller, and was a man apparently infinitely patient in his research (either that, or infinitely inventive). We believe the stories are generally correct, at least in their basic details. We consider the book was well worth reprinting

AFTER FORTY YEARS,

for the incredible index if nothing else. We think the publishers, in their brief introduction, bring well into focus the message (probably unintended by the author) that it may, indeed, take violence to bring law and order out of violence—a thought to-day's law enforcers around the country could ponder well and long.

The Rio Grande Press of Glorieta, N. M. herewith has our vote of thanks for reprinting this book, and this rather lengthy review (or notice, or whatever) in to-day's Epitaph sort of makes up for our predecessors' oversight forty years ago. Better late than never, we say.

—Wayne Winters.

TOMBSTONE'S YESTERDAY

BY

LORENZO D. WALTERS

WITH ILLUSTRATIONS

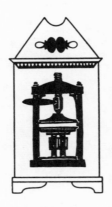

The Rio Grande Press, Inc.

GLORIETA, NEW MEXICO · 87535

© Copyright 1968
The Rio Grande Press, Inc.,
Glorieta, N.M. 87535

Copy from which
this edition was reproduced
was supplied by
INTERNATIONAL BOOKFINDERS
Box 3003
Beverly Hills, Calif.

A RIO GRANDE CLASSIC
First published in 1928

LIBRARY OF CONGRESS CARD CATALOG
68-25392

1968

GLORIETA, NEW MEXICO 87535

PUBLISHER'S INTRODUCTION

One of the more rewarding aspects of publishing our kind of books is the great variety of reading we have to do. For every book we select to reprint, we read and reject at least ten. We have two main (and equally important) criteria in the selection of a title: (1) is it good reading? and, (2), is it authentic source material?

In the case of *Tombstone's Yesterday*, we were practically hypnotized as the marvelous tales roared on and on through the pages, spinning a saga of violent adventure the like of which is hard to match in American history. . . up until now.

As to its authenticity as source material—well, we read it with a box of salt handy. Generally speaking, it is authentic enough for citation if it be remembered that the man who put the book together was not himself an eyewitness to the events he describes so graphically. I suppose we ought to mention, too, that when this book was first published in 1928, it appears that neither the author nor the printer did any proofreading. The printed text is replete with errors, presumably typographical, and there may be errors of fact as well. But nevertheless, and all things considered, *Tombstone's Yesterday* is quite the most lively book we have reprinted. We feel constrained, however, to add some comments we believe pertinent on the subject of law and order.

We hear much these days of violence in the streets and lawlessness, of bad men killing good men, and of bad men killing bad men, too. Personal, physical violence is nothing new to Americans. This country was born in domestic violence, it has lived nearly two centuries with domestic violence, and it may well die of domestic violence. The big difference between the past and· today is that until now, lawlessness in an American community was never tolerated as a legitimate part of our social order. It was always, as it was in Tombstone, eventually curbed by angry citizens.

We visited Tombstone June 12, 1968, in the aftermath of the murder of the late Senator Robert F. Kennedy, and we chanced upon an editorial relating to the personal ownership and use of firearms, and the reasons therefor. While the editorial touches on the theme of this book, it is pertinent to the great national issues of 1968; it could well have been written about the issues that beset Tombstone in the years immediately subsequent to 1880. With the permission of William R. Matthews, Editor and Publisher of the Arizona Daily Star (Tucson), we have reproduced this editorial facsimile in the front matter of this edition.

When Tombstone was at its wildest, 1875-1890, Washington, D. C., was a capital city practically without crime. It is supremely ironic that nearly one hundred years later, after virtually a century of "progress", Tombstone has come to be almost a model of civic virtue while the nation's capital is the most vicious, dangerous, crime-beset city in the United States. In Tombstone, in 1968, crime and punishment are very nearly synonymous, so there is very little of either. In Washington, the very seat of our national government, a malodorous Congress sits impotent and intimidated in a veritable jungle of lawlessness, willingly tolerating and even encouraging a crime wave of unbelievable proportions. Political hacks at all levels of government coddle criminals and excuse lawlessness past all human understanding in a blind, idiotic pursuit of 'bloc' or 'ethnic' votes; this, in the parlance of 1968, is known as "The Great Society".

A century ago, men like the Earp brothers put their lives on the line to bring law, order and decency out of the anarchy inherent in a frontier community like Tombstone. Today, the law enforcement agencies and courts of justice of the United States make a mockery of their constitutional missions; they not only condone, but are the maudlin apologists for crime unprecedented in the history of this nation—gutless officers of the government tolerate and make excuses for violence in the streets, arson, looting, murder, and even sedition and treason. Never in its wildest days was Tombstone as dangerous a place for the law-abiding citizen as the nation's capital today—in this strange year of our Lord, 1968. This book should be mandatory reading for national policy-makers, in our opinion, for here alone is documented proof (if any be needed) that vigorous enforcement of the law brings a quick end to lawlessness anywhere. In Tombstone, about a century ago, the arbitrary end of real and alleged trouble makers soon brought tranquility to a community of law-abiding citizens; in Washington, today, the only thing seemingly important to the professional politicians is a vote—nothing is more important, apparently, not even the fabric and the destiny of the United States of America. How a century of "progress" could have brought men like these into public life is simply beyond understanding.

We find it difficult to hold our indignation in check as each day we read the newspapers to find things worse.

Tombstone's Yesterday (the 38th title in our continuing line of basic source books of American history) was brought to our attention by Richard (Dick) Mohr, International Bookfinders, Beverly Hills, Calif., and he loaned us the precious first edition from which we reprinted this edition. In our research for supporting data on the author, we had the prompt and amiable assistance of Mrs. Margaret Sparks of the Arizona Pioneers' Historical Society in Tucson, and of Mrs. Lynne M. Phillips of the Reference Section of the Tucson Public Library. When we visited Tombstone for contemporary photographs and research, we met Mr. and Mrs. Burt Devere, owners of the world's largest rosebush (it really is) and sellers of Americana and rare books. We talked Mrs. Devere (a native of Tombstone) into writing a few words from her huge store of memories and knowledge.

We also dropped in on Mr. Wayne Winter, present editor of *The Tombstone Epitaph* and found him so cooperative we were able to include in this edition a review of *Tombstone's Yesterday*—the same review will be published in the Epitaph the week we release our edition to the public. Mr. Winter borrowed Mrs. Devere's copy of the book to prepare the review, and of course, we supplied him with a copy of our introduction. All this, we consider, is cooperation—plus, and we thank Mr. Winter and *The Tombstone Epitaph* very much.

We have always found Western chambers of commerce to be wonderfully helpful, and in Tombstone, this was the case as a matter of course. We found the president of the local chamber to be W. J. (Jack) Way, manager of the Wagon Wheel Bar and Restaurant and himself a spare time publisher of good Arizoniana. No visit to Tombstone hereafter will be complete without a call on Jack Way at the hospitable and historic Wagon Wheel. Jack has in print two books of his own, *The Tombstone Story* and *Ghosts and Ghost Towns* (of Southeastern Arizona), so naturally we swindled a swap in line with old western traditions.

Probably we ought to mention a word about the big index for this title, or several words, as a matter of fact. Making an index is pure and simple hard work, the kind of work that has a tendency to put the indexer to sleep. Mr. Walters must have named two thousand men by their last name only, hence we have a number of similar names apparently sometimes related and sometimes not. Where the author eventually gave an identifiable first name to a previously-mentioned last name, we have tied the two together; where no first name was ever mentioned, we merely noted the fact with an underline blank. We can say, as an understatement, that Mr. Walters had an abiding passion for names. It is likely that he himself never knew the first names of many for whom he recorded a surname, but it is just as likely that his intense familiarity with his research material made him suppose that his readers would be likewise as well informed. It may be, too, that he saw no great need for given names, an idea supported by the index which shows many names mentioned (or dropped) just one time. Anyway, an index of surnames should be both interesting and helpful to readers and researchers of Arizona history.

Despite our somewhat bitter comments herein, we are pleased to present this exceptionally timely title as another beautiful Rio Grande Classic.

Robert B. McCoy
President

John T. Strachan
Vice President

Glorieta, New Mexico
July, 1968

AN OLDTIMER'S PREFACE

When Lorenzo D. Walters wrote *Tombstone's Yesterday* in 1928, he had the advantage of being able to talk to many of the people who had lived through and been a part of Tombstone's early history. Today this generation is gone. In years gone by, not enough attention was paid to the then-old-timers, and now they are gone and their stories are gone with them. Here we are deeply indebted to one man (although there are others) who, though not a writer by profession, saw the need to record the old tales—and did so.

First editions of *Tombstone's Yesterday* have been very rare and much sought after by collectors for many years, and we of Tombstone are grateful to the Rio Grande Press for again making it available to the many thousands who are now interested in Western Americana. We are very pleased to see pictures included of Tombstone as it is today, for to us—descendants of the original settlers of Arizona—Tombstone is our proud heritage.

Mrs. Burton (Jeanne Macia) Devere

Tombstone, July 1968
The Rosetree Inn

The Arizona Daily Star

THE ARDEN PUBLISHING CO.   ★   ESTABLISHED 1877

PUBLISHED EVERY MORNING OF THE YEAR
William R. Mathews, Editor and Publisher
P.O. Box 5058
TUCSON, ARIZONA 85703

Subscription Rates: City Carrier Delivery 55ᶜ per week; $28.60 Yearly: Outside Carrier Delivery 55ᶜ per week; $28.60 Yearly

Mail Rates: Payable in advance: State of Arizona: One month $3.25; One Year $39.00 Outside Arizona including Canada & Mexico: $3.75 per month and $45.00 per year.
Phone 622-5855

CHARTER MEMBER OF THE ASSOCIATED PRESS. The Associated Press is entitled exclusively to the use for republication of all the local news printed in the newspapers, as well as all AP news dispatches. All rights of republication of special dispatches are also reserved.

MEMBER AUDIT BUREAU OF CIRCULATION

EDITORIAL PAGE   WEDNESDAY, JUNE 12, 1968

The Role Of Firearms

Some 80 to 90 years ago it was common practice in Tucson and most other places in the new West for men to carry revolvers or pistols. They did it to protect themselves from assaults by others. They did it also, because of weak administration of justice.

At times they would form themselves into groups of vigilantes, and administer justice, after it had broken down, in a definitely certain way. The stories of Tombstone describe this in a spectacular way.

There are very, very few individuals left who saw those days of gun play gradually fade away, as they did as soon as the administration of justice became certain and responsible. When the people of the old Tucson community saw that take place, they stopped carrying their guns. Their lives were no longer in danger.

To this day the laws relating to guns of all kinds in Arizona are lenient. One forbids carrying any concealed weapon. Because hunting abounds in Arizona, many men do keep rifles and shotguns. Many fathers take their sons hunting and teach them how to use guns. Many other men enjoy the sport of trap shooting, and belong to the trap shooting club east of the city limits. Despite the fact that firearms of all kinds abound in Arizona, the administration of justice in Arizona measures up to relatively high standards.

Obviously this discussion has to do

with the pending gun-control legislation in Congress. Because three notable public leaders have been assassinated since 1963 by rifle or pistol fire, a widespread public movement has developed demanding new legislation by Congress to regulate the sale and ownership of all firearms.

Emotions are running high. The contention is that such regulation would reduce the hazards and chances of future assassinations and of crime in general.

The Star cannot support this belief, because it believes history and experience prove to the contrary. When a man plans an assassination of a high public official, he knows that the chances are heavy that he will lose his life. Most assassins have been men holding deep grudges of one kind or another that urged them on. No kind of law will reduce the chances of future assassinations. Such dedicated personalities will get the firearms they need in one way or another, despite all laws to the contrary.

If there is legislation that should be adopted, it should be of a kind that will help the peace and judicial officers track down criminals. New York City has a tight law forbidding the carrying of guns of any kind. Evidently the police think it is helpful. There are possibly other communities that do the same thing. Laws that forbid the carrying of concealed weapons are quite common throughout the country. So far this matter of control of firearms has been left to the states, and in many cases to the cities.

The people should be told the truth, although it may be unpleasant to many of them. Firearms are a result, not a cause. The cause today is the paralysis, at least the befuddling, of the administration of justice. Criminals and law-breakers can slow down the administration of justice and certainly discourage its administration. They know that their chances of escaping punishment have greatly increased.

Washington D. C., our capital city, furnishes the best proof of this. Sen. Paul J. Fannin in his May letter to constituents writes:

"It is a sad commentary on our present situation when constituents must be advised to plan summer trips to the capital with an eye to possible riots and violence, but this is the case.

"Those in charge of the national capital apparently lack the will to ensure the safety of all visitors this summer. There are risks presently involved in a visit to the nation's capital and you should keep yourself aware of the changing situation."

No later than Monday of this week has this warning been confirmed in its truth. While returning to his home late Sunday night after the funeral service of his employer, the chauffeur for the late Robert F. Kennedy was stopped on the streets of Washington where he was assaulted and robbed by a group of three men. This kind of an incident has become common in Washington. The streets of Washington are not safe at night.

Who is responsible for this shocking deterioration of the administration of criminal justice in this city?

Congress is responsible. It refuses to furnish sufficient money to employ and train sufficient policemen.

The mayor of Washington, who happens to be a Negro, finds his hands tied as effectively as his predecessor, a white man, did.

In the final analysis, the President is responsible, for not seeing to it that Washington, D. C., is a model city in the administration of criminal justice.

The administration of criminal justice in Washington, D. C., has become so uncertain and ineffective, that criminals with firearms can carry out their depredations in the streets with comparative ease.

To the contrary, wherever the administration of justice is effective, and certain, the easy ownership of firearms, becomes an insignificant fact.

TOMBSTONE'S YESTERDAY

True Chronicles of Early Arizona

TOMBSTONE'S YESTERDAY

BY

LORENZO D. WALTERS

WITH ILLUSTRATIONS

ACME PRINTING CO.
TUCSON, ARIZONA
1928

LORENZO D. WALTERS

TOMBSTONE'S YESTERDAY HAS BEEN APPEARING AS A
SERIAL IN THE "PROGRESSIVE ARIZONA AND THE GREAT
SOUTHWEST," A WARD SHELBY PUBLICATION, DURING
THE PAST TWO YEARS AND HAS NOW BEEN REVISED AND
ENLARGED AND OFFERED TO THE PUBLIC IN BOOK FORM

DEDICATED TO THE PIONEERS OF ARIZONA, PAST AND
PRESENT, WHO MADE REAL HISTORY WHICH IS HEREIN
HANDED DOWN TO THEIR POSTERITY.

CONTENTS

CONTENTS

ILLUSTRATIONS

ED SCHEFFELEIN

TOMBSTONE'S
YESTERDAY

PREFACE

It seems to be the custom of authors and near authors, to preface their literary efforts with some kind of an apology. I have no apology to offer, but, will offer the following alibi; that this literary effort was prompted by an eastern tourist's question of: "What became of all of the bad men who used to live in and around Tombstone in an early day?"

I have made an honest effort to obtain the real facts surrounding many of the old time gun-men, both good and bad, who practically dominated the destinies of Cochise and surrounding counties of Arizona and Grant County, New Mexico, back in the '80's. I have checked nearly every item against the newspaper reports of that period and am satisfied that the information contained herein is as nearly correct as is possible to obtain after so much elapsed time.

In my extensive search for information I have learned that it is almost impossible to get any two old timers to agree upon the vital details of any certain event; they will even dispute court records and deny the truthfulness of absolutely reliable newspapers of the dates in question. For the verification of nearly every event chronicled in this book, I am indebted to the "Tucson Citizen," "The Arizona Star," "The Tombstone Nugget," "The Tombstone Epitaph," and other early day publications.

In my writeup of Tom Horn, I have quoted nearly altogether from his life's history which he wrote himself while awaiting the execution of his sentence and same is supplemented by statements of his many friends who still reside in Arizona.

I wish to thank my many friends for their contributions of valuable information and pictures which have played such an important part in the construction of this book, the most prominent of whom are: Colonel William Breakenridge who, in the early '80's was known as Deputy Sheriff Billy Breakenridge, Mrs. George Kitt, M. F. Shaw, M. Q. Hardin, L. Burr Hall, C. A. Wien, C. Urbana, Filemino

Santa Cruz, Mrs. Lyman Wakefield, Mrs. Charlie Shibell, Carter Crane, Herbert Drachman, Carmen Mungia and Jack Benton, all of Tucson, Ariz., B. B. Ownby and Charles Keppler of Lordsburg, New Mexico, Judge J. S. Lea of Roswell, New Mexico, E. A. Wittig and Pete Crane of Bisbee, Jeff D. Milton of Fairbanks, Ariz., John A. Rockefellow of Cochise, Ariz, Doug Lemmon of Willcox, Ariz., William Sparks of Globe, Ariz., Ross Sloan of Skeleton Cañon, Ariz., E. B. Foster of Arizona at Large, Walter Noble Burns of Chicago, Ill., Wyatt S. Earp of Los Angeles, Calif., James Converse of San Diego, Calif., Charlie Siringo of Venice, Calif., E. H. Barton, Tucson, and E. P. Lamborn of Leavenworth, Kansas.

I wish to especially thank Herbert Cody Blake of Brooklyn, N. Y., for many true facts which kept me from straying from the straight and narrow paths of truthfulness in some of my writeups, where I had been given erroneous information concerning some of my subjects. The value of the excellent pictures which he furnished me, absolutely free, cannot be estimated in dollars and cents.

I am presenting this book with malice toward none and goodwill toward all.

LORENZO D. WALTERS.

Tucson, Arizona,
May 15, 1928.

THE SETTING

FROM the latter part of 1877 until about 1887 there were probably more real gun-men in Cochise County, Arizona, and its adjoining counties, than were ever gathered together in any one locality or territory of that size in the United States, either before or since.

The bad men were a law unto themselves, and settled their mutual differences without recourse to the courts of law. It was a case of the survival of the fittest. Coroner's juries oft times rendered a verdict of "suicide" in favor of the party of the second part on the grounds that he should have known better than to have attempted to get the drop on a man whom he knew was faster than he.

It has been repeatedly stated by old timers, that Tombstone was not a bad town; that there were not many killings perpetrated therein. It is not believed that such statements were made with any misleading intentions, but that in those days human life was held with such light regard that many killings actually took place that were forgotten quickly.

Nearly every killing chronicled within the covers of this book can be proven by articles appearing in the local papers covering those dates. The balance can be proven by the word of reputable witnesses. Not all of them occurred right in the town of Tombstone, but were perpetrated by men who claimed Tombstone as their post office and recreation grounds.

With the birth of Tombstone Mining Camp in October, 1877, there appeared from all parts of the United States, a conglomeration of men, good, bad and indifferent, with a predominance of the bad and indifferent. They were numerous and active, and scarce ever could a conviction be obtained against any of them, on account of the fact that juries were made up wholly or in part, of their own kind.

If an honest man should have found his way into the jury box, he was considered a maverick, afraid to express his own convictions, and, not wishing to antagonize the accused or his friends, would swing over to the majority and the prisoner would usually be acquitted on the grounds of "insufficient evidence."

Along about 1881 and '82, based on a conservative estimate, it is believed that there were not less than 200 known to be outlaws within the sparsely settled county of Cochise, and perhaps twice that number of men who declared themselves neutral, which did not benefit the law but did benefit the outlaw.

Stage holdups were of almost daily occurrence, and many short stage routes were abandoned on this account. Cattle rustling and horse stealing, interspersed with frequent murders, were the most popular forms of occupation indulged in by the lawless element.

Many of these outlaws posed as cattlemen, and owned or occupied small tracts of land at the various springs around in the foot-hills and back up in the mountains, and would steal horses and cattle from the bonafide ranchers with which to stock their own ranges, oft times crossing the international line into Mexico and bringing back large herds of cattle and horses which they would locate on their own ranges in Cochise County.

One of these men would usually homestead, or "squat", on a piece of land at some spring and gather around him any number of questionable characters who would pose as his cowboys. The gang would rustle cattle from any and all sources, and the cattle would be disposed of by the gang captain to some unscrupulous cattle buyer, and the funds divided.

These men never hesitated to kill any one who stood in their way when making loot collections. A congregation of so many questionable characters in any one location was explained by the fact that Cochise County was at that time infested by warlike Apaches under such leaders as Naña, Geronimo, Cochise and others, who were always ready to clean house at any time of the year.

Peace officers were unable to cope with the situation, as these outlaws usually traveled in gangs, and their code of game laws declared open season on peace officers the year around.

Occasionally one of their number would be arrested for disturbing the peace, and be fined, but seldom were any of them ever arrested and punished for their greater offenses, as it was almost impossible to get a jury to return a true verdict against the accused; and thus it was that they flourished and took toll of human lives to their hearts' content.

Matters, legal and otherwise, jogged along in a haphazard manner for several years. Officers were content to take only such action as was absolutely necessary, and scarce ever actually looked for trouble. John Slaughter, who appeared on the scene when Cochise County was about ten years of age, was the first sheriff who actually went out and hunted trouble. He invaded the outlaw range and served notice on known outlaws to get out of Cochise County or be killed. Many of them faded away. Many of them were killed while resisting arrest. Many were killed in fights among themselves as feuds existed between the various camps and different members of these camps often met and shot it out with disastrous results to both sides.

Cochise County was cut off Pima County in 1881, and Tombstone made the county seat. The activities of the outlaw element extended all over Cochise County and overflowed into Pima County on the west, with Tucson as county seat; into Grant County, New Mexico, on the east, with Silver City as county seat and with Lordsburg and Shakespeare as the two nearest towns in that direction.

Bisbee appeared on the scene shortly after Tombstone was organized. Douglas was not then on the map. Graham County, north of Cochise County, was cut off Pima and Apache Counties in 1881, with county seat at Solomonville. Gila County was also formed from portions of Pima and Pinal Counties in 1881, with Globe as county seat. It appeared that the outlaw element invading this territory, had its headquarters at Tombstone.

In Cochise County, the outlaw element was distributed around at various well known camps, the most important of which were: Rustler Mountain Camp, Double 'Dobe Camp, Rucker Cañon Camp, Davis Mountain Camp, Galeyville (afterwards rechristened Paradise), and many other

smaller camps located at advantageous points along the
border where Mexican smugglers could be intercepted with
the greatest facility as they came across the line into the
United States with pack trains of gold bullion and Mexican
silver dollars looted from reduction plants, banks, stores
and individuals below the line, with now and then a diamond
smuggler coming across the line to dispose of his wares on
this side, to those who asked no questions and paid cash on

NAÑA

delivery.   There can be no question but that the loot of the
outlaw gangs amounted to millions of dollars each year.

Indignant citizens became wearied of outlaw rule, and
Law and Order Leagues, or similar organizations, were
formed in Cochise County, also in Grant County, New
Mexico, and when an outlaw was caught red handed in the
commission of any crime, he was accorded a hearing before
the League and, if found guilty as charged, the result
would always be an attack of acute suspended animation.
Many petty offenders were ordered out of the country.

This drastic mode of proceedure had more to do with the cleaning up of the undesirables than the fear of a permanent home in the State Penitentiary at Yuma. No reflections are intended to be cast upon the officers of the law, who were honest in their efforts to enforce the law, but there were so few of the really honest kind that they were unable to accomplish their purpose.

Just as soon as the people began to get busy and co-operate with the officers, the result was very gratifying. Cochise County was considerably handicapped by the fact that some of her peace officers deserted the straight and narrow paths of rectitude in favor of the wild bunch, and the man higher up never knew just which of his subordinates could be trusted to carry out his instructions.

It has been reported that upon one occasion a bunch of 19 outlaws were rounded up at the head of Texas Cañon and all hanged in one juniper tree. This report is denied by men who claim that such an occurrence could not have taken place without their knowledge, but a man who occupies a high government position has stated that when he first came to Cochise County as a boy in 1884, that this was the first sight of interest which met his eye; that the remains of the bodies were still hanging suspended in this juniper tree at that time—and his word is as good as any other man's word.

It is also claimed that a large overhanging limb of a giant cottonwood tree, standing on the bank of the San Pedro River at Charleston, had served as a gallows for 18 or 20 outlaws during the turbulent days of the early '80's, but this is denied by some and affirmed by others. Be this as it may, the tree in question has been undermined by the San Pedro River until it has toppled over, and it now lies in stately majesty as a memory of the past.

Ed Scheffelein has been called the Father of Tombstone, as he made the original discovery of ore there in October, 1877. This strike caused much excitement and people thronged into the new mining camp, to find that the original discovery was only a pocket, and it dwindled to a memory only. In February, 1878, a new strike was made and this strike was substantial, whereat Tombstone flourished.

For many weary months Scheffelein had prospected the Burro Mountains in search of mineral wealth which he declared was there and that he was going to find it. In his daily travels he always drifted back into the foothills to

OLD COTTONWOOD AT CHARLESTON   *Photo by L. Burr Hall*

RUINS AT OLD CHARLESTON   *Photo by L. Burr Hall*

make his nightly camp among the immense boulders about two miles north of where the town of Tombstone now stands. Apache Indians were numerous and always on the warpath in those days, and as cattle ranches were few and far between, they were always kept well supplied with guns, ammunition and men, and the cowboys usually traveled in bunches, well armed and ready to play a hand in any game which the war-like Apache might suggest.

An army officer once asked Scheffelein what he was always looking for, and he replied,—"I'm looking for stones." The officer answered,—"The only stone you will ever find will be your tombstone." A few months later when the strike was made and a new town sprung into existence, Scheffelein remembered this conversation and named the new town "Tombstone." This name met the approval of the most fastidious of miners, cowboys and outlaws.

Tombstone, in the prime of her life, boasted of 8,500 souls, which included many who apparently laid no claim to the possession of souls. It is doubtful if a careful census today would show much more than one-tenth of that number. The slump in silver was responsible for the shrinkage of Tombstone's population.

Charleston, nine miles to the south, was the headquarters of the Clantons, with the McLowery Boys as their support-ers, while the Earps and Doc Holliday had their headquar-ters in Tombstone, and between these two factions there ex-isted a deadly feud, which resulted in the Earp-Clanton gun battle one day at the O. K. Corral, of which more will be mentioned in another place. The slump of silver and the earthquake of '87 put Charleston out of business, and one night the cowboys, miners and outlaws literally shot Charles-ton off the map, and everybody moved away, and the one time prosperous town of Charleston, with its population of perhaps four or five thousand inhabitants, is now a city of adobe ruins, over-grown and shadowed by mesquite trees, shaded by giant cottonwoods, grand in the intenseness of its own solitude.

Tombstone was made famous by Alfred Henry Lewis in his popular novel entitled "Wolfville", wherein Tombstone is presumed to have been his Wolfville and Charleston his Red Dog. Inasmuch as Jim Wolf is the old timer who furnished him with much of his information, he called his new town Wolfville in his honor.

Jim Wolf is a typical old-time cowhand and exceedingly eccentric in his verbal expressions, and has lived in the vicinity of Tombstone for perhaps fifty years. He is still living, and a short time ago, some one asked him what he had done with all of his land. Jim replied,—"Oh I sold off all of it, but I "conserved" ten acres for my own use." "No Jim, you mean "reserved", don't you?" "No, I don't mean reserved, I mean just what I said." Jim then went on to say,—"I am going to build a "congregated" iron house on that ten acres and live in it." "No Jim, you mean a "corrugated" iron house, don't you?" Jim very indignantly came

O. K. CORRAL GATE

Photo by L. Burr Hall

back with,—"Hell no, I mean just what I said; I am a man of my word; I have just as much right to make new words as Nora Webster."

Tourists passing through Tombstone may still have the pleasure of viewing such historic points of interest as The Bird Cage Opera House, which is still standing, in excellent state of preservation when considering its age and the fact that it has not been used for many years; The Can Can Restaurant, with the original sign painted on it as in days of yore; The Crystal Saloon and Gambling House which is now known as the Crystal Opera House; The Scheffelein Monument, which was erected at a later date; the O. K.

Corral, which was made famous in less than one minute, as the starting place of the Earp-Clanton feud fight.

Tombstone's Boot Hill holds the remains of scores of notorious outlaws who flourished in those days, their last resting places marked only by mounds of stones, erected above them at the time of their burial for the purpose of preventing coyotes and other wild animals from precipitating a premature resurrection. There is standing today, only one head board in Boot Hill, and it is very doubtful if there are any records in existence today to show where any particular body rests in this notorious abode of the dead.

In later days there were two new cemetaries established, and many bodies were transferred to these. Of course there were many good citizens laid to rest in Boot Hill, as, at that time, there was only the one cemetery, and the good and bad were laid to rest side by side. Old Boot Hill is located on a long ridge to the northward of town, and is fast becoming a dumping ground for city refuse.

Just a few words, in passing, regarding the Scheffelein Monument, which is located two miles to the north of town. Ed Scheffelein had always said that he wanted to be laid to rest among the huge boulders where he had camped during the strenuous Indian days while prospecting in that vicinity. Scheffelein made two or three fortunes from his Tombstone holdings, but spent it all on worthless mines. He also made a strike in Alaska. He died shortly after his return from Alaska and his body was buried in his old home town in Oregon.

Tombstone friends remembered that Scheffelein had most emphatically declared that he wished to be laid to rest among his old Tombstone boulder friends, with his pick, shovel and canteen to keep him company. About 1914, his Tombstone friends succeeded in getting his body transferred to its present resting place which was his old camping ground of years gone by.

An imposing monument of boulders was erected over his remains and on one side, set in the face of one of the large boulders, is a metal plate bearing the following inscription:

ED SCHEFFELEIN
Died May 12, 1897
Aged 49 Years 8 Mos.

A Dutiful Son
A Faithful Husband
A Kind Brother

SCHEFFELIN MONUMENT

Photo by L. Burr Hall

TOM HORN

TOM HORN was born in Memphis, Scotland County, Missouri, in December, 1860. Tom attended school in the little old country school house, just as all country boys do, alternately trying to interest himself in things educational and playing hookey.

One day when Tom was about fourteen years of age, he and his father became involved in an argument in which Tom came out second best. His father had used a tug out of a buggy harness with which to enforce his argument and Tom himself said,—"Dad had done his work well."

It was several days before Tom had fully recovered from his interview with his father, but when he had, he informed him that he was going to leave home. His father instructed him to ask his mother for a lunch so that he would not miss his dinner as he would expect him home by night.

Tom started west on foot. Day after day he walked until he reached Newton, Kansas, where he worked on the railroad until he had saved $21.00. He then threw in with a man named Blades, who was freighting to Santa Fe, and landed in Santa Fe late in 1874.

Tom said,—"By the time I reached Santa Fe, I was a different boy from what I was when I left home; I was getting wisdom—and graybacks." In January, 1875, he hired out to Mr. Murray, Superintendent of the Overland Mail Route from Santa Fe to Prescott, to drive stage. After driving stage for two months at $50 per month, he was promoted to the position of guard, which position he held until May of that year when he was sent with another man to take a bunch of mules down on the Verde River, in Arizona, into the heart of the Apache country.

After the mules were delivered, he went down to Camp Verde and hired out to George Hansen, to night-herd oxen which were being used in hauling wood into Camp Verde for the government. All of the time which Tom had been in Arizona he had been busy learning the Mexican language and by this time was quite proficient in its use.

After working for Hansen for three months at $75 per month he went to Ft. Whipple and hired out to the quartermaster at that place to herd a bunch of horses which was being held there for distribution to the different military posts and camps in that department.

After the horses had all been distributed, Tom was once more out of a job but Al Sieber, Chief of Scouts for the department, came to Whipple just at that time and taking a

TOM HORN

liking to the boy, hired him to go back with him to Ft. San Carlos to act as interpreter at a salary of $75 per month. Quite needless to say, Tom accepted this offer and in July 1876, after a ten days' journey through Apache infested country they arrived at the San Carlos Indian Agency, where he was installed as interpreter of the Mexican language.

Just as soon as Tom was fairly settled he began the study of the Apache language and it was not long until he could carry on a fairly good conversation in that language and, although he was never considered in the light of an Apache interpreter, was often called upon in an emergency and always managed to deliver the goods.

During the late summer of 1877, there being no more funds available from the government appropriation for the payment of civilian employes, they were all laid off. Al Sieber was included in the cut and he, Tom Horn, Archie MacIntosh, Sam Bowman, Frank Monic, Charlie Mitchell, Long Jim Cook, Frank Leslie, Frank Bennett, Big Ed Clark and eleven others, including Mexican scouts and packers, headed for Tucson.

Upon arrival there most of the gang obtained work with different freighting outfits until only five or six of the original crowd were left. When Ed Scheffelein came through from California and stopped in Tucson to outfit for the purpose of prospecting the country now known as the Tombstone Mining District, Al Sieber, Tom Horn and Buckskin Frank Leslie joined him and in company of about 60 more seasoned prospectors, they started for what they called "Cochise Country," as Cochise had been born in that country and ruled it until the time of his death and the dictatorship had descended to Geronimo, who was busily engaged in keeping out invaders.

Six days after their start, they landed on the ground where now stands the town of Tombstone and where the Indians had killed Scheffelein's partner, Lenox. Scheffelein, according to Tom Horn, stated that as the initial monument of his first claim was right at the grave of Lenox, he would call the camp "Tombstone."

Some time in October, 1877, they made a strike which looked to be a very rich one, and the Mining Camp of Tombstone began to grow with leaps and bounds and during its hectic career, it was probably one of the most important mining camps in the United States.

Sieber and Horn made some locations and were sitting back awaiting developments when they were notified that their services were once more needed by the government and for them to report for duty at Ft. Whipple. They sold their holdings to Charlie Leach for $2,800 and departed for Ft. Whipple. Upon arrival there, Sieber, as

Chief Scout, organized the scouting force, with Tom Horn
as interpreter at a salary of $100 per month.

In the Spring of 1878, Naña sent word to Major Chaffee,
that he and Geronimo, who had been living in the Sierra
Madres of Mexico, wanted to come back into the United
States and live on the reservation and that they would meet
and talk to Sieber whom they knew and trusted. Naña
instructed Sieber to come into Mexico and to the Terras
Mountains, where one of his men would meet the latter
and guide him into the hostile camp.

Sieber took Horn and a Mexican named Merijilda and
started out, and after many days of hard riding they were
met by an Indian who guided them into Geronimo's camp.
Horn acted as interpreter upon this occasion and stated that
Geronimo appeared to have more grievances than a railroad
switchman and talked steady for an hour or two, asking for
everything he could think of. After he had completed his
tale of woe, Sieber informed him that he had forgotten to
ask that the mountains where he was then located, be moved
up into the United States, and then notified Geronimo to be
ready to move back into the United States in four days.
Geronimo was ready and with him were Naña, and Old Loco
who must have then been upwards of 80 years of age. Just
before the start was made for the United States, Geronimo
came to Tom Horn and said—"You are a young man and
will always be at war with me and mine; but war is one
thing and talking business is another and I will be just as
pleased to meet you in battle as in council." The envoys
reached San Carlos in due time with this bunch of renegade
Indians.

In June, 1879, the appropriation for the payment of civilian employees once more became exhausted and Horn was
out of a job and of course, went to Tucson. There he hired
out to Tully and Ochoa, who had a contract with the government to deliver 2000 head of beef steers to the Indian agent
at the San Carlos Agency for distribution among the Apaches
and Tom was on the job at a salary of $175 per month
until the distribution was completed

In the spring of '80 Tom once more found himself back

MERIJILDA

on the job with Sieber, in the government service as interpreter.   Chief Ju (pronounced Who) jumped the reservation with his bunch of renegades and Major Tupper with
a command of about 25 men, accompanied by Sieber, Tom
Horn and a half breed scout named Mickey Free, started
in pursuit, and overtook them at Media (Middle) Mountain across the line in Mexico and in the fight which took
place, five Indians were killed.

Shortly after the fight at Media Mountain, Major Forsythe arrived on the scene with five troops of cavalry and
the pursuit of Ju was resumed.   The Apaches rode down
into Carretas Cañon and met a large force of Mexican soldiers under Colonel Justo Garcia of the Fifth Chihuahua
Cavalry and in the fight which followed this meeting, Garcia's forces killed one hundred and sixty-seven Indians.

By the time that Forsythe arrived in Carretas Cañon,
Garcia had done his work and done it well.   Forsythe introduced himself to Garcia and informed him that the bunch
of Indians which he had just wiped out, was the same bunch
which he had been following for days.   Garcia informed
Forsythe that he and his command should consider themselves under arrest, but that they could retain their arms
for the time being.   Tom Horn, acting as interpreter, Forsythe addressed Colonel Garcia as follows:

"I know that I am violating an international agreement
and I knew what I was doing when I came in here and I
know what I am going to do now.   I am going to mount
my men and go back as I came here, and that was without
order or command; I will not submit to go anywhere with
you and your command, and I will now bid you good day."

Forsythe ordered his men to hold themselves in readiness
to meet any act which might arise from the situation and in
a very few minutes he and his command were moving back
toward the international line.

After resting for a few days at Ft. San Carlos, after returning from Mexico, Chief Scout Al Sieber was ordered to
take Tom Horn, Mickey Free and a detachment of 30 soldiers and go to Cañon Creek, arrest and bring back five

Cibicu Apaches who were making war talk and trouble among their own people.

The adjutant had instructed that Dead Shot and Dandy Jim, sergeants of the scout company, should go along to identify the outlaw Indians. Both Sieber and Horn knew that these two Indian scouts were members of the Cibicu family and that they would not hesitate to lead them into an ambush but they could not help themselves as they had received their orders.

Upon arrival at Cañon Creek they learned that the Indians whom they desired to arrest were at Cibicu Creek, so they camped that night near a bunch of Apaches which had already been camped there before they arrived. In this bunch of Indians was a Mexican named Suneriano, who had been captured when quite small and had been raised among the Apaches, had taken two Apache squaws for his wives and had raised a considerable family of children.

That night Suneriano sent one of his children over to the soldier camp to tell Tom Horn that the Indians had laid a trap which was to be sprung at Cibicu Creek and that Dead Shot was going to lead them into it.

At daylight, Tom told Sieber of this trap and together they went to Captain Hetig, who was in command of the detachment, and told him of the trap, but did not tell him where the information came from. Hetig informed Sieber that if they were afraid, that he, Horn and Mickey Free, might turn back to Camp Apache.

They reached Cibicu Creek about noon. Sieber had instructed Horn to keep close to, and watch, Dandy Jim and for Mickey Free to do the same by Dead Shot. It was not long until Dead Shot realized that Horn and Free were watching him and he went to Captain Hetig and informed him of his suspicions. Hetig ordered Horn and Free to drop back to the rear of the command and thus it was that Dead Shot and Dandy Jim had free rein.

Hetig marched the little command right up to the door of the trap, but the Apaches, believing that the soldiers could not escape, did not wait until all of them had gotten down into the cañon to open fire. The fight lasted about ten

minutes and eleven soldiers were wounded. The only soldier killed was Hetig. Their five scouts deserted them and
went over to the enemy. As the weather was warm, they
were forced to bury Captain Hetig near where he fell. As
they had eleven out of about twenty-five men wounded, it
was more than useless for them to make any attempt to pursue the Indians further, so they returned to Camp Apache.

Colonel Eugene Carr arrived at Camp Apache with two
more troops of cavalry and, being ranking officer, he took
command of the situation. Many Indians began coming in
from Cibicu and Cañon Creeks and making camp near the
post, saying that they did not care to be classed among those
taking part in the killing of Captain Hetig and later firing
on the post.

Horn was ordered by Colonel Carr to take his scouts and
locate the outlaw Apaches. The trail lead them in the direction of Green Valley and they learned that they had
supplied themselves with horses from Tweeksbury Ranch
and also some from Al Rose's ranch. They found that the
Indians had killed two men named Louie Huron and Charlie
Sigsbee.

Horn had sent an Apache scout back to inform Colonel
Carr that he was still on the trail of the Indians and for
him to follow him. Major Chaffee, who had been ordered
out from Ft. McDowell, and who was accompanied by Al
Sieber, Pat Kehoe and a small command of soldiers, had
met the scout and learned Horn's location and they came
direct to him. At daylight the following morning Major
Chaffee left the pack train and went ahead light.

They headed toward the Meadows Ranch which they
reached at about ten o'clock and found Old Man Meadows
killed and his sons, Henry and John, badly shot to pieces,
but still alive. Mrs. Meadows informed them that the Indians could not be more than half a mile ahead of them
so, leaving a doctor and four men to take care of the wounded
at Meadow's Ranch, they pushed ahead.

They overtook the Indians at Chevelon's Fork and as
this creek cuts through a deep cañon, the Indians were
hurrying to get up the opposite bank before the soldiers

arrived, but they were doomed to disappointment. Tom Horn described the fight which followed thus:

"As we came to the banks of the cañon, the renegades were just coming up on the opposite side. We opened fire on them, of course. About half way up the side of the cañon, on the opposite side, the trail would have to run around on a wide bench for a ways to find an opening in the bench to allow them to pass through. Then there would be a place in the trail leading straight away from us. The distance was just about six hundred yards, and when they came to the place which led straight away from us, it made fine shooting.

"Going up over the last rim was a place about sixty feet long, and no one could get out of the cañon without going through this place. Sieber and the First Sergeant of I Troop (Chaffee's), whose name was Woodall, and who was a famous shot, took up a position with me to command this last slide and to stop as many Indians as possible.

"It was a deadly place for the renegades. We had been at them for an hour, at least, before they got up to this place and they were pretty badly demoralized. Pat Kehoe had gotten his five men down in the cañon below them and they could not go that way. Up the cañon it was impossible for them to go, so up the side they must go. Not a horse ever did get up to that place. There were three started up at first and the one in the lead was a gray. I suppose that we all thought the same thing and that was, if we hit the lead horse, he would fall back on the others and knock them down like ten-pins. We all fired at the gray horse and down he came, struggling and knocking down the two behind him. We all felt good, for if Sieber and Woodall felt as good as I did, each of them thought his shot had done the work.

"'Good work, men!' cried Major Chaffee; 'keep that hole stopped and we have got 'em.' He did not use just those words, for Chaffee, in a fight, can beat any man swearing I ever heard. He swears by ear, and by note in a common way, and by everything else in a general way. He would swear when his men would miss a good shot and he would swear when they made a good shot. He swore at himself for not bringing more ammunition and he would swear at his men for wasting their ammunition or shooting too often. Then, when an Indian would expose himself, he would swear and yell: 'Shoot, you damned idiots! What do you suppose I give you ammunition for—to eat?'

"The gray horse stuck in the trail and no other horse could get up until he was gotten out of the way. Several renegades tried to get him out of the way, but it was an awful place to work to much advantage, for we were all good shots, and while the distance was close to six hundred yards, we had the range down so fine, and we were perhaps fifty feet above them, so that for that distance the spot for us was ideal. After they saw that they could not get the gray horse away from the place where he had fallen, another one tried to lead his horse over the top of the gray one, and down that horse went; not on top of the gray but nearly so, and that blocked the trail completely. No more horses tried to get through, but several Indians ran up on foot."

Still further in quoting from Tom Horn's statement; in part he said that just at this stage of the game there came up a heavy rain and hail storm, the heaviest that he had ever seen and it was impossible for them to see across the cañon and the fight was all over, but that at about six o'clock that evening, the pack train, which had not seen any rain or hail, came up and after getting hot coffee and a good feed, they all felt better. A young lieutenant of Chaffee's troop in telling about this storm, said,—"Why, Major Chaffee got so cold and wet that he had to stop swearing."

The following morning investigation showed that out of about one hundred horses that the Indians had with them, there were only about twenty of them alive, all of the rest having been killed in the fight. Twenty-one dead Indians were found, more than likely there were as many more carried down the cañon by the torrent caused by the storm of the night before. A wounded squaw, who was found on the battle field the next morning, told them that there were forty-five warriors in the party and that nearly all of them were killed.

This photo of GERONIMO was made at Slaughter's Ranch in 1896. Had surrendered, but soon after made his escape.

GERONIMO

Horn played a part in the apprehension of Dandy Jim, Dead Shot, Loco and one more Indian who took part in the uprising and the murder of Captain Hetig. These Indians were hung at Ft. Grant in 1882.

In the early part of 1883, Geronimo, who was camped down in Mexico on Rio Viejo, sent word to General Crook, who was in command of the military department, that he wished to have a talk with him and make arrangements to come back into the United States, surrender and be taken back into the fold once more. Geronimo was evidently out of flour, sugar and coffee.

General Crook, taking a large escort of soldiers and Sieber and Horn, made the trip down into Mexico and the meeting was arranged. The talk lasted two or three days and as Geronimo did not like the Apache interpreter nor the Indian interpreter, and refused to let them act, also making a special request that Tom Horn, whom he knew and trusted, should act as interpreter, Tom acted in the capacity of official interpreter.

After Geronimo had made a bombastic speech in which he, as usual, had demanded everything which he could think of and had offered nothing, General Crook informed him that he could have his choice of either going back onto the San Carlos Reservation or fight. Crook was an old hand at handling Indians and did not waste very many words in issuing orders as to what should be done.

Geronimo took council with Al Sieber who was also an interpreter, Chief of Scouts, as well as a man whom Geronimo liked. Sieber of course, advised him to yield to the will of General Crook and go back into the United States. Geronimo, after a dignified delay bordering on mutiny, gathered his people together and accompanied the soldiers back to San Carlos and was happy once more. Geronimo was an expert at burying the hatchet, especially when the opportunity offered to bury it in a white man's head.

In the fall of '83, Sieber's old enemy, rheumatism, returned and in November he had Tom Horn appointed Chief of Scouts. Sieber knew the Apaches so well that he divided his time between Whipple and San Carlos and acted as official adviser until the surrender of Geronimo which put an end to the Indian troubles in Southern Arizona.

During the latter part of December, '83, Tom was instructed to take his scouts and intercept a party of about twenty renegade Apaches who had been raiding in Mexico and were about to return to the United States. Taking his company of twenty-five scouts, with Mickey Free as their first sergeant, they made camp at the international line. As Tom could not take his scouts, which would have been classed as an armed body, into Mexico, he went by himself. Making his lonely camp in the top of Terras Mountains, he kept a close lookout for Indian signs. His vigil was at last rewarded when he saw smoke signs in the distance, which he easily read and which meant,—"Answer" or "Communicate." These signals were repeated in an hour and then, from a point far in the distance came the reply,—"All right, will wait here for two days." This meant that the main body would wait two days for the party who signaled to join them and it was presumed that the entire party would then start back into the United States.

Tom lost no time in getting back to his scouts across the line. His scouts were somewhat scattered and he set about getting them together. He rode into Slaughter's Ranch at daylight on the following morning and after partaking of a good substantial breakfast, John Slaughter gave him one of the best horses on his ranch and he pulled out for Camp Rucker. He met one of his scouts who was with a small party some distance away and, after intructing him to see that all of the scouts were gotten together at Tex Springs without delay, he went to that place and waited. This was at two o'clock in the morning, but all of the scouts were there by shortly after daylight.

The scouts were joined at Tex Springs by Lieutenant Wilder, of the Third Cavalry, in charge of twenty troopers, under orders from General Crook to stay with Horn and take command of the expedition. The following morning, while they were headed for the line to wait for the renegade Apaches to appear, they were joined by six San

Simon cow boys, well armed and well mounted, anxious for something to start.

Just as the command was starting out, a scout rode hurriedly into camp and announced the approach of a band of some kind of mounted men, coming across the flat. These turned out to be five cow boys from Slaughter's Ranch who were also anxious to get into a scrimmage with the renegade Apaches.

Shortly after daylight the following morning the Indians were sighted. Arrangements were quickly made for Lieutenant Wilder and his command to strike them head on and the cowboys, headed by Mickey Free to slip down and take a stand where they could close in on them from behind as soon as the soldiers had opened fire on them. As the Apache scouts were not mounted, Horn held them in reserve.

The renegade Indians came up to within two hundred yards of Wilder's soldiers before they sighted them. They were driving a large bunch of horses (stolen of course), and the dust prevented them from seeing the white men until it was too late. Just at the last minute the Indian scouts were given soldier blouses by Wilder's men, so that when they got into the fight, they could be distinguished from the renegade bunch, as to the crazy soldiers and the still crazier cow boys, an Indian was an Indian, and when excited by the shots of battle they would not take time to ask an Indian to identify himself to them. The identification always came after the fight.

After a five minutes' fight there appeared to be no more renegade Indians in sight, so a check up of casualties was made. They had captured one of the renegade Apache squaws and she informed them that the party had consisted of eleven men and three women. Twelve dead Apaches were found and these with the prisoner, accounted for thirteen of the original party. As the fourteenth Indian never showed up at the reservation for rations, it was presumed that he was wounded and crawled away to die.

The casualties on the attacking side amounted to one dead Mexican cowboy from the San Bernardino Ranch, and two wounded cowboys of the San Simon force. Mickey Free had a long slash in his left arm, one soldier was shot through the neck and one through the stomach. The captured horses amounted to 118. The San Bernardino Mexican cowboy had roped an Indian and pulled him off his horse; the Indian got up and killed him. Everybody concerned was apparently satisfied with this short little fight and its results, and all divided up and returned home by their various routes. They did not get back to Ft. Bowie until some time in January, 1884.

In 1885 General Crook came out from Washington, armed with a treaty which permitted him to campaign in Mexico just the same as in the United States. One hundred Apache scouts were enlisted for a six months' campaign in Mexico. It was in December, 1885, before all arrangements had been completed for the trip into Mexico.

A line of heliograph stations had been installed during the summer and these proved to be invaluable in the campaign which came later. Settlers were instructed to report to their nearest helio station all Indian signs.

After several Indian engagements of minor importance along the line, Horn, with a bunch of his scouts, dropped down into Mexico and began to scout for the main bunch of renegade Indians, which he finally located on the Rio Arras. He sent two of his scouts back to inform Captain Crawford, who was in charge of the detachment of soldiers who had followed Horn, to come ahead, prepared for business.

This soldier command was divided into four parties. Captain Crawford on the north, Horn on the east side next to the Arras River, Lieutenant Maus on the south side, and Lieutenant Shipp on the west side, and all were in position before daylight.

Just at daylight, two Apache bucks from the renegade camp came directly to where Horn and his twenty-five scouts were stationed. They came right up to within twenty yards of them and then it seemed as though every scout in the company shot at one or the other of those two Indians and at that short range it is doubtful if any of those twenty-five shots missed.

Horn states,—"Well, there were big doin's in that camp

for the next half hour! Geronimo jumped up on a rock and yelled, 'Look out for the horses!' And a minute afterwards he yelled,—'Let the horses go and break toward the river on foot! There are soldiers and Apache scouts on both sides and above us. Let the women and children break for the river and the men stay behind.' "

Lieutenant Shipp and his men lay perfectly quiet until the renegades, who had started west, had gotten within ten feet of them and then, as Horn said, "They did good work and plenty of it." Horn personally captured Naña, an old Apache chief who, at that time was over ninety years old. Naña took the situation very calmly and, raising his gun over his head, brought it down on a rock, breaking it. He then said to Horn, in Spanish,—"Para sirvir usted." (At your service.) It is not known how many Indians were killed in this fight, but evidently the majority of them ran away.

Shortly after daylight the next morning, they saw Mexican soldiers coming toward them and although the Mexicans were hailed in their own language, they kept coming right ahead and their officers could be plainly heard, giving orders to prepare for a charge. As they executed the order, Captain Emmett Crawford jumped up on a large rock, with a white handkerchief in his hand. However, the Mexicans paid no attention to his signals of peace, but kept right on advancing, and firing into Crawford's command. A glancing bullet struck Captain Crawford in the forehead and he fell, with brains oozing out of the opening. He lived three days. Horn was wounded in an arm also, but not seriously.

When the advancing Mexicans paid no attention to peace signals, Horn commanded his scouts to open up on them, and they did so with a vim which paralyzed the Mexicans. In a check-up later, it was learned that the Mexicans suffered thirty-six killed and thirteen badly wounded.

Old Chief Naña went to Horn and begged him to release him and give him a gun and ammunition, that he might have a chance to get back at some of his hereditary enemies. Horn did as he was asked, and Naña was happy.

The Mexicans soon had enough and one of them called

out for the white man who spoke Mexican, and Horn answered them. They professed ignorance of the existence of a compact whereby the United States soldiers were permitted to campaign on the south side of the international line. The American force had left Ft. Bowie on December 1st, 1885,

GEN. NELSON A. MILES

and as it was now January 11th, 1886, Horn stated that in view of the fact that they had not had much communication with the outside world since starting on this winter campaign, for a little while he thought perhaps Mexico had declared war on the United States.

The wounding and subsequent death of Crawford gave the command to Lieutenant Maus. After considerable talk at long range, two Mexicans came over to the American camp to talk over matters and they admitted that they had made a mistake and did not know that they were firing upon American soldiers. They claimed they saw only the Apache scouts and thought they were hostiles. About the middle

of the day, a Mexican came over and asked Lieutenant Maus
if he could spare a doctor to go over and attend to their
wounded.   Dr. Davis went over and dressed the wounds of
many of them and upon his return stated that he saw one
Mexican who had been wounded eight times.

Lieutenant Maus went over to the Mexican camp and
was made a prisoner.   The Mexicans sent over word that
the Americans must divide their rations with them and give
them mules with which to carry their wounded away, and
informed the Americans that they intended taking Maus to
Chihuahua with them.

Horn sent over word that if they would send over four
or five men they would see what they could do regarding a
division of rations and mules.   Five Mexicans soon arrived
and Horn made them prisoners.   Standing all five of them
on a large rock, he called to his scouts to shoot them when
he gave the word.   He then shouted across to the Mexicans, that if Lieutenant Maus was not released immediately, he would order his scouts to shoot the five Mexicans.
It was only a matter of a few minutes until Maus came
walking into camp.

Chihuahua, an Apache chief who was with Geronimo,
sent a squaw over to the camp, with instructions to say that
he would like to make arrangements for a talk with General
Crook; that he was tired of following Geronimo, who was
all of the time running away from the white soldiers or else
engaged in drinking mescal.   Chihuahua was one of Cochise's grandsons.   Horn accompanied the squaw to Chihuahua's camp and had a talk with him and asked him to
try and get Nachez, his half brother, to come in also and
surrender, and that he would try and get General Crook
lined up for a big pow-wow to take place at San Bernardino
Peak at the time of the March full moon.

They broke camp and went back north to their base camp
at Nacori.   It was here that they buried Captain Emmett
Crawford.   His body was taken up later and shipped to his
home in Lincoln, Nebraska.

The meeting at the time of the March full moon was
arranged, and at the appointed time all concerned were on

hand. Chihuahua said that he had no talk to make, that he was willing to go to the guard house and stay there until Geronimo came in. While they were talking the situation over, Geronimo at the head of a large party of renegades, came into sight. Geronimo had the reputation of being the champion Apache hot air merchant, and could not resist a chance to make a long-winded peace talk and it was this magnet which drew him to San Bernardino Peak, twelve miles below the international line, at this time.

Upon arrival at camp, Geronimo demanded that he be permitted to see General Crook. He was primed for a life-sized gab fest, but General Crook cut him short by informing him that he could do just one of two things and that was, he could go to Ft. Bowie as a prisoner or fight it out; that he would hear his decision in the morning.

Geronimo started in to talking with the Indians who had come in with Chihuahua, and Chihuahua came at once to Horn and asked him to place him and his band under close guard as he wanted to go back to Ft. Bowie, and that if Geronimo were permitted to talk to them, he might persuade many of them to desert.

Geronimo asked the reason for such precautions and was informed that all of the Chiricahuas who went back to Ft. Bowie would be placed in the guard house and kept there. Geronimo replied that this was a hard proposition, and that no more of his people would surrender under such conditions. In the morning, he and his band were among the missing.

Shortly after the delivery of two hundred Apache bucks, squaws and papooses, to the commanding officer at Ft. Bowie, Horn was notified that the office of Chief Scout would be abolished and that from that time he would be known as an interpreter. This was a severe blow to Tom's pride. When General Miles arrived to take command of the department, the newspapers came out with the information that matters Apache would be handled in a very much different manner from what they had in the past; that Horn was as much of an Apache as Geronimo; that he entered Geronimo's camp at will and departed in the same manner.

Tom felt the injustice of this newspaper comment to such an extent that he resigned and went over into the Arivaipa country where he had some mines and many real friends.

In August, 1886, General Mines sent word to Horn that he would like to have him come to Ft. Huachuca to see him and have a talk with him. The result of the proposed meeting was that Tom was once more appointed Chief of Scouts, with instructions to Captain Lawton to do all that he could to help him. Captain Lawton, afterwards General Lawton, was killed in the Philippines.

Horn found Lawton camped down in Sonora, Mexico, at a place called Sierra Gordo. Lawton had two troops of cavalry, twenty-five Apache scouts and four or five white scouts. Leaving the two troops of cavalry in camp, they took the twenty-five Apache scouts and soon picked up the trail of the renegades and, with the entire co-operation of the Sonora, Mexico, state troops, they pushed Geronimo ahead of them for five weeks, not giving him time to supply himself with either food or fresh horses.

When the American force reached Fronteras, a squaw came in and said that Geronimo wished to see and talk to Horn. After considerable controversy, per helio, Horn was instructed to go into Geronimo's camp and make any arrangements he might see fit to make, as long as it would have a tendency to end the campaign against Geronimo.

Lieutenant Gatewood accompanied Horn on his trip to Geronimo's camp. They were met on the Bavispe River by Geronimo, who came to meet them, and arrangements were soon made for Geronimo to meet General Miles in Skeleton Cañon, in the United States, in twelve days. When this information was received by Geronimo, he asked if the message was sent direct to him, and when he was informed that it had been sent to Captain Lawton, who was in command of the expedition, Geronimo informed Horn that if General Miles sent a message to him through him (Horn) that he would meet him in Skeleton Cañon in twelve days, he would be there, otherwise, not.

In reply to a helio message sent Miles the latter stated that Captain Lawton was in command and he could do no business with a civilian. When Geronimo was informed of this message, he and his gang of 136 lost no time in getting away from that locality. Horn informed Lawton of the situation and, mounting his horse, rode north across the international line, stopping at John Slaughter's San Bernardino Ranch, where he ate a hearty meal and laid down to get some very much needed sleep.

There was a troop of soldiers camped at Slaughter's Ranch and about noon, the lieutenant in command, came to the ranch house and asked Slaughter if Horn was there. Slaughter replied that he had ridden in about daylight and that he was then asleep. The lieutenant informed Slaughter that he had a message for him from General Miles and that it was of the utmost importance. Slaughter took the message and gave it to Tom. This was what it contained,—"Make any arrangements you want to for me to meet Geronimo. I will go where and when you say to meet him."

Since leaving Geronimo, Horn had ridden forty miles to the north and Geronimo had probably ridden a like distance to the south. Horn sent a message to Miles to hold the soldiers where they were and that he would try and locate Geronimo, and in just one week he had the renegade chief back to the same neighborhood and sent word to Miles to meet him in Skeleton Cañon in four days.

Needless to say that Miles was there and Geronimo surrendered without any ceremony. Whey they arrived at Bowie, there was a special train waiting and Geronimo and his entire band were loaded into it, the doors locked, guards posted and Geronimo was taken away from his lifetime range, never to return. He was taken to Florida and later to Oklahoma, where he died at Ft. Sill but a few years ago.

After the disposal of Geronimo, there being no more scouting to do, the scout company was disbanded and Horn was once more out of a job. He went over into the Aravaipa country and worked in his mines all of the winter of '86 and '87.

Early in April, 1887, Horn went into the Pleasant Valley Country where there was a life sized rustlers' war going on, in which there were probably as many as twenty-five men

killed on each side.   Buckey O'Neill, who was sheriff of
Yavapai County at that time, called on Horn to act as
mediator and appointed him one of his deputies.   After
peace had been restored between the warring factions, Tom
returned to his old range and spent the winter of 1887-88
in the Aravaipa County, working his mining claims and visiting with Al Sieber at Ft. Grant and San Carlos.

He was appointed deputy sheriff by Sheriff Glen Reynolds, who was the first sheriff of Gila County.   At the time
that Apache Kid was tried for the murder of "Rip," another
Apache Indian, Horn was to have acted as interpreter, but
decided that he would attend the Arizona Territorial Fair
at Phoenix during the fall of '88 and consequently was not
present at the Kid's trial.   Tom won the steer roping con-
test at Phoenix in 1891 in 49½ seconds.

Tom worked around the Arivaipa County until some time
in 1890, when he sold his claims to some eastern company
for $8,000. He then went to Denver and went to work for
the Pinkerton Detective Agency and the first case he was
given was the running down of two train robbers known as
Burt Curtis and Pegleg Watson, whom he trailed around
over a large portion of Colorado, Utah and Texas before
landing them.   He quit the Pinkertons and went to work
for the Swan Land and Cattle Company of Wyoming.
While Horn states that he did not go to Wyoming until
1894, it is believed that he meant to say 1892, as he was in
Johnson and Converse Counties during the Cattlemen's
War in the early part of 1892 and known as Tom Hale.

He worked in Wyoming for the next five or six years,
and at the breaking out of the Spanish-American War, General Maus, who, as a lieutenant, had campaigned all over
Southern Arizona and Northern Mexico with Horn during
the Geronimo chase, looked him up and made him chief
packer of Shafter's Army and a short time later appointed
him Master of Transportation with the rank and pay of
colonel.

During his service in Cuba he contracted Cuban fever and
was returned to the United States.   After spending many
weary weeks in the hospital, he so far recovered his health

as to be able to get to the ranch of John Coble, a warm friend of Tom's who lived in the Iron Mountain Country of Wyoming. By the time he had recovered his health the Iron Mountain Rustlers had grown very bold and active and the cattlemen in that vicinity hired him to look after their interests and apprehended those who were rustling their cattle.

On the morning of July 19th, 1901, Willie Nickell, the 14-year-old son of Kels Nickell, was found dead about three-quarters of a mile from his home, having been shot twice in the back, one bullet having pierced his heart. There was some talk made by Tom's enemies that he had committed this cold blooded murder but neither he nor his friends paid any attention to this passing rumor.

It is stated that Horn was on friendly terms with the Nickell family and had no reason whatsoever for killing Willie Nickell, as it was a well known fact that Tom liked children and besides, no one who ever knew Tom Horn would ever accuse him of shooting any one in the back, especially a boy who was scarcely more than a child in years.

Scraps of evidence filtered into local conversation which indicated that Horn was going to be made the goat in this deal but none of his friends placed any credence in the rumors, but, in January, 1902, Tom Horn was arrested on a charge of having killed Willie Nickell and later a Deputy United States Marshal, named Joe La Fors, testified that Horn had confessed to him in the presence of witnesses that he had done the deed.

At his preliminary examination on May 10th, Charles Ohnhaus, who was district court interpreter, and Leslie Snow, a deputy sheriff, testified that they were stationed behind a door leading into the Marshal's office and and had heard Tom make this confession to Joe La Fors.

Horn's trial was set for October 13th and his testimony was to the effect that he was drunk at the time of his socalled confession and that La Fors had boasted to him about the different men that he had killed and that he (Horn) had told of the killing of Willie Nickell, the wounding with intent to kill, of Kels Nickell, also the killing of two more men, just to keep pace with La Fors. It seems that it was customary with these men to "tell 'em wild and wooly" whenever they got together and this was the reason why Tom told what he did. His statement was not made under oath at the time but was used as evidence against him because Snow and Ohnhaus, who were hidden in the Marshal's office, heard the drunken boastings of Horn. They did not make any record of the killings which La Fors boasted of having committed, in order to get Tom to talking. They only made a record of one side of the story.

The confession was full of profanity and vulgarity and it was a well known fact that Tom Horn never used such language when either drunk or sober. It was stated by those who were acquainted with both men that the language quoted in the so-called confession was more like that of Snow than it was like that of Horn's.

Even the unfriendly newspapers predicted either an acquittal or a hung jury and great was the surprise at 5:00 p. m. of October 26th, when the jury returned a verdict of guilty.

After the trial it was discovered that Horn and his two friends, Duncan Clark and Sam Moore, had recovered stolen stock from some of the jurymen while they were acting as officers. It will plainly be seen that Tom Horn, a cattle detective, had been tried before a jury of men, the majority of whom were actually stock rustlers. During the trial, a prominent stock man publicly stated—"Show me a cattleman who is against Tom Horn and I will show you a rustler."

Although the attorneys for the defense cited seventy-nine errors, they could not procure a new trial. Horn was sentenced to be hanged on November 20th, 1903. On the 31st day of October an appeal was made to Governor Chatterton, but with no favorable reply.

Miss Gwendolyn Kimmel, a school teacher in that district, made statement that she had heard three different conversations between two well known local men, wherein one of them was incriminated in the killing of Willie Nickell and that she had informed one of them that she had heard such conversations and that he admitted that the other one had committed the deed, but that she had agreed not to say anything about the matter as long as no attempt was made to side track the crime or to frame it upon Tom Horn, which she had already heard some talk of.

After all of the evidence, perjured and otherwise, had been submitted, and it became an assured fact that Tom was to be railroaded to the scaffold, Miss Kimmell made a written statement of what she knew and had heard, and called upon the Governor, but he did not appear to be interested in the matter sufficiently to re-open the case and at half-past three of the afternoon of November 14th, 1903, announced that he would not interfere with the execution of (so-called) justice and at 11:00 a. m. of November 20th, 1903, Tom Horn was legally murdered.

Tom's straightforward story as told on the stand, carried conviction of his innocence, and his friends were confident of his acquittal, but their hopes were crashed when a jury of his enemies returned a verdict of "Guilty." The presiding judge could have recommended clemency, or a new hearing, but he took no action or interest in Tom's behalf after having pronounced the death sentence.

It was afterwards stated that two men, riding horses of the same description as horses owned by the men who Miss Kimmell accused of having a guilty knowledge of the crime, were near where the murdered boy was afterwards found and this information entered into her statement to the judge, but the judge, likened unto Pilate of old, having already pronounced sentence, washed his hands of the affair. This judge afterwards committed suicide and it is believed that his act in so doing was due to his brooding over his unjust decision in the Tom Horn case.

Thomas N. Wills, ex-sheriff of Pinal County, Ariz., worked on the roundup with Tom and knew him probably as no other man in Arizona ever did, made a trip to Wyoming several years after the execution of Tom's sentence, to attend and participate in the Cheyenne Frontier Day Celebration. One of Cheyenne's daily papers issued the following statement:

"Thomas N. Wills, the sheriff of Florence, Ariz., who is in the city to participate in the Frontier Celebration, says that he knew Tom Horn, the notorious Wyoming cattle detective, in Arizona 23 years ago and was well acquainted with him for many years.

"Sheriff Wills states that Horn was a hard working industrious man during his residence in that section; a quiet, peaceable man and was never in any trouble of any kind.

"So far as I know," said Sheriff Wills, "the only man Horn ever killed, was a Mexican bully and he shot him in self defense, being promptly exonerated by a jury from any blame in the matter. The reports sent out at the time of Horn's trial here, and before his hanging, in regard to crimes committed in Mexico and southern states, were without foundation. I knew Horn personally, almost up until the time he left for Wyoming, and the sensational story in regard to Horn killing a Mexican officer as the result of a love affair over a senorita, was without foundation. I know nothing about Horn's career in your state, but would have accepted him as an honest, industrious man in my section, and one who would not commit a willful murder."

Al Sieber, one of the best known old time Indian scouts, and under whom Tom Horn worked as interpreter and assistant, writes under date of April 7th, 1904, in part, as follows: "Tom went to work for me in the government pack train in 1882; he was with me for three years. A more faithful or better worker or a more honorable man I never met in my life.

"During the period of three years, I made numbers of scouting expeditions, and oftentimes needed the help of a man I could rely on, and I always placed Horn in charge; for it required a man of bravery, judgment and skill, and I ever found Tom true to the last letter of the law to any and every trust confided to his care.

"In making my side scouts alone, I would always place Horn in charge of all Indian scouts left behind in camp. This required a man who was cool and had judgment to control and handle these scouts. Also, on other side trips, when I took a few pack animals with me, as it very often

AL SEIBER

required me to have a man that I could rely on in every way, as I oftentimes had to split my crowd after being out and I ever made it a point to take Tom with me. At these times I would always put Horn in charge of one set of scouts, tell him where, and the time, to meet me and what came up—rain or snow, clouds or sunshine—Tom was there to meet me and true to the trust."

In writing further of Horn and his work during the Geronimo campaign, Sieber says—"Horn's part in the war deserves the greatest praise for his services and the handling of his Indian scouts. Shortly after this, Horn quit the government service. I saw him frequently afterwards. He went to work in Pleasant Valley as a ranch hand. After this, there was a fierce war in this section, known as the Pleasant Valley War, between cow-men and sheep-men. There were between twenty and thirty men killed during the fight. Tom took no part with either side, although every inducement was offered him to take sides.

"Now, I wish to state that during the time of three or four years he was around me, and with me, I never once saw him under the influence of liquor. The most he ever drank, was a glass of beer, when out with a gang of the boys. And, knowing him, as I do, and taking all into consideration, I can not, and will not, ever believe that Tom Horn was the man the papers tried to make the world believe he was. These words and sentiments can not be put too strong, for I can never believe that the jolly, joval, honorable and whole-souled Tom Horn I knew was a low-down miserable murderer."

John C. Coble, for whom Tom Horn worked for about two years, and who had been his friend for several more years, writes: "Tom Horn was seldom profane, and this assertion will be sustained by those who really knew him —a fact which alone serves to disprove that so-called 'confession' the language of which smacks very much more of the talk of those who edited the notes taken on the spot."

In referring to his preparation and publication of Tom Horn's "Life," Mr. Coble further states—"The fact that such a 'Life' had been written, had no sooner become known

than I was beseiged by his personal friends and acquaintances, and by interested readers of the published reports of
the trial, for the publication of the autobiography prepared
by Tom Horn. Letters reached me by every mail from almost every state and territory of the Union; and I may be
permitted here to state that there was scarcely a letter among
them all which did not declare a belief in the innocence of
Horn, 'after carefully considering the details of the case'."

F. M. Ownbey of Loveland, Colorado, one of the men
who knew Tom Horn best, in a letter written by him to Tom
from Denver, Colorado, under date of January 24th, 1902,
is quoted in part, as follows: "I see by the papers that you
are in serious trouble. After reading an account of the
charge preferred against you, I can not for the life of me
believe it to be true. Knowing you so long and knowing
you so intimately I can not comprehend how a man of your
sense and ability could be guilty of so great a charge as is
preferred against you.

"Tom, I do not believe you are guilty of the crime. I
am writing this in all justice to you and the community at
large; knowing you as I do, and knowing your ability and
sense. I can not believe you would stoop so low as to murder a fourteen year old boy for the small sum of five hundred dollars, when you could, in all probably have made
that amount in a week legitimately. I live in Loveland,
Colorado, and if there is anything I can do for you, or aid
you in any manner as far as it is right, I am at your service."

In conclusion, here will be shown a copy of the last letter
which Tom Horn wrote. Read it and ask yourself if the
man who wrote it, could be guilty of the crime of shooting
a fourteen year old boy in the back.

"Cheyenne, Wyoming, Nov. 20th, 1903.
"John C. Coble,
"Cheyenne, Wyo.,

"As you have just requested, I will tell all my knowledge
of everything I know in regard to the killing of the Nickell
boy.

"The day I laid over at Miller's Ranch, he asked me to
do so, so that I could meet Billy McDonald.

"Billy McDonald came up and Miller and I met him up the creek, above Miller's house. Billy opened the conversation by saying that he and Miller were going to kill off the Nickell outfit and wanted me to go in on it. They said that Underwood and Jordan would pay me.

"Miller and McDonald said that they would do the work. I refused to have anything to do with them, as I was not interested in any way. McDonald said that the sheep were then on Coble's land and I got my horse and went up to see, and they were not on Coble's land.

"I promised to stay all night again at Miller's, as McDonald said he would come up again the next morning.

"He came back next morning and asked me if I still felt the same as I did the day before, and I told him I did.

" 'Well,' he said, 'we have made up our minds to wipe up the whole Nickell outfit.

"I got on my horse and left, and went on about my business. I went on, as John Brae and Otto Plaga said I did, and on to the ranch, where I got in on Saturday. I heard there of the boy being killed. I felt I was well out of the mixup."

"I was over in that part of the country six weeks or two months later and saw both McDonald and Miller, and they were laughing and blowing to me about running and shooting the sheep of Nickell. I told them that I did not want to hear of it at all, for I could see that McDonald wanted to tell me the whole scheme. They both gave me the laugh and said that I was suspicioned of the whole thing.

"I knew that there was some suspicion against me, but did not pay any attention to it that I should.

"That is all there is to it so far as I know. Irwin, who swore that I came into Laramie on the run on that Thursday, just simply lied.

"All that supposed confession in the United States Marshal's office was prearranged, and every thing sworn to by those fellows, was a lie, made up before I came to Cheyenne. Of course there was talk of the killing of the boy, but La Fors did all of that. I did not even make an admission, but allowed La Fors to make some insinuations.

"Ohnhaus, La Fors and Snow, and also Irwin of Laramie, all swore to lies to fit the case.

"Your name was not mentioned in the marshal's office.

"This is the truth, as I am going to die in ten minutes.

"Thanking you for your kindness to me, I am, Sincerely yours, TOM HORN."

Several years ago the writer was told by a close friend of Tom Horn's, that Tom had told that he did shoot Willie Nickell, but that he had done so, believing that he was shooting Willie's father, Kels Nickell, but this story does not hang together very well for the reason that Willie Nickell was shot twice through the body, one bullet passing through his heart; either shot would have been fatal and the second one would have been delivered at such short range that recognition of Willie by Horn would have necessarily taken place as the boy would have been lying on the ground beyond any reasonable doubt, and his executioner standing over him for the second shot.

It was stated that Willie was wearing his father's coat and hat and was riding the horse usually ridden by his father and this was why he was killed instead of his father.

In the April 15th, 1928 issue of the Denver Post, appears an article from the able pen of Edwin Hunt Hoover, a well known writer of western stories, who states that C. W. (Doc) Shores, a one time partner of Tom Horn's, has stated recently that a few hours before his execution, Tom told a friend of his that he did shoot Willie Nickell, but that he had done so through a mistake; he thought that he was shooting Willie's father, Kels Nickell.

Tom Horn was known in Arizona as a square shooter and his many friends are firm in their belief that he could not have killed Willie Nickell. It is a well known fact however, that whether guilty or not, he did not get a square deal at his trial, that the evidence was more or less framed. He was considered a dangerous man by his enemies and apparently they decided to get him out of their way and so the jury was packed with enough of his enemies to insure a conviction and Tom Horn paid the penalty of their hatred.

WYATT EARP

AFTER Wyatt Earp, as City Marshal, assisted by Bat Masterson, Doc Holliday and others, had succeeded in making Dodge City a safe place to live, he decided to make a change in his location and went to Prescott, Ariz., where the U. S. Marshal for that district persuaded him to act as his deputy with location at Tombstone.

Wyatt Earp arrived in Tombstone some time later, armed with full authority to act as United States Deputy Marshal in the Tombstone sub-district. During his first eight months' residence in this new and hilarous town he acted as shot-gun messenger for the Wells-Fargo Express Company and was quite successful in discouraging the operations of several hold-up gangs and, in his official capacity, made good men out of several offenders against the peace and dignity of the express company.

Soon becoming wearied of the routine work of his new position, he turned the shot-gun messenger job over to his brother Morgan, and entered into a partnership with the managers of the Oriental Gambling House which was at that time the largest and most important mansion of the Goddess of Chance in Tombstone. It appears that the tougher element had taken a violent dislike to Rackabaugh, one of the partners, and the owners of the establishment believed that having a deputy United States Marshal in the firm would lighten their troubles to a noticeable extent.

Morgan Earp held down the shot gun messenger job for the Wells-Fargo Express Company for about six months and then resigned in favor of a position in the Oriental with Wyatt.

Virgil Earp arrived in Tombstone about this time and was soon appointed city marshal. Jim Earp also appeared about the same time and took employment in the Oriental with Wyatt and Morgan. Warren Earp came along later, making five representatives of the Earp family in Tombstone at the same time.

A bunch of wild ones held up a stage near Tombstone

and killed the driver. They also shot a passenger who was simple minded enough to resist donating to the unholy cause. Wyatt Earp, Virgil Earp and one more man, whose name is unavailable at this late date, took the trail of this outlaw gang and followed them for seventeen days over and through the mountains.

The outlaws were well acquainted with the country over which they were traveling and had many friends along the route who furnished them with food and fresh horses. The

ORIENT GAMBLING HOUSE, BREWERY GULCH, BISBEE

pursuing posse could never secure fresh horses, for when they would ask the ranchers for them they would be most emphatically informed that there were no horses available for their use.

Their hard riding for seventeen days brought them no results and upon their return to Tombstone, Wyatt Earp went to Ike Clanton, who was a sort of a leader of the rustlers, and offered him the entire reward of $6,000 if he would only lead him to a place where he could arrest this outlaw bunch. Clanton, however, would not close the deal until assured that he would receive the reward for them, either dead or alive. After much talk on both sides, Ike finally agreed to the proposition and sent one of his lieutenants, Joe Hill, out to lead the gang, under some pretext or another to some point within 25 miles of Tombstone.

As this transaction would require several days to consummate there was nothing further for Wyatt Earp to do but patiently wait. Marshal Williams evidently suspicioned that Wyatt Earp was using Ike Clanton for some purpose or another and, one day while Clanton was drunk, tried to pump him dry. Clanton became panic stricken at the thought of a third party sharing their secret so he proceeded to get drunk, or drunker than usual, and then accused Wyatt of having taken Williams into the deal.

Earp denied having ever mentioned the matter to Williams and then Ike accused him of having told Doc Holliday and this Earp denied too. Clanton then went to Holliday and spilled the beans to him. Holliday berated Clanton very vigorously for his treachery to his friends and the conversation was heard by several people. Doc Holliday was always loyal to his friends and thought every one else should be also, regardless of which side he represented.

Ike Clanton realized that it was now up to him to either kill Wyatt and Virgil Earp or be killed by some one of his gang. The following morning Wyatt and Virgil were informed by friends that Ike Clanton, armed with a Winchester and six-shooter, was out looking for them with murderous intent. Wyatt and Virgil Earp both started out looking for him, each going in a different direction. As Virgil was walking down Fourth Street, keeping a sharp look-out for the enemy, Clanton came out of a door-way and chanced to look in the opposite direction and did not see Virgil, who walked up behind him and said, "I want you, Ike." Clanton threw his gun around as though to take a shot at Virgil but the gun was knocked away and he was covered by Virgil's gun.

Ike was taken before the justice of the peace and fined $25 on a charge of disturbing the peace. Wyatt Earp states that as soon as Ike had paid his fine and cleared the court room, he sent a message to his brother Billy, who was at Charleston, to bring Tom and Frank McLowery and Billy Claibourne to his assistance.

Thereupon these men, being regular he-men looking for trouble, loaded up their artillery and, taking an ample supply of ammunition, came galloping into town at daylight of September 26th, 1881, swearing to kill every one of the Earps and their friends as well.

Virgil Earp asked Wyatt, "What shall we do?" Wyatt replied, "Go and arrest them." Ike Clanton, Billy Clanton, Frank McLowery, Tom McLowery and Billy Claibourne had taken their stand between the two adobe buildings which formed the entrance to the O. K. Corral and then sent word to Wyatt and Virgil Earp to come and get them and that if they did not come and fight it out with them that they would waylay them and kill them.

Wyatt Earp, Virgil Earp, Morgan Earp and Doc Holliday walked down to the entrance of the O. K. Corral where they found the Clanton-McLowery Gang with their backs to one of the adobe buildings just inside of the gate. Virgil Earp informed them that they had come to arrest them and the fight was on without any preliminaries.

Here is Wyatt Earp's description of what followed: "Frank McLowery fired at me and Billy Clanton fired at Morgan and both missed. I had a gun in my overcoat pocket and I jerked it out and fired at Frank McLowery, hitting him in the stomach at the same time that Morgan shot Billy Clanton in the breast. So far, we had gotten the best of it, but just then Tom McLowery who had gotten behind a horse, fired a shot under the animal's neck which bored a hole through Morgan sideways, having entered one shoulder and come out through the other. 'I've got it,' said Morgan. 'Then get behind me and keep quiet' said I, but he didn't.

"By this time the bullets were flying fast and I could not keep any track of them. Frank McLowery had given a yell when I shot him, and made for the street with his hand over his stomach. Ike Clanton and Billy Clanton were shooting fast and so was Virgil. Ike Clanton and Billy Clanton made a break for the street. I fired a shot into Tom McLowery's horse and made it break away and Doc Holliday took the opportunity of pumping a charge of buck-shot, out of a Wells-Fargo shot-gun, into Tom McLowery who promptly fell dead. Doc Holliday in the excitement of the moment did not know what he had done and flung the shot-gun away in disgust, pulling his six-shooter instead.

"Then I witnessed a strange spectacle. Frank McLowery and Billy Clanton were sitting in the middle of the street, both badly wounded, but emptying their six-shooters like lightning. One of them shot Virgil through the leg and then Virgil shot Billy Clanton, then Frank McLowery started to his feet and staggered across the street although he was full of bullets. On his way he came face to face with Doc Holliday and said, 'I've got you now Doc.' 'Well, you are a good one if you have,' said Holliday, with a laugh, and with that they both aimed. But before you can understand what happened next, I must carry you back half a minute.

"After the first exchange of shots in the lot, Ike Clanton had gotten into one of the buildings from the rear and, when I reached the street, he was shooting out of one of the front windows. Seeing him aim at Morgan I shouted, 'Look out Morg, you're getting it in the back.' Morgan wheeled around and in so doing, fell on his side. While in that position he caught sight of Doc Holliday and Frank McLowery aiming at each other and with a quick drop, shot McLowery in the head. At the same instant McLowery's pistol flashed and Doc Holliday was shot in the hip.

"That ended the fight. Ike Clanton and Billy Clanton ran off and made haste to give themselves up to the sheriff for the citizens were out one hundred strong to back us up. It may, or it may not, surprise some of the readers to learn that from the first to the last shot fired, not more than a minute elapsed."

Wyatt Earp and Doc Holliday were arrested by Sheriff Johnny Behan and charged with the murder of Tom Mc-

Lowery, Frank McLowery and Billy Clanton. Virgil and Morgan Earp were temporarily exempt from arrest on account of being badly wounded and disabled. They were all acquitted at their preliminary examination but were re-arrested on another warrant charging the same offense, but this time the preliminary was held at Contention, nine miles south of Tombstone. Wyatt Earp claims that undoubtedly he and Doc Holliday would have been killed enroute, had it not have been for a large body of their friends who insisted upon accompanying the sheriff as a guard. The preliminary hearing was never completed as they were released upon a writ of habeas corpus and in the meantime the grand jury had refused to indict them.

The Clanton element appeare dto be determined to, assassinate the Earps and one day, about three months after the fight at the O. K. Corral, as Virgil was crossing the street enroute to his hotel, he received several charges of buckshot from ambuscade. One charge shattered his left arm, while another passed through his body. Wyatt Earp, acting in the capacity of an officer, arrested several of the would-be assassins and they stood trial, but their friends swore to air-tight alibis and they were all acquitted.

About three months after Virgil Earp had been shot, and was still suffering from his wounds, Morgan Earp was playing a game of pool when some one shot him through the glass door of the pool room. He lived only a few minutes after the shot was fired. This murder was supposed to have been committed by Frank Stilwell or a half-breed Indian known as Freeze or Indian Charlie.

Wyatt, Virgil, Jim and Warren Earp, accompanied by Doc Stillwell, Doc Holliday, Texas Jack and McMasters, started to California with Morgan's remains and had reached Tucson. While waiting for the train to pull out they spied Frank Stilwell standing under a tree a short distance away. As one man they all drew their guns and fired at him. Some of the lot must have missed because there were only six bullets holes found in his body, according to the findings of the coroner's jury.

Virgil, who was at that time a total wreck from wounds

received at the hands of the Clanton-McLowery sympathizers who bombarded him with shot-guns, went on with the body of Morgan, while the other men returned to Tombstone.

Upon Wyatt's return to Tombstone, Sheriff Johnny Behan attempted to arrest him but Wyatt refused to be arrested and informed Behan that he had better not look like he wanted to arrest him.   Behan gave the arresting business up as a bad job.   For several months Wyatt Earp occupied the unenviable position of being a fugitive from justice from the state authorities and being a deputy United States Marshal conscientiously discharging the duties of his office with the full consent and sanction of his superior officer.

On one occasion, Wyatt and several of his friends had ridden 25 miles over the mountains and intended camping at a certain spring.   But as they neared the spring in question, Wyatt had a presentiment that all was not well so he drew his double barreled shot-gun from its scabbard and no sooner had he done this than nine cow-boys jumped up from behind the bank of the spring and began firing at him and his companions.

Wyatt jumped from his horse and returned the fire, supposing that his friends would do the same, but they retreated.   Curly Bill, a notorious character and stage robber, whom Wyatt had been looking for with a warrant in his pocket, was one of the attacking gang and was doing his best to start a lead mine in Wyatt's person, but had failed to connect.   Wyatt states that he fired both barrels of his shot-gun at Curly Bill, literally tearing him to pieces.   It was then that the attacking party retreated into the brush, though they continued firing.

Wyatt retreated, keeping his horse between himself and his enemies.   His horse was a very high strung animal and every time that Wyatt tried to get his Winchester out of its scabbard, the horse would jump and try to run.   It had been a hot day and Wyatt had loosened his cartridge belt for comfort and it had slipped down over his thighs so that every time that he tried to mount his horse, the belt held his legs together so that he could not slip down into the saddle.

Finally he threw his weight into one stirrup and holding the bridle reins in one hand, tried to pull up his belt. While in this position, the horn was shot off his saddle. As they had traveled up high in the mountains and evening was approaching and the weather had become quite chilly, Wyatt

JOHNNIE BEHAN, FIRST SHERIFF OF COCHISE COUNTY

had slipped his overcoat on and although he escaped bodily injury in the fight just described, the skirt of his overcoat was completely riddled, but he was not even scratched.

Wyatt claimed that Sheriff Johnny Behan trailed him with a large posse of rustlers but that was said to only be a bluff as Wyatt had sent word to Behan where he might find him at any time he might want him. But Behan never came. Wyatt's friends advised him to get out of the state so he went to Colorado. While he was there Behan tried to get a requisition for him, but the Governor of Colorado would not honor it.

Wyatt Earp finally located in California, his home state, where he is still living. Jim Earp who was living in California at last report, now over 80 years of age if living, appears to have been the only one of the brothers who was never drawn into the turmoil and strife of his environment in Tombstone.

Virgil Earp died of pneumonia at Goldfield, Nevada, October 19th, 1905 and his body was shipped to Portland, Oregon, for burial. He was 65 years of age at the time of his death.

Warren Earp went to Willcox, where he hired out to drive stage between Willcox and Ft. Grant. He was a good worker and easy to get along with when sober but when drunk, he was very quarrelsome. One day during the summer of 1900, while laying over in Willcox he became drunk and it is reported that he made war talk against Johnny Boyett, who "heeled" himself and, meeting Warren on the street later, shot him. On account of the drunken threats made by Warren, a coroner's jury exonerated Boyett on the grounds of self defense.

In the preliminary examination beginning October 29th, 1881, following the Earp-Clanton fight at the O. K. Corral on October 26th, Sheriff Behan testified that Frank McLowery had told him that he and his gang would not give up their guns unless the Earps and Doc Holliday would do the same, as he anticipated trouble. He was standing in the street, holding his horse, at the time and assured Behan that he did not want any fight.

Sheriff Behan saw the Earps coming and met them, at the same time telling them that he was there for the purpose of disarming the Clantons and McLowerys but they paid no attention to him but went right on until they met the Clantons just inside of the entrance of the O. K. Corral.

Billy Clanton told him that he did not want to fight and Tom McLowery threw open his coat to show that he was unarmed. Frank McLowery and Billy Clanton appeared to be the only ones who were armed.

W. C. Claibourne testified that while he was talking to Billy Clanton, Johnny Behan walked up the street and then the Earps and Doc Holliday appeared; That Virgil Earp walked up to the Clantons and addressed them in a vile manner, adding, "You have been looking for a fight and now you can get it, throw up your hands." Ike and Billy Clanton and Frank McLowery put up their hands and Tom McLowery took hold of the lapels of his coat and pulled his coat open and back and showed them that he was unarmed.

Claibourne further testified that Doc Holliday and Morgan Earp then fired, the former dropping Tom McLowery and the latter getting Billy Clanton as he had his hands in the air and saying, "Don't shoot me, I don't want to fight."

Sheriff Behan then took Billy Claibourne and placed him in Fly's photograph gallery and instructed him to stay there. While in the photograph gallery a bullet came through the wall and passed through his pant's leg. Claibourne stated that he was not one of the gang at all and his story was substantiated by the survivors of the gang. He said that he was talking to the Clantons and that all they were talking about was "going home," that Billy Clanton and Frank McLowery were the only ones armed. Billy Claibourne is the man whom Wyatt Earp refers to as Billy Clayton.

W. A. Cuday testified that he heard Ike Clanton tell Sheriff Behan, "They will have no trouble with us, Johnny; we are going to leave town now." He passed on and shortly afterwards the shooting began and that when he went back he saw the dead bodies and heard Behan say to Wyatt Earp, "I will have to arrest you," and Wyatt Earp replied, "No man can arrest me now," then added, "We had to do it and you threw us Johnny; you told us that they were disarmed," Behan said that he was not afraid to arrest Wyatt Earp and Earp said that as soon as the excitement was over that he was willing to be arrested.

B. H. Fallehy testified, "I heard some stranger ask Ike Clanton what the trouble was and Ike replied, 'There will be no trouble.' Ike then went into Dolan's Saloon. I then looked over to where the Marshal and the Sheriff were talking and heard the Sheriff ask the Marshal, 'What's the trouble?' The Marshal replied, 'Those men have made their threats and I will not arrest them, but will kill them on sight.'

"I then crossed the street and saw three Earps and Doc Holliday walking in a bunch down Fourth Street toward Fremont. When the shooting started, Doc Holliday was in the middle of the street and Virgil Earp about three feet from the side walk and both men were shooting at a man who was standing behind a horse. They also fired at a man who ran by on the opposite side of the street; then the man who was holding the horse let go, staggered and fell; he still had his pistol when he fell.

"I did not see the two older Earps and did not know where they were located. I went to the man who fell and picked up his revolver which was laying about five feet from where he fell. Man never spoke, but moved his lips. Then Doc Holliday came running up and applied a vile epithet to the dying man, said, 'He has shot me and I mean to kill him.' I could not say who fired the first shots."

Ike Clanton testified that he saw the whole shooting. That night before the killing, he went into the lunch room of the Occidental Saloon and while in there, Doc Holliday came in and raised a row with him, calling him vile names and abusing him, having his hand on his gun all of the time and telling Ike to pull his gun. Ike informed him that he had no gun.

Ike Clanton further stated that Morgan Earp was standing behind Holliday and that they both cursed and abused him and that when he turned to go out of the door he met Virgil and Wyatt Earp and that Morgan then said to him, "If you want to fight, turn yourself loose." He again told them that he was not armed and Doc Holliday then applied a vile name to him and said, "Go and arm yourself." He did so and when he returned he saw Virgil Earp, Tom McLowery and some others playing poker and Virgil Earp had his gun in his lap.

They played poker until daylight and when the game

broke up, Virgil took his gun and slipped it inside of the waistband of his pants. Ike had sat in the game also and when the game broke up, he followed Virgil and informed him that he had been cursed and abused the night before and that he was still in town. Ike cashed in his chips and stayed around until 8 or 9 o'clock of the morning of October 26th.

He further stated that Virgil and Morgan Earp slipped up and disarmed him and a short time later he met his brother Billy and they decided to go home; that just then they met the man who had their team and as they were ready to go, the Sheriff came up and told them that he would have to arrest them and take their guns. He told the Sheriff that he had no gun on and that they were going home. The Sheriff then told Billy to go to his office and leave his gun and Billy told him that they were just leaving town. The Sheriff then told Frank and Tom McLowery to take off their guns and Tom opened his coat and showed him that he had no gun on, and Frank told him that he was going right home but would disarm if the Earps would do the same, that he had some business that he would like to transact which would only take him a few minutes and he would then be ready to go.

Ike Clanton went on to testify that just then, Doc Holliday and the Earps appeared on the scene and the Sheriff stepped out to meet them telling them that he had the party in charge, but they walked right on by him.

Ike says that he stepped out and that Wyatt Earp pointed his six-shooter at him and said, "Throw up your hands." The Marshal, (Virgil Earp), then told the other boys to throw up their hands, and Frank McLowery and Billy Clanton threw up their hands and Tom McLowery threw open his coat to show them that he was unarmed and some one of the gang, prefacing his remarks with a vile appelation, said, "You came here to make a fight," at the same time Doc Holliday and Morgan Earp shot. Morgan's bullet struck Billy Clanton but he does not know who Holliday's bullet struck. He saw Virgil Earp shooting too. He grabbed Wyatt Earp and pushed him around a corner and as he ran into Fly's photograph gallery he looked back and saw Billy Clanton fall, and then he got away.

He stated that all of the boys threw up their hands when ordered to do so, except Tom McLowery, who opened his coat to show them that he was unarmed; that he and the Earps had trouble over some business transaction but that there was no trouble between them and any of the rest of the gang.

He said that the Earps had met Billy Clanton fifteen minutes earlier, shook hands with him and remarked that they were glad to meet him; that they did not expect any attack as they had already disarmed him; did not know whether Doc Holliday or Morgan Earp had fired the first shot; after Sheriff Behan had ordered them to give up their arms and they informed him that they were leaving town, did not think that they were under arrest as Behan had said it was all right if they left town.

Mrs. M. J. King testified that she stepped into Bauer's meat market to get some meat and that every body in the market appeared to be excited and no one offered to wait on her. When she asked what was the matter, she was informed that there was going to be a fight between the Earps and the cowboys. She then stepped to the door and right back again and then some one said, "There they come," and she saw Doc Holliday and three other men coming down the street. Doc Holliday had a gun, (probably meaning a shot gun), under his coat. As they neared the cowboys, one of the three men who were with Holliday, and walking on the outside of the walk, said, "Let them have it," Holliday said, "All right." Believing that shooting would ensue, she ran back inside of the meat market just as the shooting began.

R. J. Coleman testified, "I saw the arrest of Ike Clanton in the morning before the shooting took place. Marshal Earp went up behind him and grabbed his gun and then there was a scuffle and Clanton fell. Didn't see Earp hit him but did see Earp have a six shooter but do not know whether he had taken it from Clanton or not.

"Clanton was taken to the police station and after his

trial was over, Marshal Earp offered him his rifle but Clanton would not take it. They had some words, during which I heard Clanton say, "All I want is four feet of ground.' Soon after this, I was standing in front of the O. K. Corrall and saw two Clantons and two McLowerys standing and talking in a stall in Dunbar's Corral. In a few minutes they came out and crossed the street into the O. K. Corral.

"Billy Clanton was riding his horse and Frank McLowery was leading his. As they passed me, Billy Clanton said to me, 'Where is the West End Corral?' I told him where it was and he passed on into the corral and I went on up Allen Street.

"When opposite the Headquarters Saloon I met Sheriff Behan and told him he should go and disarm the men, that I thought they meant mischief. I soon after met Marshal Earp and told him the same thing. I then walked down Allen Street again and passed through the O. K. Corral, where I saw the Clantons and the McLowerys talking with Sheriff Behan and I heard one of them say, 'You need not be afraid of us Johnny, we will not make any trouble.'

"Billy Clanton had his horse with him. I then turned and went up Fremont Street. When I got as far as Bauers' Butcher Shop, I met Virgil, Morgan, and Wyatt Earp and Doc Holliday, walking down the center of the street. Sheriff Behan walked up to them and said, 'I don't want you to go any further.' I don't think that they made any reply, but passed on down the street until they came opposite the Clanton party.

"The Earp party addressed them and I heard vile language passed out but do not know who was doing the talking. Some one of the Earp party then said, 'Throw up your hands,' or 'Give up your arms!' I thought that I was too close and as I turned around I heard two shots, and then the firing became general.

"Ike Clanton ran up the street and through Fly's Gallery. I think that there were two shots fired at him. After the first two shots, Tom McLowery ran down Fremont Street and fell. Billy Clanton stood in the same position as when I first saw him; I saw him fire two or three shots while in a crouching position, one of which hit Morgan Earp, who stumbled or fell. He jumped up again and commenced shooting.

"About that time, Frank McLowery came out in the street toward Doc Holliday, and some words passed between them. Frank said, 'I've got you now,' firing a shot at the same time, which struck Holliday on hip or scabbard. I helloed at Holliday, saying, 'You've got it now.' He answered, 'Yes, I am shot through.' Frank then passed across the street and fell.

"I think that Billy Clanton must have been struck but he was down in a crouching position, using his pistol across his knee and fired two shots, one of which struck Marshal Earp. Wyatt and Morgan were still firing at him, then he raised himself up and fell, still holding his pistol in his hand.

"After the shooting I heard Sheriff Behan and Wyatt Earp talking and Behan said, 'I ought to arrest you,' and Wyatt said, 'I won't be arrested; you deceived me Johnny when you said that they were not armed; I won't be arrested, but am here to answer for what I have done, I am not going to leave town.'

"I could not tell from where I was whether they threw up their hands or not, except Billy Clanton, who had his hand on his pistol which was in the scabbard, I can't swear how many Clantons were armed; don't think that Ike was. Can't say that I saw a shot-gun. Don't think that Billy Clanton was shot until after the two first shots. Don't think that he was hit until after he had shot. Did not see Tom McLowery have a pistol. My impression is that he started to run to get away from the shooting."

Coroner H. M. Matthews then testified that he had examined the bodies of the three dead men and that William Clanton came to his death from bullet wounds, one through the lungs and one beneath the 12th rib. That Frank McLowery had come to his death from bullet wounds, one shot just under one ear and one through the abdomen. Tom McLowery had come to his death as the result of receiving twelve buckshot in right side of body.

Sheriff Johnny Behan then testified that he was acquainted with John H. Holliday, Wyatt, Virgil, Morgan Earp, Tom McLowery, Frank McLowery and William Clanton. That at about half past one or two o'clock p. m. of October 26th, 1881, as he was sitting in a barber shop, being shaved, that someone said that there was liable to be a fight between the Clantons and the Earps. That there was considerable said and he asked the barber to hurry up and get through as he intended going out to disarm or arrest the parties; that when the barber had finished shaving him, he passed out of the shop and crossed over to Hafford's Corner, where he saw Marshal Earp standing and asked him what was the excitement and he replied that there were a lot of unprintably described individuals in town looking for a fight.

Behan advised Marshal Earp to go and disarm them as that was his duty as city marshal and he replied that he would not, as he wanted them to have a chance to make a fight, also that Marshal Earp then had a shot gun.

Behan then walked down Fourth Street to Fremont where he met Frank McLowery and informed him that he would have to disarm him as there was liable to be trouble in town. Frank told him that he would not give up his arms as he did not intend having any trouble. Behan then told him that he would have to give up his gun, (meaning his six shooter), and they walked on down the street to where Ike, Billy Clanton, Tom McLowery and Billy Claibourne were standing and said, "Boys, you have got to give up your guns." Frank McLowery objected, saying, "I do not want to give up my arms unless the other party is disarmed." Ike said that he was not armed and was searched then and there by Sheriff Behan who found no arms on him. Tom McLowery opened his coat and showed Behan that he was not armed either.

Billy Claibourne stated that he was not one of the party and his statement was corroborated by the other four men. He said that he was going home.

Behan then told them to go to his office and stay there until he came as he was going to disarm the other party; then, seeing the Earps and Doc Holliday coming down Fremont Street, he told the Clantons and the McLowerys to wait there. He walked up and met the Earps in front of Bauer's Meat Market and told them they should go no further, that he was down there for the purpose of disarming and arresting the Clantons and the McLowerys. They paid no attention to him and started to pass on when he threw up his hand and said, "Go back! I am sheriff of this county and I am not going to allow any trouble if I can help it." They brushed on by him and he followed them, trying to get them to turn back, but they kept on until they met the Clanton and McLowery Boys just inside of the entrance of the O. K. Corral.

As they met, one of the Earp party said, prefacing his remark with vile and indecent language, "You have been looking for a fight and now you can have it." Then followed an order for them to throw up their hands. Billy Clanton said, "Don't shoot me, I don't want to fight." At the same time Tom McLowery threw open his coat to show them that he was unarmed and then the firing commenced, by the shots from the Earp party.

Sheriff Behan states that he saw Frank McLowery staggering and holding his left hand over his stomach and his gun in his right hand, saw him shoot at Morgan Earp but the bullet went into the ground, short. He fired two shots at Morgan Earp and then started across the street. Heard two shots from that direction but did not know who fired them, but as Clanton fell on his head, heard Morgan say, "I got him."

Behan stated that Frank McLowery and Billy Clanton appeared to be the only ones of the Clanton bunch who were armed. Ike ran away; could not say as to where he was going, but appeared to be wanting to get away very badly. Doc Holliday carried a shot-gun under his coat. Stated positively that Ike Clanton and Tom McLowery were not armed as he had just searched them.

Andy Mehan stated that Tom McLowery left his gun in his saloon between one and two o'clock that afternoon and that he had placed it in his safe and that it had been there ever since.

Westley Fuller testified that when the Earp party met the Clanton party, that some one of the Earp party said, "Throw up your hands," and that Billy Clanton threw up his hands and said, "Don't shoot me, I do not want any fight," that the Earp party opened up by firing two shots almost together.

He further testified that Frank McLowery was standing, holding his horse, and did not have any gun in his hands, but did, later, pull his gun and shoot, after seven or eight shots had been fired by the Earps and Holliday. That each and every one of the Earp party was armed. That Morgan Earp and Doc Holliday fired the first two shots but as the shots were fired very close together, he could not tell which one of them fired the first one.

Billy Claibourne testified and corroborated all events leading up to the shooting and stated that Doc Holliday and Morgan Earp fired the first shots, Doc Holliday shooting at Tom McLowery and Morgan Earp at Billy Clanton. That Tom McLowery staggered back and Billy Clanton fell up against the corner of a building and then laid down and that, after six or eight shots had been fired, he drew his six-shooter and, resting it across his arm, began shooting. That Frank McLowery did not pull his gun until six or eight shots had been fired by the Earp party.

Claibourne further testified that Morgan Earp and Billy Clanton were both at the same corner of a house, one on each side, and that they were only about three feet apart and that Morgan Earp, placing the muzzle of his six-shooter within a foot of Billy's breast, pulled the trigger. Claibourne said that a stray bullet cut his pant's leg at the knee and then Behan took him and placed him in Fly's Photograph Gallery and instructed him to stay there.

Billy Claiborne also stated that he saw Sheriff Behan search Ike Clanton and Tom McLowery and that they had no guns on them. Claiborne in his summary of shots, stated that the first shot was fired by Doc Holliday, the

second by Morgan Earp and the next three shots by some
of the Earps.

J. H. Halliman, a saloon keeper, testified that Ike Clanton had left both his Winchester and six shooter in his saloon some time before the fight.

Ike Clanton's testimony corroborated all events leading
up to the fight and that when the Earps came up to them
inside the O. K. Corral gate, both Wyatt and Virgil Earp
applied vile names to them and one of them said, "You have
been looking for a fight and now you can have it."

As they threw up their hands, Morgan Earp and Doc
Holliday fired two shots and Frank McLowery had his
hands in the air when Morgan Earp shot him and that Billy
Clanton had his hands up when Doc Holliday shot him.
Also that Tom McLowery was holding his coat open to
show them that he was unarmed as Virgil Earp had taken
his guns and put them behind the bar in the Grand Saloon.
Clanton then identified the Winchester and six shooter as
being the property of Tom McLowery.

Ike Clanton further testified that in the early morning
of the day of the fight, Virgil Earp had walked up behind
him and struck him over the head with his six shooter,
knocking him against the wall of a house, and that Virgil
and Morgan Earp had taken his guns away from him and
taken him to Judge Williams' office, cursing him all of the
time; that he was fined and released at about 10 a. m. of
that date.

J. H. Bacher testified that on the day of the fight, October 26th, 1881, he saw Wyatt Earp strike Tom McLowery over the head with his six shooter after they had met
and talked a while and had heard Tom assure Wyatt that
he had always been his friend and had never done anything
against him, but said, "If you want to fight, I am with you."
Then Earp pulled his gun and said, "Are you heeled?"
Could not hear what Tom said, but Earp struck him first
with the palm of his left hand and then across the head
with his six shooter. Tom fell down and Earp walked away.

A. Bauer also testified to the foregoing statement of J.

H. Bacher and added that when Wyatt Earp asked Tom McLowery if he was heeled, that Tom had replied, "No, I am not." Thomas Keefe also corroborated the foregoing statement in full.

Wyatt Earp then testified that he was 32 years of age on the 19th day of March, 1881 and that he had come to Tombstone December, 1879. That he had put up a job with Ike Clanton to get Leonard, Crane and Head, the three men who attempted to hold up a stage near Fairbanks in which Bud Philpot was killed, and who were then at Eureka Springs, New Mexico. That Ike was to lure them to Soldiers' Hole, near the McLowery Ranch where a posse would be waiting for them.

Ike was to tell the outlaw gang that there was shortly to be made a paymaster trip from Tombstone to Bisbee with money to pay off the miners and that they could easily get the money. Joe Hill was the messenger who was sent to confer with the outlaws. He returned and informed Ike that they were too late, that Leonard and Head had been killed by a bunch of horse thieves the day before he had reached their camp. The horse thieves were later killed by the Clantons and McLowerys.

Wyatt Earp further testified that he and his brother Morgan had assisted in the arrest of Stilwell and Spence, who were alleged to have held up and robbed the Bisbee stage, and that this act had so angered Frank McLowery that when he met Morgan Earp on the streets of Tombstone a few days later, he said to him, "If you ever come after me, you will never get me." Morgan informed him that if he ever wanted him that he would surely get him. McLowery replied, "I have threatened you boys' lives and a few days ago I took it back, but since the arrest (of Stilwell and Spence) it now goes."

Earp also testified that he met Ike Clanton in the Eagle Brewery in Eagle Gulch and that Ike had said that this fight talk had been going on too long and that in the morning he would have man for man and the fight business would come to a close. That Ike walked away saying, "I will be ready for all of you tomorrow morning."

The following morning he and his brother Virgil arrested Ike Clanton, whom he claimed was around with a Winchester and a six shooter looking for them. That they took him before Judge Wallace who fined him for carrying concealed weapons. That while they were in the court room waiting for Judge Wallace to come in, Ike had said to him, "I'll get even with you for this. If I had a six shooter I would make a fight now with all of you." Morgan Earp then replied, "If you want to make a fight right bad, I'll give you this," at the same time offering him his (Ike's) own six shooter. Clanton started to take it but Deputy Sheriff Campbell interfered and the fight talk was ended.

Wyatt stated that after Ike Clanton had paid his fine and had been released, that he (Wyatt) had walked out of the court room and met Tom McLowery who said to him, "If you want to make a fight, I will make a fight with you anywhere." And that he (Wyatt) had replied, "All right, make a fight right here," at the same time slapping Tom in the face with his left hand and drawing his gun with his right. McLowery had his gun in plain sight but made no attempt to draw it, that he (Wyatt) struck him over the head with his six shooter and then walked on down the street.

That he (Wyatt Earp) walked down Fourth Street, stepped into Hafford's and bought a cigar. Saw Tom and Frank McLowery and Billy Clanton in a gun store where they were joined by Ike Clanton and that they were changing the cartridges in their belts.

Wyatt Earp continued his testimony by saying that Virgil Earp was city marshal, that he (Wyatt Earp) was deputy city marshal and Morgan Earp was special police. That he (Wyatt) had been sworn in as deputy city marshal to act as city marshal during Virgil's absence from Tombstone serving as a witness in the Stilwell and Spence case which was being tried in Tucson and then went on to say that the Clantons and McLowerys came out of the gun store and went on down to Dunbar's Corral and that parties had come to him and told him that the Clanton-McLowery outfit were out for trouble.

Virgil said to Wyatt and Morgan that they had better go down to the corral and disarm these men. Morgan said, "They have horses, had we not better get horses ourselves so that if we have a running fight we can catch them?" but that he (Wyatt) replied, "No, if they try to make a running fight of it, we can kill their horses and capture them."

Wyatt Earp concluded his testimony by stating that he was city marshal of Dodge City, Kansas, from some time in 1876 until December 1st, 1879, and that he was a member of the Wichita, Kansas, police force from 1874 until 1876.

Bob Hatch, Ned Boyle, J. E. Kelly and H. S. Sills testified that Ike Clanton was not armed just previous to the fight, Boyle having testified that Ike Clanton had on his six-shooter at 8:00 a. m. of the date of the fight and that he had said that just as soon as the Earps and Doc Holliday showed up on the streets, the ball would open. That he went to Wyatt Earp's house and told him what Ike had said and then he went home and went to bed.

Many other witnesses were examined but their testimony was only a re-hash of what had already been offered. On November 30, after a thirty days' session, court was adjourned and Judge Spicer set about reviewing the evidence and drafted his decision which was delivered to the public on the following day.

Judge Wells Spicer in the case of The Territory of Arizona vs. Wyatt Earp, et al., rendered the following decision:

"Defendants Wyatt Earp and John H. Holliday; two of the defendants named in the above entitled action were arrested upon a warrant issued by me on the 29th day of October, 1881, on a charge of murder.

"The complaint filed, upon which the warrant was issued, accuses said defendants of the murder of William Clanton, Frank M. McLowery and Tom McLowery on the 26th day of October, 1881, at Tombstone, in this (Cochise) county."

"The case has now been on hearing for the past 30 days, during which time a volume of testimony has been taken and legal talent employed on both sides.

"The great importance of the case, as well as the general interest taken in it by the entire community, demands that I should be full and explicit in my findings and conclusions, and give ample reasons for what I do.

"From the mass of evidence before me, much of which is upon collateral matters, I have found it necessary, for the purpose of decision, to consider only those facts which are conceeded by both sides or are established by a large preponderance of testimony. Viewing it in this manner, I find that on the morning of the 26th day of October, 1881, and up to noon of that day, Joseph I. Clanton, or Isaac Clanton, the prosecuting witness in this case, was about the streets and in several saloons of Tombstone, armed with Winchester rifle and revolver, declaring publicly that the Earp Brothers and Doc Holliday had insulted him the night before, when he was unarmed, and now that he was armed, he intended to shoot or fight them on sight.

"These threats were communicated to defendants Virgil Earp and Wyatt Earp. Virgil was at that time Chief of Police of Tombstone and charged, as such officer, by the City Ordinances, with the duty of preserving the peace and of arresting, with or without warrant, all persons engaged in any disorderly act whereby any breach of the peace might be occasioned and to arrest and disarm all persons violating the City Ordinances which declare it to be unlawful to carry on the person any deadly weapon within the city limits without first obtaining a permit in writing.

"Shortly after noon of October 26th, 1881, the defendant, Virgil Earp, as Chief of Police, assisted by Morgan Earp, who was at that time a special policeman in the pay of the city, and wearing his badge, arrested said Isaac Clanton and, in such arrest and disarmament, inflicted upon the side of his head a blow from a pistol. Whether the blow was necessary or not is not material here to determine. Isaac Clanton was then taken to justice, or Recorder Wallace, where he was fined and his arms, consisting of a revolver and Winchester rifle, were taken from him and deposited at the Grand Hotel, subject to his order.

"While in Justice Wallace's Court and awaiting the coming of Judge Wallace, some hot words passed between Isaac Clanton and Wyatt Earp, Earp accusing Clanton of having previously threatened to take his life, and then proposing to make a fight with him anywhere, to which Isaac Clanton assented, and then declared, 'Fight is my racket,' and that when he was arrested and disarmed, if Earp had been a second later, 'There would have been a coroner's inquest in town.'

"Immediately subsequent to this, a difficulty occurred in front of Judge Wallace's court room between Wyatt Earp and the deceased, Tom McLowery, in which the latter was struck by the former, with a pistol, and knocked down. In view of these controversies between Wyatt Earp and Isaac Clanton and Tom McLowery and, in further view of the quarrel of the night before, between Isaac Clanton and J. H. Holliday, I am of the opinion that the defendant, Virgil Earp, as chief of police, by subsequently calling upon Wyatt Earp and J. H. Holliday to assist him in arresting and disarming the Clantons and McLowerys, committed an injudicious and censurable act, and although in this he acted incautiously and without proper circumspection, yet when we consider the condition of affairs incident to a frontier country; the lawlessness and disregard for human life; the existence of a law defying element in our midst; the feeling of insecurity that has existed; the supposed prevalence of bad, desperate and reckless men who have been a terror to the country and kept away captial and enterprise, and considering the many threats that have been made against the Earps, I can attach no criminality to his unwise act. In fact, as the result plainly proves, he needed the support and assistance of staunch and true friends upon whose courage, coolness and fidelity he could depend in case of an emergency.

"Soon after the conclusion of proceedings in Judge Wallace's Court, Isaac Clanton and Thomas McLowery were joined by William Clanton and Frank McLowery, who had arrived in town. In the afternoon these parties went into a gun shop where they were seen by Wyatt Earp, who reported same to Virgil Earp, Chief of Police, said Wyatt Earp at the time being a sworn policeman. After this, the Clantons went to the Dexter Stables, on Allen Street, and shortly after, crossed the street to the O. K. Corral and passed through to Fremont Street. With what purpose in view they crossed through to Fremont Street will probably never be known.

"It is claimed by the prosecution that their purpose was to leave town. It is asserted by the defendants that their purpose was to make an attack upon them, or at least to feloniously resist any attempt to arrest or disarm them that might be made by the Chief of Police or any of his assistants.

"Whatever their purpose may have been, it is clear to my mind, that Virgil Earp, the chief of police, honestly believed, (and from information of threats that day given him, his belief was reasonable), that their true purpose was, if not to attempt the death of himself and brothers, to at least resist with force of arms, any attempt on his part to perform his duty as a peace officer by arresting and disarming them.

"At this time, Virgil Earp was informed by one E. A. Sills, who had arrived in town only the day before and was totally unacquainted with any persons in town, or the state of affairs existing therein, that he (Sills) had overheard armed parties, just then passing through the O. K. Corral, say, in effect, that they would make sure to kill Earp, the marshal, and would kill all of the Earps. At the same time, several citizens and a committee of citizens came to Virgil Earp, the city marshal, and insisted that he should perform his duty as an officer, and arrest and disarm these cowboys, as they termed the Clantons and McLowerys.

"Was it for Virgil Earp, as chief of police, to abandon his clear duty as an officer because his performance was likely to be fraught with danger? Or was it not his duty that, as such officer, he owed to the peacable and law abiding citizens of the city, who looked to him to preserve peace and order and their protection and security, to at once call to his aid sufficient assistance to proceed to arrest and disarm these men?

"There can be but one answer to these questions, and that answer is such as will divert the subsequent approach of the defendants toward the deceased of all presumption of malice and illegality. When, therefore, the defendants, regularly or specially appointed officers, marched down Fremont Street to the subsequent scene of the homicide, they were going where it was their right and duty to go; they were doing what was their right and duty to do; they were armed, as it was their right and duty to be armed, when approaching men whom they believed to be armed and contemplating resistance. The legal character of this homicide must, therefore, be determined by what occurred at the time and not by the precedent facts.

"To constitute the crime murder there must be proven, not only the killing, but the felonious intent. In this case the corpus delicti or fact of killing, is in fact admitted, as will be clearly proven. The felonious intent is as much to be proven as the corpus delicti, and in looking over the mass of testimony for evidence upon this point, I find that it is anything but clear .

"Witnesses of credibility say that each of the deceased, or at least two of them, yielded to a demand to surrender. Other witnesses of equal credibility testify that William Clanton and Frank McLowery met the demand for surrender, by drawing their pistols, and that the discharge of firearms from both sides was almost instantaneous.

"There is a dispute as to whether Thomas McLowery was armed at all, except with a Winchester rifle that was on the horse beside him. I will not consider this question because it was not of controlling importance. Certain it was, that the Clantons and McLowerys had among them, at least two six shooters in their hands and two Winchester rifles on their horses. If Thomas McLowery was one of the party who was thus armed and making felonious resistance to an arrest, and in the melee that followed, was shot, the fact of his being unarmed, if it be a fact, could not of itself incriminate the defendants, if they were not otherwise criminal.

"It is beyond doubt that William Clanton and Frank McLowery were armed, and made such quick and effective use of their arms as to seriously wound Morgan Earp and Virgil Earp.

"In determining the important question of whether the deceased offered to surrender before resisting, I must give as much weight to the testimony of persons unacquainted with the deceased, as to the testimony of persons who were companions and acquaintances, if not partisans of the deceased, and I am of the opinion that those who observed the conflict from a short distance and point of observation that gave them a good view of the same, to say the least, were quite as likely to be accurate in their observations as those mingled up in, or fleeing from the melee.

"Witnesses for the prosecution state unequivocally that William Clanton fell, or was shot at first fire, and Claibourne says, was shot when the pistol was only about a foot from his belly. Yet, it was clear that there were no powder burns or marks on his clothes and Judge Lucas says he saw him fire, or in the act of firing, several times before he was shot, and he thinks two shots afterwards.

"Addie Boland, who saw distinctly the approach of the Earps and the beginning of the affray from a point across the street where she could correctly observe all their movements, says she cannot tell who fired first; that the firing commenced at once from both sides upon the approach of the Earps, and that no hands were held up; that she would have seen them if there had been.

"Sills asserts that the firing was almost simultaneous, he

cannot tell which side fired first.   Considering all the testimony together, I am of the opinion that the weight of evidence sustains and corroborates the testimony of Wyatt Earp
and Virgil Earp, that their demand for a surrender was met
by William Clanton and Frank McLowery drawing,   or
making motions to draw their pistols.   Upon this hypo-
thesis my duty is clear.   The defendants were officers charged with the duty of arresting and disarming brave and determined men who were experts in the use of firearms, as
quick as a thought and certain as death, and who had previously declared their intentions not to be arrested nor disarmed.   Under the Statutes, as well as the common law,
they had a right to repel force by force.

"In coming to this conclusion, I give great weight to
several particular circumstances connected with the affray.
It is claimed by the prosecution that the deceased were shot
while holding up their hands in obedience to the demand of
the Chief of Police, and on the other hand, the defense
claims that William Clanton and Frank McLowery at once
drew their pistols and began firing simultaneously with the
defendants.

"William Clanton was wounded on the wrist of the right
hand on the first fire, and thereafter used the pistol in his
left.   This wound is such that he could not have received
it with his hand thrown up, and the wound received by Tom
McLowery was such as could not have been received with
his hands on his coat lapels.   The circumstances being in-
dubitable facts, throw great doubt upon the correctness of
witnesses to the contrary.

"The testimony of Isaac Clanton that this tragedy was
the result of a scheme on the part of the Earps to assassinate him, and thereby bury in oblivion the confessions
the Earps had made to him about tipping off the shipment
of coin by Wells-Fargo & Co., falls short of being a sound
theory, because of the great fact being most prominent in
the matter, to-wit: That Isaac Clanton was not injured at
all, and could have been killed first and easiest.   If he had
been the object of attack, he would have been the first to

fall, but as it was, he was known, or believed to have been unarmed, and was suffered, so Wyatt Earp testified, to go away and was not harmed.

"I also give just weight in this matter to the testimony of Sheriff Behan, who said on one occasion, a short time ago, that Isaac Clanton told him that he had been informed that the Sheriff was coming to arrest him and that he had armed his crowd with guns and was determined not to be arrested by the sheriff, or words to that effect. And Sheriff Behan further testified that a few minutes before the Earps came to them that he, as sheriff, demanded of the Clantons and the McLowerys that they give up their arms and that they had 'demurred' as he said, and did not do it, and that Frank McLowery refused and gave as reason that he was not ready to leave town just then, and would not give up his arms until the Earps were disarmed, that is, that the Chief of Police and his assistants be disarmed.

"In view of the past history of this country and the generally believed existance of desperate, reckless men in our midst, banded together for mutual support, living by felonious and predatory pursuits, regarding neither life nor property in their career, and at this time for men to parade the streets, armed with repeating rifles and six shooters and demand that the Chief of Police of the city, and his assistants should be disarmed, is a proposition both monstrous and startling. This demand was made by one of the deceased only a few minutes before the arrival of the Earps.

"Another fact that rises up pre-eminent in the consideration of this sad affair, is the leading fact that the deceased from the very first inception of the encounter were standing their ground and fighting back, giving and taking death with unflinching bravery. It does not appear to have been a wanton slaughter of unresisting and unarmed innocents, who were yielding graceful submission to the officers of the law, or surrendering to, or fleeing from their assailants, but armed and defiant men, accepting the wage of battle and succumbing only to death.

"The prosecution claims much on this point, as they alleged that the Earps acted with criminal haste; that they precipitated the triple homicide by a felonious anxiety and a quickness to begin the tragedy; that they precipitated the killing with a malice aforethought, with the felonious intent then and there to murder the deceased and that they made use of their official character as a pretext.

"I cannot believe this theory, and cannot resist the firm conviction that the Earps acted wisely, discreetly and prudentially to secure their own self preservation; they saw at once the dire necessity of giving the first shot to save themselves from certain death. They acted; their shots were effective, and this alone saved all of the Earps party from being slain.

"In view of all these facts and circumstances of the case; considering the threats made, the character and position of the parties, and the tragical results accomplished in manner and form as they were, with all surrounding influences bearing upon the res gestae of the affair, I cannot resist the conclusion that the defendants were fully justified in committing these homicides, that it was a necessary act in the discharge of an official duty.

"It is the duty of an examining and commiting magistrate in this territory to issue a warrant of arrest in the first place, whenever from the depositions given them there is reasonable grounds to believe that the defendant has committed a public offense. After hearing the evidence, however, the Statute changes the rule, and he is then required to commit the defendant only when there is 'sufficient cause to believe' him guilty.

"My interpretation is, that the rule which should govern the examining magistrate is the same as that which governs the conclusion of a grand jury. That such is prescribed by Statute is: the grand jury ought to find an indictment when all of the evidence before them taken together is such as in their judgment will, if unexplained or uncontradicted, warrant a conviction by the trial jury.

"The evidence taken before me in this case would not, in my judgment, warrant a conviction by a trial jury, of any

offense whatever. I do not believe that any trial jury that
could be gotten together in this Territory would, on all the
evidence taken before me, with the rules of law applicable
thereunto given them by the court, find the defendants
guilty of any offense.

"It may be that my judgment is erroneous and my view
of the law, incorrect, yet it is my own judgment and my
understanding of the law as I find it laid down, and upon
these I must act and decide, and not upon those of any other
person. I have given over four weeks of patient attention
to the hearing of the evidence in this case, and at least four-
fifths of my working hours have been devoted all this time
to an earnest study of the evidence before me, and such is the
conclusion to which I am forced to arrive.

"I conclude the performance of the duty imposed upon
me by saying in the language of the Statute: 'There being
no sufficient cause to believe that the within named Wyatt
Earp and John H. Holliday guilty of the offense mentioned within, I order them released.'

"(Signed), WELLS SPICER,

"Magistrate."

JOHN H. HOLLIDAY, ALIAS
DOC HOLLIDAY

THE following information regarding Doc Holliday, one of Tombstone's gunmen de luxe, was given to the San Francisco Weekly Examiner by Wyatt Earp, who was probably better acquainted with him than any other man living today. The interview was published under date of August 6th, 1896, and the following is an abstract.

John H. (Doc.) Holliday was born in Virginia, probably about 1850. There is no available information regarding his social standing in his home state, but it is a well known fact that he was a man of excellent education and a dentist by profession. Unfortunately he developed lung trouble and, believing that a permanent residence in the southwest would assist in the arrest of his malady, he came to Ft. Griffin, Texas.

While sojourning at Ft. Griffin, he formed the acquaintance of Kate Fisher, better known around Ft. Griffin as Big Nose Kate. This acquaintance ripened into sincere friendship and upon state occasions, Doc would introduce her as Mrs. Doc Holliday.

Wyatt Earp, acting in the capacity of Deputy United States Marshal from Dodge City, having occasion to trail a bunch of cattle thieves through to Ft. Clark, passed through Ft. Griffin and made a brief stop there to rest up before pursuing his journey. Nearly all such journeys, at that time were made on horse back. It was while recuperating at Ft. Griffin that Wyatt Earp first met Doc Holliday and the meeting resulted in a staunch friendship between them until Doc's death and although Doc passed over many years ago, Wyatt Earp still reveres his memory as a real pal.

While Wyatt Earp was enroute from Ft. Griffin to Ft. Clark and return, Doc Holliday was seriously contemplating a move and the events of a poker game caused him to decide in a very speedy manner that the quicker he moved the better.

Doc, who was an inveterate gambler, was hopelessly entangled in the alluring meshes of a poker game with several

more men of similar inclinations. A man named Ed Bailey
was sitting on the right of Doc and insisted upon holding
post mortems over the deadwood and this, in the parlance
of the gambling fraternity is not only a discourteous act,
but a dangerous pastime, inasmuch as when a hand is thrown
into the deadwood it is so dead that it cannot be resurrected and flirting with the discard is positively prohibited
in all well regulated poker games.

Doc had advised Bailey several times to "play poker"
which, being translated into the plain unvarnished language
of the common people, means, "stop cheating." Bailey did
not pay any attention to these timely warnings but kept right
on disinterring dead hands and turning them face up and
making caustic comments upon their value or the manner in
which their owners had played them.

Finally there appeared upon the scene, a goodly pot and
all of the players dropped out but Doc Holliday and Bailey.
Inasmuch as Bailey had been fumbling the discard, Doc
reached out and garnered in the harvest without going
through the formality of showing down his hand, which
was playing good poker, according to poker etiquette. When
a man is caught trying to handle too many cards at one time
he forfeits his equity in the pot.

Bailey made an abortive attempt at getting his artillery in
action but Doc beat him to it by producing a knife of business
like dimensions, which he had concealed about his person
and, to use Doc's own words, he caught Bailey "just below
the brisket" with it and Bailey quickly lost all interest in
earthly poker games and had no use for discards where he
went.

It goes without saying that the poker game was broken
up right way. Doc was arrested by the city marshal and
placed in charge of two policemen to prevent a hundred or
more drink infuriated miners and gamblers from stretching
his neck after a manner not employed by chiropractors. Doc
had not been in Ft. Griffin very long and Bailey was a very
popular man among the crooked element and the situation
became exceedingly tense.

Big Nose Kate investigated the situation and decided that

quick action was absolutely necessary or she would lose her meal ticket. There was a horse stabled in a shed behind the hotel where they were holding Doc as prisoner. Kate, being a very kind hearted girl, took the horse out and tied him in the alley before setting fire to the shed. As the fire blazed up she shouted, "Fire! Fire!! Fire!!!," and everybody, except Doc's guards, rushed out to the fire.

Kate was armed with two six shooters and she walked boldly in and covered the officers before they realized what it all meant. Handing one of the six shooters to Doc, she said with a laugh, "Come on Doc." They backed out of the hotel, keeping the officers covered until clear of the door and then faded away into the darkness of the night. They remained in hiding among the willows all night and in the morning, a friend brought them two horses and some clothing which he had managed to sneak out of Doc's room.

Kate dressed in a suit of Doc's clothing and together they rode 400 miles to Dodge City, Kansas, and were there to greet Wyatt Earp upon his return from Ft. Clark. Doc Holliday, although a Virginian and possessed of the instincts and habits of the same, preferred to be a vagabond. Quoting the exact words of Wyatt Earp, "He was a philosopher, but preferred to be a wag. He was lean, long and an ash blonde and the quickest man with a gun that I ever knew."

Shortly after Doc's arrival in Dodge City, he chanced to save Wyatt's life. A man had sneaked up behind Wyatt's back with a drawn six shooter, but before he could use it Doc shouted, "Look out Wyatt," and, with a motion which baffled the eye, he pulled his gun and shot the would-be assassin dead. This friendly and timely act on the part of Doc, cemented the ties of friendship more strongly than ever between them.

In 1879 Doc and Big Nose Kate had decided to play quits and Kate departed for parts then unknown. Later in the year Wyatt and Doc decided to go to Tombstone, which at that time was just getting out of short dresses into pants. They came by way of Las Vegas, New Mexico, where they found Big Nose Kate and she and Doc soon patched up their differences of opinion and she accompanied them to Tombstone.

Doc Holliday reached Tombstone in due time, accompanied by Kate, his tuberculosis, an ever ready six shooter and a hair trigger temper. Seeming to realize that his days were numbered and that the back numbers were unobtainable, he appeared to be utterly devoid of fear, and when it came to gun fighting he enjoyed himself to the limit.

With Wyatt Earp as Deputy United States Marshal, Virgil Earp as City Marshal, and Morgan as an assistant, Doc always, when possible, made it a point to be present whenever there was any gun fighting to be done.

Doc Holliday was said to have been implicated in the Fairbanks stage robbery with Harry Head, Billy Leonard and Jim Crane. Bud Philpot was the stage driver on this occasion and Bob Paul was the shot-gun messenger or guard. Some one on the inside who had access to the information was tipping off the gold shipments to the wild bunch and stage holdups were of common occurrence whenever the picking was good.

Upon this particular trip Bob Paul changed places with Bud Philpot for the purpose of driving, as the day was cool, Philpot sitting back on top of the stage and acting as guard in place of Paul.

As they neared the spot about where the stage was usually held up, the masked bandits appeared and, according to custom shot the guard, as they supposed, but in fact it was Bud Philpot who was shot. Bob Paul, knowing of the unusually heavy shipment of gold aboard undertook to get himself an outlaw or two and in the melee which followed, dropped the reins of equine government and the horses, frightened at the shooting, ran away and did not stop until they reached Fairbanks. Although the outlaws pursued the stage for a considerable distance, Paul's defense, the speed of the horses and their proximity to Fairbanks, prevented them from splitting the $80,000 worth of gold four ways.

Harry Head alias Harry the Kid and Billy Leonard, after the foregoing event, believing that they had been recognized by Paul and that some form of retribution would surely follow, decided to change their range for a while. They went to Owl City, over in Grant County, New Mexico, and while there the Haslett Brothers ambushed them and killed them both.

Jim Crane made himself scarce and showed up in Hatchita where he undertook to show the natives over there how to play poker, but his best directed efforts in that direction failed to offset their winning ways and he was soon a financial wreck.

The only commodity obtainable in Hatchita without price, was whiskey or a fight. This being the case he got busy and tried to drink the town dry but failed, said failure causing him to become very peevish and hard to get along with, so he tried to pull the town apart to see what caused the big noise but met with much opposition and, having considerable of an alcoholic impediment in his draw, be fell for the town and remained a permanent fixture in Boot Hill.

Doc Holliday and Big Nose Kate lived more or less together as man and wife, until Kate became peeved at him to such an extent that she went before the District Attorney and spilled the beans as to how Doc Holliday was the one who shot Bud Philpot, thinking that he was shooting Bob Paul. On the strength of her information, a warrant was issued for the arrest of Doc Holliday on a charge of murder and he was arrested and given a preliminary hearing and bound over in a bond of $5,000 to appear for trial at the next term of District Court. Bond was promptly furnished and Doc was released from custody.

Shortly after the bond had been furnished, Kate once more went before the District Attorney and made sworn statement that at the time she filed the murder information against Doc, she was both drunk and mad and did not know what she was doing. She had no trouble in proving that she was drunk, so the murder charge against him was dropped.

Ike Clanton made a sworn statement later, that Doc Holliday had told him that he (Holliday) had shot Bud Philpot through the heart, believing him to have been Bob Paul, also that Holliday had offered him $6,000 to kill Billy Leonard, Harry Head and Jim Crane, the three men who had been with him in the stage holdup.

Doc Holliday departed Tombstone about the same time that Wyatt Earp and several of his friends did and it is supposed that they all went to Colorado together and then separated. The next that was heard of him was in Deadwood, Dakota. It is related that when he landed in that town, his initial act was to enter the first saloon he saw, in search of old friends, but that he found no one whom he knew.

He tarried there a short time after sampling some of Deadwood's most approved brand of "jig juice." During his delay in this drink emporium, the bar tender, a big coarse bulley, attempted to make a miner purchase a drink and when the miner mildly advised him that it was not yet his drink time, the bar tender reached down under the bar and came up with a six shooter in his hand, at the same time threatening to shoot the miner unless he purchased a drink. He further announced in loud and lurid language that the miner had insulted him and that he was going to shoot him anyway. He moved quickly but, before he could pull trigger, a shot rang out from the side of the bar-room and his six shooter fell to the floor. A timely and well placed shot through the wrist of the bad, bad man, permitted considerable of his bad, mad blood to escape. Doc Holliday had, by his quick gun play, saved the life of the miner.

A bunch of the tough citizens began to close in on the slender, sickly appearing man who stood with his back to the wall. During the momentary lull which usually preceeds a crisis, he remarked, "Gentlemen, my name is Doc Holliday and I'm from Tombstone." These few quietly spoken words had an electrical effect on the crowd and they began to apologize for horning in on his deal. The bartender apologized and Doc dressed his wounded wrist and the drinks were on the house.

Soon afterwards, Doc drifted back into Denver and it is reported that he spent some time in a sanitarium there and recovered his health to such an extent that he lingered along for several years and finally died at Glenwood Springs, Colorado.

At the time of his death, Doc Holliday was about 35 years of age and was credited with having killed 23 men.

BAT MASTERSON

W. H. (Bat Masterson was born in or near Danville, Illinois, in either 1854 or '55 and when he was about 16 years of age, his people moved to Kansas and settled on a farm about seven miles from Wichita. Evidently Bat did not take kindly to farming, so he attached himself to a bunch of buffalo hunters who were working the Panhandle Country and it is stated that he took active part in the Adobe Walls fight against hostile Comanche Indians in 1872.

In the spring of 1875, Bat became tired of buffalo hunting and drifted back into civilization once more and landed in Dodge City, being at that time about 21 years of age. At the time of Bat's arrival in Dodge City, Wyatt Earp was City Marshal and he appointed Bat as one of his assistants.

Wyatt Earp's famous organization of peace commissioners consisted of himself, Bat Masterson, Luke Short, W. H. Harris, W. H. Petillion, Neal Brown, Sam McNeil and Charlie Bassett, with changes from time to time, but these men were the principals of the organization and to them belongs the credit of making Dodge City a safe place in which to reside.

In the fall of 1876 Bat became a candidate for the office of sheriff and was elected. Even in those days, when boys were men, the office of sheriff was a heavy one for a young man of twenty-one, but he filled the office in a manner which reflected credit upon himself.

He came to Tombstone in the spring of 1881, but only remained about six or eight months and then returned to Dodge City and from there to Denver, where he remained for several years, then coming back to the middle west and from there further east and finally landing in New York City.

About the time that Bat landed in New York City, he met and became acquainted with President Roosevelt, who took a fancy to him and appointed him a deputy United States Marshal for that district, which position he successfully filled until Roosevelt was succeeded by William Taft

BAT MASTERSON, IN 1876

as chief executive of our nation and, as a general political change was made in the personnel of the United States Marshal's office, Bat was once more footloose.

His success as a federal officer in the New York District made Bat a very popular man and he accepted a position on the New York Morning Telegram as sporting editor, which position he held for seventeen years until his death, which occurred in 1926.

Bat passed away while sitting at his desk, as though asleep. His loss was keenly felt by the sporting world because he was known as a square shooter in all of his decisions and writeups.

It is stated upon good authority that in the execution of his duty as a peace officer, Bat accounted for the lives of 28 bad men.

W. H. Harris   Luke Short   Bat Masterson
Charley Bassett   Wyatt Earp   L. McLean   Neal Brown
DODGE CITY PEACE COMMISSIONERS IN EARLY '80'S

THE CLANTONS

THE·CLANTONS, posing as cattle buyers, had their headquarters at Charleston and the "gang" consisted ofOld Man Clanton, his sons, Ike, Phin and Billy, with Frank and Tom McLowery as able assistants, while the many others of the outlaw element threw in with them from time to time, forming a very formidable gang. This gang was usually referred to by the people in that locality, as the "Cowboy Gang." Curley Bill was the executive head, while John Ringo was the general manager and brains of the gang.

It has been stated that Old Man Clanton was killed in a fight with Mexican smugglers over in Skeleton Canon. It has also been stated that a survivor of the Mexican smuggler party, a boy of about 16, followed Old Man Clanton until he succeeded in ambushing him and shooting him at short range.

William Sparks of Globe, who was perhaps as well acquainted with the Clantons as any one else, says that Old Man Clanton was freighting over on the San Pedro River not far from Charleston and that he and the boy swamper who was with him, made camp one night, and in the early morning they were killed by a party of Mexicans from Old Mexico, who said that they were in pursuit of some horse thieves and thought that Old Man Clanton and the boy were the guilty men. They were shot as they lay rolled in their blankets. It is possible that this party of Mexicans may have been connected with the party of smugglers which Old Man Clanton and others of his gang wiped out over in Skeleton Canon some time before. Quien sabe?

Billy Clanton, Tom and Frank McLowery were all three killed in the Earp-Clanton fight at the O. K. Corrall on September 26th, 1881, the particulars of which event are recorded elsewhere in this book.

Soon after the death of Old Man Clanton and Billy, Ike went north and took up his residence in the Globe District where he continued to handle cattle. One day in 1887,

Deputy Sheriff Parnell, from Apache County, and a Cattle-mens' Association detective named Brighton, desiring to question Ike regarding some of his livestock transactions, went over on Eagle Creek to see him. They located him at Cy Wilson's cabin down on Lower Eagle Creek. Ike resented some of their insinuations regarding his truth and veracity and went for his gun. He did not start soon enough and Brighton beat him to it. Walter Fife and Warren Snow came along just as it was all over and buried him.

Soon after Ike's death, Phin Clanton was overtaken by the strong arm of the law and sent to the State Penitentiary for a term of years. His health was so poor in Yuma that Governor Zulick pardoned him. Phin went back to Globe and worked for the Old Dominion Mining Company long enough to get himself a stake, which he invested in a small bunch of cattle, married, settled down and made good. He died of heart disease in about 1908.

JOHN RINGO

JOHN RINGO, who was a second cousin of the Youngers of the well known Jesse and Frank James Gang, was a well educated man of excellent family and was credited with being the real brains of the wild bunch around Tombstone. He was a periodical drinker and these periods of debauchery were always followed by acute attacks of remorse. California was his native state and from there he drifted into Texas and took part in many of the cattle country feud wars which constituted the favorite out door sports of Western Texas during the '70's and early '80's. Ringo became so popular in Western Texas that when he left there, he headed a long procession out, consisting of the sheriff and several deputies. They sure did hate to see him leave there but he chanced to be riding a faster horse than any of the posse and he made good use of his mount.

Ringo landed in Tombstone just about the time that Cochise County was shaved off the eastern extremity of Pima County and turned over to the wild bunch to do as they pleased with. This was in '81, and Ringo threw in with the wild ones and soon became their acknowledged brains.

At one time Wyatt Earp, in his official capacity as Deputy United States Marshal, committed some act which particularly exasperated Ringo. The latter walked across the street in Tombstone one day and, facing the Earp party, challenged Wyatt Earp or Doc Holliday to step out into the street and shoot it out with him and settle the difficulty once for all.

It is stated that neither Wyatt Earp nor Doc Holliday accepted the challenge. Inasmuch as the nerve of neither one of these men had ever been questioned, it is not known by any one except themselves just why his challenge was not accepted by one of them. It is possible that there may have been some justification for his anger and they, realizing it, permitted the incident to pass unnoticed.

Upon one occasion, Ringo rode over to Galeyville to confer with Curly Bill, his able lieutenant, and while there inserted himself into a poker game which was in progress within the walls of the chief drink emporium of that robbers' roost. The Galeyville gang believed that when a stranger came to their town that they should take him in. They lived up to this Biblical advice and "took him in" and he was soon broke and talking to himself.

Ringo pondered over the situation for a minute and then produced his solid gold watch and handed it over to Kettle-bellied Johnson with a request that he advance him one hundred dollars upon it. Johnson refused and advised Ringo to go out and steal a bunch of cattle and then come back.

Ringo got up and left the room without having made any comment. He went to the corral, saddled his horse, led him out in front of the saloon, "tied him to the ground" and walked back into the saloon. No one paid any attention to him until he had walked back to the poker table and "thrown down" on the gang with a mild request that they elevate their hands high and quick. Knowing him as well as they did there was not the least hesitation in the execution of his command. He then gathered unto himself everything in sight and after calling them "a bunch of damned robbers," backed out of the room, mounted his horse and rode away. As this was a crooked game and the crooks knew it, there was no pursuit.

A few days later, Kettle-bellied Johnson rode over to Tombstone and, while narrating his hard luck to the entire universe, it came to the ears of the Law and Order League and they caught Johnson before he had a chance to get too drunk, and persuaded him to file the information against Ringo, charging him with the hold-up.

A warrant was issued and placed in the hands of Deputy Sheriff Billy Breckenridge, who rode over to where Ringo was camped, and informed him that he was under arrest on a charge of highway robbery. Breckenridge informed Ringo that as his horse was already tired and that he wanted to get back to Tombstone that night, that he (Ringo) would have to make haste in his preparations for the return trip.

Ringo told Breckenridge to go ahead, that he would

catch him at Sulphur Springs. Ringo was a man of his word
and he overtook Breckenridge right where he said he would
and they rode on into Tombstone together.

The Law and Order Party believed that with Ringo in
jail they could go to Charleston and get Curly Bill, who
was Ringo's lieutenant, and this would be a long step toward cleaning up the outlaw bunch; that, with the two head
men in jail, the balance of the bunch would break up and
drift out of the country.

It being late at night when Breakenridge and Ringo arrived in town, it was not possible for Ringo to arrange bail
that night so he was held in durance vile for a period of
about ten hours. He finally succeeded in getting in touch
with his attorney and it was then that he was informed of
the intention of the Law and Order League to go to
Charleston for the purpose of bringing back Curly Bill or
any of his henchmen with whom they came in contact and
did not kill.

Ringo believed that Curly Bill was equal to the occasion, if the Law and Order Party reached Charleston
early enough in the morning, before Bill had a chance to
get well started on his daily drunk. Ringo's attorney came
into Sheriff Behan's office and announced that all arrangements had been made for Ringo's bail. Everything had been
arranged for except the money. Behan, being an easy going officer, presuming that this formality was all that was
necessary and, as such proceedings had been in vogue for a
long time, he informed Ringo that he was free to go. In
the meantime, some friend had saddled Ringo's horse and
brought him to the Sheriff's office and Ringo lost no time
in missing himself from that immediate vicinity.

Some time later in the morning, the Law and Order
League to the number of about 50, so it is related, took their
departure from Tombstone with perfectly good intentions
and rpoceeded in the direction of Charleston. When they
reached the bridge which crossed the San Pedro River into
Charleston, they were met by just one man, who was stationed at the opposite end of the bridge, and that one man

was John Ringo. There were just six words spoken and they were spoken by Ringo when he said: "Come on, I'm waiting for you." That remark was evidently sufficient to cause the Law and Order Representatives to back up and they kept right on backing up until they once more reached Tombstone.

When Judge Stilwell came to the court house about the middle of the day, and informed Sheriff Johnnie Behan that he was ready to take up the matter of John Ringo's bail, this was the first intimation that Behan had received which would indicate that the district attorney had objected to the bail which had, apparently, been arranged for early that morning.

John Ringo was out and with his own gang and no bail money in sight. When Law and Order League arrived from Charleston and learned Johnny Behan's predicament they kept their secret as to the whereabouts of Ringo, and Judge Stilwell informed Sheriff Behan that he would be ready to take up the matter of Ringo's bail the following morning and that he would expect Ringo to be present in person.

That night more than fifty members of the Law and Order League, armed with guns and liquid enthusiasm, once more departed in the darkness for Charleston on the San Pedro. Charleston was the headquarters of the Clanton Boys who were at the head of the outlaw gang which was located at that place and governed by Curly Bill and John Ringo. Ringo and Curly Bill had been informed of this prospective move of the Law and Order League and prepared themselves by keeping every man who came into town during the day.

When the Law and Order party arrived at the San Pedro Bridge, confident that they would be able to cross the bridge and capture Ringo and Curly Bill, they found themselves surrounded by more outlaws than any of them had ever seen before in one bunch. Their arms were taken from them and they were herded across the bridge into Charleston, where they were taken into Charleston's most commodious drink emporium and invited to drink much and often;

this they did, fully believing in the old motto of "Safety First."

John Ringo learned of the tight position into which Sheriff Behan had wedged himself and, believing that if Behan lost out, Deputy Sheriff Billy Breakenridge would also lose out, he saddled his horse and rode back to Tombstone and quickly located Billy Breakenridge. As badly as he hated Behan, he smothered his hatred in order to do a favor for Billy Breakenridge, for whom he had formed a strong friendship.

The following morning when court was convened, many of Sheriff Behan's enemies were present for the purpose of witnessing his downfall. John Ringo walked into court and no one was more surprised than Sheriff Behan himself. Ringo's bond was arranged to the satisfaction of all parties concerned and he was released from custody.

Along in the afternoon the Law and Order Party came straggling in through the foothills from Charleston where they had been entertained all night under guard of Curly Bill and the rest of the gang under willing protest.

John Ringo was a marked man from that date, more than ever. Many of the Law and Order Party would have been glad to have heard of his death, but not one of them was possessed of sufficient nerve to take the responsibility of his death upon himself. Thus it was that John Ringo went his way, which passed many saloons which he never failed to patronize. His periods of debauchery became more frequent and of longer duration.

One hot summer's day, Deputy Sheriff Billy Breakenridge met John Ringo in the Middle Pass of the Dragoon Mountains. Ringo had been into Tombstone and was supplied with plenty of liquor. After exchanging commonplace greetings, Ringo offered Breakenridge a bottle, accompanied by an exceedingly pointed invitation to take a drink. Breakenridge, not wishing to anger him, took the bottle and pretended to take a drink and then handed the bottle back to Ringo who accepted it and, turning it up, drained it to the last drop and threw the bottle from him, with the remark, "Got another quart." He then rode on toward San Simon Valley.

The next that was heard of John Ringo was when Buckskin Frank Leslie rode into town and informed the authorities that he had met John Ringo and that they had fought it out and he had killed Ringo.

A party of officers at once went out and viewed the remains of John Ringo which they found, in the place described, the body seated on a rock between two small trees, away out in San Simon Valley, with a bullet hole between his eyes.

Sign readers stated that some distance out of Middle Pass, Ringo had dismounted, taken off his boots, tied them together, hung them over the saddle horn and lain down in the shade of some desert growth and gone to sleep. His horse strayed away and was later found at the Sulphur Springs Ranch, with the boots still tied to the saddle horn. When he awoke he walked for some distance in his sock-feet and then took off his shirt and wrapped his feet in pieces of it. This frail protection soon wore out and he discarded it in favor of his undershirt and wandered on until he came to the stone between the two trees where he was found.

A coroner's jury verdict rendered on the ground, stated that he had come to his death as the result of a self-inflicted wound. This reason was generally accepted as the cause of his demise, in spite of the very vehement declaration of Buckskin Frank Leslie that he was responsible for his death; that he met Ringo and Ringo had shot at him and missed and that he had shot and killed him. There was one empty shell in Ringo's six shooter.

Some state that the wound in Ringo's head was powder burned and there are still several witnesses living who declare that the wound was not powder burned. Be that as it may, there are only two people who knew how John Ringo came to his death and they are Ringo and Leslie, and both of them are dead.

A young boy named Billy Chadbourne, some times called Billy the Kid on account of his youth, attempted to assassinate Leslie and Leslie shot him. Chadbourne only lived a few minutes, but with his last breath he said: "Leslie shot John Ringo, for I was along with him and saw him do it."

WILLIAM GRAHAM ALIAS WILLIAM BROSCIUS ALIAS CURLEY BILL

WILLIAM GRAHAM, alais William Broscius, alias Curly Bill, who was known to have killed eight men, and claimed to have killed thirty-two, was one of the best known, best liked and worst feared man in the main outlaw gang. He always went after big game and never was known to take anything from any one who was not able to stand the loss. John Ringo was the brains of the Charleston Gang, which included the Clantons and Mc-Lowerys, but Curly Bill was the chief executive and supervised, more or less, all of the main camps which included Charleston, Galeyville and the old Hughes Ranch, and was always present when there was a transaction of any magnitude to be pulled off.

On one occasion, learning that there was a bunch of Mexican smugglers coming across the line, via Guadalupe and Skeleton Cañons, Bill took Old Man Clanton, Billy Clanton, Rattlesnake Bill, Frank McLowery, Tom McLowery and Jake Gauze out to receive them. They went over into the mouth of Skeleton Canon, just above where Ross Sloan's Ranch House now stands, lay in ambush behind the big rocks, and waited until the Mexicans appeared.

As the smuggler band came down the canon, Curly hastily assigned each man to a stand which would cover as much territory as possible. He instructed his men not to fire a single shot until he had fired the signal shot and then one man was to take the first man, another was to take the second and another one the third and so on down the line, and then all join in on the chorus and kill those who were left.

Bill rode boldly down into the bed of the cañon and turned up the canon and met the gang. He, being a lone horseman, did not excite their suspicions and as he could talk their language fluently, he chatted a bit with the captain of the smuggler band and rode on, greeting each man in his own language as he met him, until he reached the last man, when he fired the signal shot and the last man fell from his horse, dead.

In less time than it takes to tell it the Mexican smugglers, who were taken by surprise, were all mowed down by the withering fire of the outlaw gang. One 16-year old boy was the only survivor and he escaped by hiding behind the rocks up on the side of the canon.

In those days it was not uncommon for outlaws to talk openly of their crimes, even unto the details thereof, and it is stated that these men, in their drunken saloon talk, boasted of obtaining 75,000 Mexican silver dollars, which at that time were worth about the same as our dollars. It was in this manner that the amount of their loot became known.

In those days, it was the duty of the Sheriff to collect taxes, but on account of the large number of outlaws infesting Cochise County, it was considered an almost suicidal act for an officer to make any attempt at touring the country for any such purpose. Cochise County, which had just been formed from a slice cut off Pima County, was woefully deficient in tax monies and it remained for Deputy Sheriff Billy Breakenridge to devise some scheme to beat the game. As Billy was a natural born diplomat, it did not take him long to decide upon a mode of operation.

Billy Breakenridge rode over to Galeyville, which at that time was Bill's headquarters. He entered the first regularly ordained thirst parlor and boldly asked the bartender where he could find Curly Bill. The bartender pointed to a man who was curled up on a pool table, asleep, and informed Breakenridge that there was the man whom he had asked for. Suspicioning possibly that Curly Bill might be wanted for something or another, the bartender, not wishing for any one to get the drop on Bill, called to him that there was a man present who wished to see him.

Bill raised himself up on one elbow and looked the situation over. The bartender turned to take a drink of water and just as he raised the tin cup to his lips, Bill flipped his six shooter into position and shot the tin cup out of the bartender's hand, with the remark, "That stuff ain't fit to drink."

Deputy Sheriff Breakenridge walked over to where Bill was, introduced himself and unfolded his plan to him, which was so original that it appealed to Bill's humor and he readily agreed to accompany Breakenridge over the country to the different ranches as a body guard on his tour of collection.

Right at this stage of the game one of Bill's friends entered the saloon and informed him that his horse, which

DEPUTY SHERIFF BILLY BREAKENRIDGE

had been standing tied to the hitch rack in front of the saloon, had been shot. Bill laughed and then said, "Hell, I shot him myself when I fired that shot a little bit ago. Oh well, horses are easy to get." It is not related just how or where he obtained a substitute horse, but he obtained one anyway and was soon ready to travel.

Curly Bill had taken a great liking to the pleasant little deputy who tried to give everybody a square deal, and they rode together, sleeping under the same blankets, fasting and feasting together, as the case might have been, for three weeks. The collection trip was a financial success and Bill accompanied Deputy Billy Breakenridge to within sight of Tombstone, bade him a cordial good-bye and turned his horse's head back toward Galeyville. Although an outlaw in every sense of the word, Curly Bill was a square shooter with his friends or any one who had ever done him a favor.

A man named Gage, living at Contention, had a fine race horse stolen from him by the Clanton-McLowery Gang, of which, at that time, Curly Bill was the executive officer. Deputy Sheriff Billy Breakenridge decided to ride out to their camp and make a diplomatic attempt at recovering the horse for Gage.

Breakenridge rode boldly into their camp and took the matter up with Curly Bill, who in turn called a short business meeting at which the Clantons and McLowery's were present. After the adjournment of this meeting Bill came to Breakenridge and told him to make himself perfectly at home, eat with them, sleep with them and that in the morning he would find the horse in question tied to the hitch rack in front of the house, but that while he would guarantee the presence of the horse there as stated, he would not guarantee just how long Breakenridge would retain possession of him as the gang had declared their intention of riding after him when he departed, and retaking the horse.

Breakenridge ate his supper with the men, slept in the same room with them, shared breakfast with them and, sure enough, when he looked for the horse, he found him just as Curly Bill had told him he would. He decided that the quicker he got on his way the better it would be for him, as he did not like the looks and actions of the Clantons and McLowerys. Curly Bill was evidently the only friend that he had in that crowd.

He made preparations for his departure by saddling the horse which he had ridden out from town and then mounting he headed for Tombstone, leading the race horse. He had no sooner cleared the gate on his home bound trip than he saw the Clantons and the McLowerys mount their horses,

which were already saddled and ready, and ride out toward
the foot hills and then turn in the same direction in which he
was going.

Right here is where Billy Breakenridge did some lighten-
ing-like calculating. There chanced to be an emigrant wagon
traveling in his direction so he rode up alongside of it, and
keeping it between himself and the outlaw gang, he dropped
to the ground and, keeping the horses moving, he changed
his saddle from his own horse to the back of the race horse.
After giving the saddle horse to the emigrant with a request
to take him into Tombstone and turn him over to the livery
stable, he mounted the race horse and started making a big
dust toward town.

Paul Revere's famous ride of Revolutionary days sinks
into insignificance when compared with the ride of Billy
Breakenridge on this memorable occasion. The gang tried
to overtake him by the liberal use of horse flesh and bullets
but they failed to connect. Billy said that the race horse
fairly outran the bullets and left them far behind.

On one occasion Curly Bill and Sandy King became involved in a heated argument with a sheriff's posse over in
the San Simon Valley and, although they both made their
escape, Sandy carried a bad wound. They were riding across
the flat below Ft. Bowie when they ran squarely into a
young lieutenant from Bowie, who was out with his pack
of hounds, running jack rabbits.

Curly covered the young officer with his six shooter until
he learned that he was not armed. The lieutenant whom we
will call Blank, took quite an interest in Sandy's condition
and suggested that he ride back to the post and send out an
ambulance to carry him in to the post hospital.

Bill, looking the lieutenant squarely in the eyes, said,
"And then, what?" Blank replied, "Why, nothing. Here's
a man who needs attention and I am going to see that he
gets it and after that you are at liberty to do as you please."
The officer rode swiftly toward the post and soon returned
with an ambulance and Sandy was carefully loaded in and
taken to Ft. Bowie where his wound was dressed and he was
made comfortable in the post hospital. In a few days he

was up and around, and one night he disappeared and the incident was considered closed.

Three weeks later, a bunch of outlaws made a run on the herd at Ft. Bowie and cut out several horses which they ran away. Lieutenant Blank was detailed to take three or four men, trail the gang and bring back the horses.

They followed the trail, which lead them to the Old Hughes Ranch, where the bunch of outlaws maintained a permanent camp. Upon arriving at the outlaw camp, they were confronted by a high adobe wall and a heavy gate. As they rode up to the gate, a man standing on a shelf on the inside of the wall, asked them what their business was there and upon being informed by Lieutenant Blank that they were after some stolen government horses which they had trailed to this gate, the man inside informed them that they were a bunch of good trailers and that they had come to the right place, that the horses were there, but that they would be in a much hotter country than Arizona before they would get them.

The situation was becoming exceedingly tense when a big head, adorned by short black curls, appeared above the top of the wall and there were then two men standing on the shelf. The late comer was Curly Bill. He immediately recognized Lieutenant Blank and exclaimed, "Hold on boys, this is the lieutenant who took care of Sandy when the sheriff shot him all up, and he can have anything in here that he wants."

The big gate was immediately swung open and Lieutenant Blank, accompanied by his insignificant little command marched triumphantly inside. Not only did they recover the horses which were stolen that morning, but several more which had been stolen on previous occasions. The members of the gang all shook hands with Lieutenant Blank and thanked him more or less expressively for his kindness to Sandy, and they departed in all of their glory, and in possession of more than they had come for.

In May, 1881, Deputy Sheriff Billy Breakenridge made a business trip to Galeyville. Curly Bill had at that time a partner named Wallace and when Breakenridge rode into

Galeyville he met Wallace, who became very much angered at Breakenridge's presence in Galeyville and, drawing his six-shooter, he made many pungent remarks at and to the little deputy. The latter however, diplomatically ignored the remarks and went about his business.

There was, as has before been stated, a warm friendship existing between Curly Bill and Deputy Sheriff Breakenridge and when the news of this insult reached the ears of Bill, he hunted Wallace up and informed him in language more forcible than elegant that he must go to Billy and apologize.

Wallace looked Breakenridge up and made a very nice apology, but Curly Bill, who had been drinking and was very quarrelsome and abusive, threatened to kill Wallace, so Wallace took station on the porch of the saloon and as Curly Bill stepped down off the porch Wallace shot him, the bullet entering the left cheek and going out through the right side of his neck.

Deputy Sheriff Breakenridge arrested Wallace and held him, pending the result of Curly's injuries. As the bullet had passed through without breaking a bone or inflicting any serious injury, Curly Bill refused to prosecute Wallace and he was released.

There has been much discussion as to just what became of Curly Bill, and the question has never been satisfactorily settled. It has been stated that he went to South America and died there.

Wyatt Earp makes the statement that he and some of his friends were ambushed at some mountain spring, the name of which was not stated, by the Clanton Gang, and that in the fight which ensued, that he literally shot Curly Bill to pieces with a double barreled shot-gun. There appeared in the Tombstone Epitaph at that time, (March, 1882) an account of a fight which had taken place at Burleigh Springs, in which Curly Bill had been killed and the account states that the Clantons had carried his body away and brought it back to Charleston.

This matter was treated with the utmost secrecy and nothing more appeared to be known than was published in the meager paragraph referred to. It is said that Curly Bill held up and robbed a ranchman named Hooker of his monthly pay roll upon two or three occasions and that Hooker had offered $1,000 for his head and that the Clantons had brought him a head in a burlap sack and that Hooker had paid the promised reward. Hooker denied this through the columns of the "Epitaph." There is a possibility that Curly Bill might have been killed just as claimed by Wyatt Earp and that the Clantons may have cut off his head and taken it to Hooker and collected the reward, if such a reward had been offered, which is exceedingly doubtful.

Others state that Wyatt Earp shot and killed Curly Bill over in the Clifton Country but there appears to be no evidence at hand to prove this story to be possessed of any more foundation than the Hooker story.

It has also been stated upon good authority that Bill went back to his home in Montana and died there and in substantiation of this last statement, a perfectly reliable citizen of Lordsburg, N. M., who is still living, states that he saw a letter which Bill's brother wrote to Billy Jackson-Jones, from some point in Montana, saying that Bill had just died of the measles and that they had, that very day, laid him to rest on the old home place.

William Sparks of Globe, who is probably one of the best posted men in the southwest, states that Bill did die at home in Montana. As none of these stories has ever been verified, one man's story is as good as another's and the public will have to judge according to the testimony presented in the case.

BILLY THE KID

THE NAME "Billy the Kid" has for many years been applied to the numerous hard boiled "Billys" who have invaded the great southwest, but there never was but one real Billy the Kid and that one was William Bonny who, it is claimed by those who knew him, was born in New York City and that his first business enterprise was founded quite early in life as that of a book-black. This has been denied by many, but as such denials have never been backed up by proofs to the contrary, we are forced to believe that, in accordance with the preponderance of testimony in the case under consideration, Billy the Kid started his business career as a manicurist of footwear at an early age.

Billy's father died while he was a mere baby and it fell upon him to help support his mother. After struggling with adverse circumstances for a few years, Billy's mother managed to save enough money to pay their way to some point in Texas, where she and Billy tarried for some time. During her hesitation in said Texas town she annexed another husband whose name was given as Antrim in that locality. Antrim brought his newly acquired family to Silver City, New Mexico, and upon arrival in that peppy little mining town, tried to drink all of the whiskey in town, but failed, as they shipped it in too fast for him. It is not herein stated what became of Antrim, but that does not matter, as he is to be represented by X in this problem.

The first authentic record we have of Billy the Kid is from Silver City, where, at the age of 12 years, he killed his first man. It is related upon what is considered good authority, that a drunken blacksmith insulted his mother and that Billy resented the insult and took the blacksmith to task regarding the matter and the man threatened to horsewhip Billy. It is stated that Billy went away and soon returned with a six shooter in his possession, which he used with such good effect that the blacksmith was permanently cured of the drink habit. Some authorities state that Billy used a knife, but it is generally believed that he "borrowed" a six shooter and used it effectively.

After the killing of the blacksmith, Billy and another boy about his age ran away from home. Somewhere in their travels they picked up an old Springfield rifle and an ancient six shooter with a limited supply of ammunition for both guns. With the aforesaid artillery they ambushed three unarmed Apache Indians and shot them and took the eleven head of horses which they had and traveled on until they had an opportunity of disposing of them. They realized enough from the sale of their live stock with which to purchase real cowboy outfits for themselves. So far as is known, this was the only time that Billy the Kid ever committed a murder for pecuniary gain.

In the course of human events Billy finally reached Lincoln County, New Mexico, and went to work for John Chisum who, at that time, probably owned more cattle than any other man in the southwest.

During the Civil War, Mexican cattle had been driven across the line into the United States and many thousands were sold to the United States Government to be used as food for the soldiers. Many of these cattle were also intended to be issued to the Indians, but with the advent of the Civil War, the native sons of Arizona were forgotten. Many thousands of cattle were turned loose in Texas and adjoining states to roam at will and for many years they multiplied almost unmolested. At the close of the Civil War there were hundreds of thousands of these cattle of the "long horn" persuasion roaming the mountains, plains and valleys of the great southwest, bearing no brands as proof of ownership. Many a prosperous cattleman of today owes his start in life to a good swift cow horse, a saddle rope and a running iron.

Chisum paid his men regular wages and promised them a split on all mavericks branded. Following a large shipment of cattle by Chisum, Billy demanded his share of the rakeoff and Chisum refused to make any split, defying Billy to collect. Billy and many of Chisum's cowboys had worked the country from Lincoln County to the Old Mexico

line and their share of the proceeds was quite a large one.
Billy claimed that Chisum owed him $5000 and that he was
out to collect same.

Just about the time Billy had demanded an accounting

BILLY THE KID

with Chisum, the Lincoln County Cattlemen's War came
into existence. This war was simply a struggle for suprem-
acy in Lincoln County between Chisum and the firm of
Murphy and Dolan. Each concern determined to be the
cattle king of Lincoln County and Billy threw in with
Murphy and Dolan and soon after, at the age of 19 years, he
found himself the leader of one faction in the greatest

cattlemen's war ever known in the United States. Many
men were killed on both sides and troops were sent into
that district, but they accomplished nothing.

In March, 1878, Sheriff William Brady and his deputy,
George Hindman, attempted to arrest Billy, but Billy and
his gang shot and killed both men. A warrant was sworn
out for Billy and he became a very much wanted man, but
as he had such a strong combination behind him, no one
appeared to have the necessary equipment of nerve to go
after him.

It is so stated, and generally believed, that John Chisum
imported a man named Pat Garrett from Louisiana, for the
express purpose of killing Billy the Kid, anyway Garret
handled this part of the business for him. Billy quietly
slipped away and came into the Tombstone country where
he remained until in the fall or early winter of that year.

Upon his arrival in Lincoln County once more he was accompanied by Charlie Boudrie, Tom O'Phaillard, John
Middleton, Frank Baker and Bill Morton, whom he had
picked up in his travels. Billy soon went to work for a
young Englishman named Turnstall and a very warm
friendship sprang up between this very much mis-mated
pair. Just because Turnstall was a cattleman, Baker and
Morton deliberately shot him. Billy the Kid hunted them
down and killed them both.

Shot-gun Roberts, who was with Baker and Morton
when they killed Turnstall, was shot and killed a day or
two later by Charlie Boudrie. Just at this stage of the game
Middleton, who had been taking an active part in all of these
stirring events, dropped down and out of the wild bunch,
going back to Texas, changing his name and becoming a law
abiding citizen.

In a short time Pat Garrett was appointed sheriff of
Lincoln County and redoubled his efforts to apprehend
Billy the Kid, Charlie Boudrie, Tom O'Phaillard, and some
other kindred spirits who had joined the gang after they had
arrived from Arizona, and who were camped at Stinking
Springs, a few miles out from Ft. Sumner. O'Phaillard and
a few more of the gang rode into Ft. Sumner one blustering

winter's day and met Pat Garret and a posse just starting out
to Stinking Springs on a tour of extermination.   Garrett,
who was some quick on the draw, did not hesitate to exchange any courtesies but got busy and O'Phaillard slid
from his horse, dead.   The balance of the gang scattered
and were quickly out of sight and beyond pursuit.

Not seeing Billy in the gang, Garrett decided that he must
have remained at Stinking Springs, so he and his posse rode
on through the storm and were not long in covering the distance between town and Billy's stronghold.   As they rode
up to the house, Charlie Boudrie heard them coming and
thinking that it was O'Phaillard and his gang returning
from town, stepped to the door and opened it to extend
greetings, only to be shot dead by Pat Garrett.   Thus in the
very short space of a few hours, Billy had lost his two most
trusted and dependable lieutenants.

After an all day's siege in a raging blizzard, Billy surrendered, after being promised that he would be accorded
a regular trial in court.   He was tried in Las Vegas and
sentenced to hang for the murder of Sheriff Brady.   He was
taken to Lincoln, the county seat of Lincoln County and
placed in a room in the second story of a building which
was being used as a county court house.   Two deputies, J.
W. Bell and Bob Ollinger, were detailed to guard him, one
of them to be with him all of the time to prevent a jail
break or a rescue by his friends.

Bell was a square shooter and well liked by everybody.
Even Billy liked him in spite of the fact that they were prisoner and guard, they were warm friends.   Ollinger was a
natural born killer and always appeared to be afraid that he
might overlook a chance to abuse, or possibly kill someone,
and between him and Billy there existed the deepest hatred.

One morning Bob Ollinger took his shot gun out of a
closet in one corner of the prison room and proceeded to
change the charges in it by reloading it with buckshot.   Calling Billy's attention to the gun, he remarked that someone
was liable to get both barrels of buckshot and went on to remark that he hoped that Billy might make a break so he
might have an excuse for trying out the gun on him.   Billy

very quietly replied to his taunts,—"You had better be careful that you don't get them yourself." Ollinger replaced the shotgun in the closet and the incident was apparently closed.

On the same day, when lunch hour arrived, Ollinger took four more prisoners down to a nearby restaurant for lunch, leaving Bell to guard Billy. Shortly after Ollinger had departed, a shot was heard from the direction of the court house, quickly followed by another one. Ollinger, accompanied by Attorney Clements, who chanced to be lunching in the same restaurant, hurried in the direction of the shots. Just as they reached the front of the building, Billy, who was standing by a window in the second story, called out,—"Hello Bob," and as Ollinger looked upward, Billy fired both barrels of the shotgun into his head and breast, killing him instantly.

Billy afterwards stated to his friends that as Ollinger had repeatedly informed him that he was hoping for him to make a break so he could have the pleasure of filling him full of buckshot, he wanted him to know just exactly who killed him and that was his only reason for calling him by name.

It is presumed that Billy intended killing Bell to get the keys to his irons, but as Bell staggered down stairs and away from the building a short distance before dying, the keys were beyond his reach and this necessitated the lengthy ordeal of filing them away. It is stated that it was an hour, or even more, before Billy had completed all the preliminaries of his escape, including the rustling of a horse. No matter how long a time elapsed, he was not molested in any manner and no one protested his departure.

There were no witnesses as to what took place between Billy the Kid and Bell after Ollinger departed from the jail room. All that is known is what various people have, from time to time, claimed that Billy had told them, as Bell was killed by two shots fired by Billy.

Charlie Siringo, an old time peace officer who operated for many years around over Northern New Mexico, Colorado and Montana, and the author of an intensely interesting book entitled, "Riata and Spurs," also a real dyed-in-the-wool cowboy of the old school, states that the story told him was to the effect that after Bob Ollinger had departed, that Bell sat down to read a paper and that Billy, who had managed to slip one hand out of its cuff, slipped up behind Bell, struck him with the cuff and then pulled Bell's own gun from its holster and shot him with it.

Walter Noble Burns, author of "Saga of Billy the Kid," has written the most complete history of Billy the Kid that has ever been published. It is written in an interesting style which holds the reader in a real grip of interest from the first page to the last one. Mr. Burns states that the story told him by a friend of Billy's was that after Ollinger had gone to lunch, he and Bell sat down to the table to play cards and that when it came his turn to deal, he purposely flipped a card across the table with such force that it skidded onto the floor, and that as Bell stooped to pick it up, Billy reached over with a lightning-like movement and snatched Bell's gun from its scabbard and shot him with it.

Judge J. S. Lea of Roswell, New Mexico, writes as follows, "I was office deputy under Sheriff Pat Garrett, also under John W. Poe who followed Pat F. Garrett as Sheriff of Lincoln County, New Mexico. I began work for Mr. Garrett on July 11th, 1881, and he killed Billy the Kid July 14th, 1881. I lived in Lincoln for five years and, of course, heard the talk, pro and con from both sides on the Lincoln County War, the killing of Billy the Kid, etc.

"The Kid killed James W. Bell and Bob Ollinger on April 28th, 1881, and made his escape. I noticed that most of the recent writers refer to the Bell who was killed, as Charlie Bell, but J. W. Bell is the correct name.

"The building where Billy the Kid was being guarded, and from which he made his escape, was a large two story adobe building, built by Major L. G. Murphy and James J. Dolan for a combination dwelling and store building, in which they had a general merchandise store, saloon, billiard and pool hall.

"They built it with a view of protecting themselves against raids from Indians and it had only one stairway, which came up from the back side out of a corral where their horses were kept for protection. The out buildings and a high adobe wall made the corral which joined onto the main building on the south and back side. It was bought by the county and converted into a court house, but no changes had been made in it at the time Billy the Kid made his escape.

"Four other prisoners, who had voluntarily come in and surrendered to the sheriff to await the action of the Grand Jury, were being guarded there with Billy the Kid, but of course they were not as closely guarded as he was. Each of these four prisoners had a Winchester rifle, a six shooter and a full belt of cartridges, which the Kid noticed were put in the room at the head of the stairway. He also noticed that the door had a flimsy rim-lock which could easily be broken.

"The prisoners were all guarded upstairs and at meal time the four and one deputy would go across the street to a restaurant for their meals and would bring back a meal for the Kid. Then the deputy who had guarded the Kid would go over for his meal.

"That evening Bob Ollinger and the four went over for supper and left J. W. Bell to guard the Kid. The Kid told Bell that it was necessary for him to go down stairs, so they went down as they frequently did and Bell evidently did not think anything much about it. As they came back up, the Kid went upstairs as rapidly as he could and got as far ahead of Bell as possible without attracting Bell's attention. When he got to the head of the stairs he whirled and lunged against the door of the closet where the guns and pistols were. As it flew open, he grabbed a pistol and hurried back to catch Bell when he came to the head of the stairs, but Bell had beat him to it and was standing there with his pistol raised, ready to fire as soon as the Kid came out of the door. He fired but missed the Kid and the bullet went out through a window at the end of the hall.

"Bell then whirled and ran down the stairway and the Kid shot him twice as he was going down. Bell ran out into the corral with his pistol in his hand and ran up to Old Man

Goss, who caught Bell in his arms and gently laid him down on the ground. Bell died without speaking.

"Ollinger and Attorney Clements had heard the shooting and came running over and met Old Man Goss at east end of court house, right under the window which had been raised for ventilation some time during the day. Mr. Goss said, 'He has killed him! He has killed him!' Ollinger said, 'Killed who?' Mr. Goss said, 'Why, Bell of course.' Just then the Kid stuck Ollinger's own double barreled shot gun out of the window upstairs and said, 'Hello Bob!' As Ollinger looked up, he said, 'Yes, and he has killed me too.' The Kid instantly fired both barrels into Ollinger's breast, ranged downward into his body and he dropped to the ground and never moved again.

"Ollinger had shown the Kid that day that he was changing the loads in the shot gun and was putting in heavier buck-shot loads. He made tantalizing remarks to the Kid about the hanging and the Kid told him that he knew that he wanted him to make a break so that he, Ollinger, would get to kill him. The Kid replied, 'I am not going to give you a show to do that for you can bet your life if I do make a break I will get away with it,' and so he did.

Attorney Clements said that he never saw such an exultant look on a man's face before, and never expected to see another to equal it again, as there was on the Kid's face as he said, 'Hello Bob.' He wanted Ollinger to see him and know who killed him. They were enemies and each wanted a chance to kill the other. The Kid said that he did not want to kill Bell, but had to in order to get away, but was glad of the opportunity to kill Ollinger.

"This is the Kid's version of the killing of J. W. Bell, as he told it to his friends and as he was the only one left who knew exactly how it happened, and as the evidence left behind corroborated his statement, and as there was no reason for him not stating it correctly; therefore, I have no doubt about it myself.

"When the Kid first made his escape, each one had his own version or surmise as to how it happened, and different accounts of it were written up before the Kid's version became known. Some were so fixed in their opinion that they would not change it, as they did not hear the Kid say it himself. This accounts for the many different versions which the public has heard."

The writer does not pretend to know which is the true story of what occurred in the jail room of the second story of the Lincoln County Court House between Billy the Kid and J. W. Bell on the 28th day of April, 1881. He has given the different versions which were told him and permits the reader to draw his own conclusions.

Billy the Kid, after having made his spectacular escape, according to Charlie Siringo, went to the house of the widow of Charlie Boudrie who kept him in hiding for several weeks, but later he decided to call upon Pete Maxwell's sister who was a sweetheart of his.

Sheriff Pat Garrett had been notified that Billy the Kid was in the country once more and knowing that he would most assuredly come to Pete Maxwell's house, he took two of his deputies, Kip McKinney and John W. Poe and went to Maxwell's house where he, leaving his two deputies outside, went in to plot an ambush with Maxwell. While they were completing the detail of arrangments and conversing in low tone, they heard some one come to the door of the room where they were, and the door was cautiously opened and there stood Billy the Kid silhouetted in the door and easily recognizable to Garrett.

As Billy stepped into the door, he evidently sensed that all was not well and, drawing his six-shooter, asked in Spanish, "Quien es?" (Who is it).

Garrett shot and Billy the Kid fell, dead, never having had a chance to surrender. It is thought extremely doubtful whether he would have done so or not as, knowing that he was already under sentence of death, there is very little question but what he would have taken the gambler's chance and shot it out to the death with any one attempting to arrest him. At the time of Billy's death he was 21 years of age and it was claimed, had killed 21 men.

On one occasion Billy attempted to kill the judge who sat in judgment at his trial for the murder of Sheriff William

Brady.   It is reported that when the judge pronounced the
death sentence upon Billy, which terminated as follows:
"I do hereby sentence you to be hanged by the neck until
you are dead! dead!! dead!!!" Billy looked him squarely
in the eyes and said, "Yes, and you can go to hell! hell!!
hell!!!"

At the time of his surrender at Stinking Springs, Billy
had with him Billy Wilson, Dave Rudabaugh and Tom
Pickett, who were tried, found guilty and sentenced to long
terms of imprisonment in the New Mexico State penitentiary.

PAT GARRETT

A FEW words here appear to be appropriate regarding Pat Garrett, the slayer of Billy the Kid. So far as is known, he never lived in Cochise County, Arizona and there is no record that he ever even visited Tombstone, but on account of the part which he played in the death of such a notorious character as Billy the Kid, it seems to be in perfect harmony with the situation to mention him briefly.

Pat Garrett was born in Louisiana and spent his boyhood days there. He came to the Pecos Country in Texas, when nothing more than a mere youth. He spent several years in the cattle business in Texas and later coming to Lincoln County, New Mexico, served one term as Sheriff of that county.

On account of the method employed by him in his dealings with the Kid, he became very unpopular in Lincoln County. It is an undeniable certainty that when the Kid stepped through the door of Maxwell's sleeping room on the night of July 14th, 1881, if Garrett had called on him to throw up his hands, he would assuredly have done so, but there would have been a six shooter in one of them, and a busy one too. Inasmuch as the Kid had his six shooter already in his hand, he would more than likely have gotten the first shot and one shot would have been sufficient. It is believed that no one realized this fact more than Pat Garrett did, and as was his constitutional right, he played safety first regardless of what others might think.

It has been stated upon good authority that when Pat Garrett made the race for a second term as sheriff of Lincoln County, he was snowed under by the public opinion represented by the popular ballot.

Garrett moved south into Dona Ana County where he was appointed and acted as a deputy sheriff for some time, until he was appointed a collector of customs and was, for several years, a familiar figure to be seen at the El Paso end of the international bridge. After his term as collector of customs had expired, he returned to Dona Ana County, New Mexico, where he engaged in ranching.

Garrett leased some land to a young rancher named Wayne Brazel, with no restrictions as to what kind of stock should be ranged upon it and when Brazel stocked it with goats, Garrett became very indignant. Being a rancher with an ingrown hatred of sheep and goats, he informed Brazel that he could not range goats on any land owned or controlled by him, but he was informed that as there was

PAT GARRETT

no clause in the contract which prohibited the ranging of goats on that land, he had no recourse and that goats would be ranged thereon.

It is quite probable that Garrett, in the heat of his passion, may have made some kind of threats against Brazel, after having been goaded into a frenzy by what was apparently a frameup on the part of his enemies. It is related that a few days later Garrett and a supposed friend of his, known as Adamson, who was negotiating with Garrett for the purchase of his ranch, started to drive out to the ranch.

Later in the day, Wayne Brazel came riding into Las Cruces and surrendered himself to the sheriff, saying that at a sudden turn of the road he had met Garrett and, knowing that he was a killer and had threatened him, he had beat him on the draw and killed him. Perhaps it might be well to mention that Pat Garrett was considered to have been one of the swiftest gunmen in the southwest, and as the writer was well acquainted with Wayne Brazel twenty-five years ago and considered him as a good natured, slow moving cow-boy who was never in the habit of going armed he must have surely picked up some speed to have beat Pat Garrett on the draw, but as his statement was corroborated by that of Adamson, and Pat Garrett was not present to defend himself, Brazel was acquitted on the grounds of self defense.

In Charlie Siringo's "Revised Riata and Spurs," published by Houton-Mifflin Company, Boston, Mass., is given the last chapter of the chain of human events involving Billy the Kid, Pat Garrett and Wayne Brazel.

Jim Miller of Pecos City, Texas, a man whose guns were always for sale to the highest bidder, was hired to come to New Mexico and kill Pat Garrett for a cash consideration of $10,000. It was arranged for Adamson to cultivate the acquaintance of Pat Garrett and offer to purchase his ranch and when the time came for him to drive out to look the ranch over, Miller was to be notified so that he might lie in wait for Pat as he should drive by the ambush.

Miller was concealed in a clump of thorny brush and just before they reached the brush, Wayne Brazel rode up and he renewed his quarrel with Garrett. When within about 100 yards of the spot where Miller was concealed, Adamson stopped the team and got out, and knowing that a shot would frighten the horses walked to their heads. Pat got out and laid the shot gun on the seat and was stretching

his legs when a bullet came from ambush, striking him in
the body, felling him to the earth. As he raised up and
tried to reach the shot gun on the buggy seat, the cow boy
fired a bullet through his head.

It was proven that Miller was in that neighborhood and
those who knew him, were satisfied that he had come for
the purpose of killing some one. Capt. Fred Fornoff, of
the State Mounted Police, made quick investigation and
found where a man had lain in ambush behind the shrubbery

HANGING OF JIM MILLER AND OTHERS

thorny timber, also found one empty rifle shell. He learned
that Jim Miller had been seen in Tularosa just previous to
the murder of Garrett.

After Miller had killed Garrett, and before he had time
to collect his $10,000 blood money, he was called on to
go to Ada, Oklahoma, and kill City Marshal Bob Gossett,
for which killing he was to receive a fancy price. While at
his ranch near Ada, Miller shot Gossett from ambush. Believing that Gossett was dead, Miller rode away, but Gossett lived long enough to make his way to a nearby ranch
where he related to friends who had shot him. Miller had
ridden up to Gossett after having shot him with a rifle, and

had his six shooter drawn to shoot him again, but for some reason or another changed his mind and rode away.

In looking for Miller, the posse captured Miller's nephew and to save his own life, as he supposed, he told all about the plot to murder Gossett and named the two men who were furnishing the money. Miller was caught in the company of the two men who had hired him to kill Gossett. There was also another man in their company and all four were taken into a barn in Ada and hung from the rafters one at a time. Each man was placed on the back of a horse, the rope adjusted and then the horse led out from under him. A well known rancher of New Mexico is authority for the statement that Miller confessed to the murder of Pat Garrett before he was hung.

THE BLACK JACKS

B ILL CHRISTIAN, alias Bill Christie, alias Bill Christianson, alias Black Jack, arrived in Arizona from Oklahoma during the latter part of 1885 and took up his residence at the Williams Goat Ranch near Globe. It was known that he and Williams, who had preceded him into Arizona from Oklahoma, had been some kind of pals back in Oklahoma, but to what extent was not known around Globe at that time.

A clipping from a Guthrie, Oklahoma newspaper, under date of June 2nd, 1895, bearing caption "Quick Justice Administered," states as follows, "Justice sometimes gets in its work in short order in Oklahoma. Ten days ago, May 24th or 25th, 1895, Bob and Will Christian, whose conduct belies their names, and John H. Maxey, killed Deputy Sheriff William Turney in the Pottawatomie County while resisting arrest. Their trial came up a week ago at Tecumseh, Okla., and on yesterday they were convicted of manslaughter and sentenced to 10, 5 and 10 years respectively, in the penitentiary."

Under date of June 30th, 1895, we read as follows: "Oklahoma City, Okla. As the result of a jail delivery at this point at 6 o'clock this afternoon, two people are dead and several wounded more or less severely. When Jailer Garver entered the corridor of the jail at the usual time today to lock the prisoners in their cells, Vic Casey, Robert Christian and William Christian made a savage onslaught on him with weapons which they had managed to secrete.

"He was struck a terrific blow over his right eye and knocked insensible; the prisoners dashed over his body and away to freedom, scattering the people on the crowded streets and keeping at bay their pursuers with a rapid discharge of revolvers which in some mysterious manner they had obtained.

"Vic Casey jumped into a passing vehicle containing a man and a woman and at the point of a pistol, compelled them to jump out. Almost before they had time to obey his command, Chief of Police Milt Jones opened fire on the escaping prisoner who promptly returned the fire.

A perfect fusillade of shots then took place between the two Christians and Casey on one side and officers on the other, in which Casey and Officer Jones were instantly killed,

BLACK JACK CHRISTIAN

one man shot through the leg and a woman slightly wounded by a deflected bullet.

"One of the Christians then mounted the dead officer's horse, while the other one compelled a man to get out of a buggy and they drove furiously out into the country,

closely pursued by a posse of infuriated citizens. Blood-
hounds were requisitioned and there is but little doubt but
what they will be captured before morning; should they
be caught, a double lynching will surely follow.

"Vic Casey was 19 years old and had killed Deputy Marshal Sam Farris at Yukon, Okla., last summer. He would
have been released on bond tomorrow. Bob and Will Christian were noted thugs and desperados and were confined
on the charge of killing Deputy Marshal Tunney of Tecumseh, Okla., several months ago."

Under date of July 1st, 1895, we read further: "The
posse which went in pursuit of the escaped Christian Brothers, are coming in one by one, chagrined over their failure
to capture the murderers. The trail of Bob Christian was
found on the bank of the North Canadian four miles east
of this city. Marks on the river bank indicate where he
entered the river but a careful scrutiny of the bank for several miles below this point shows no place where he came
out and the prevailing belief is that owing to his weak-
ness from loss of blood and the high stage of the river which
is a boiling torrent, he was drowned.

"Officers are hot on the trail of Bill Christian and it is
only a question of hours until he is brought back to dangle
at the end of a rope. He is a desperate criminal and
thoroughly armed and it is very probable that more blood-
shed will ensue before he is captured. The weapons which
the prisoners had obtained were supplied by confederates
on the outside and secreted over the ceiling of the jail corridor from where they were taken at an opportune time and
so effectively used.

"Gus White, who was shot in the abdomen and the leg,
lies in a critical condition and is not expected to recover.
Jailer Garver's wound is not serious and he will be ready for
service in a few days. Mrs. Hurst, the occupant of the
buggy and who was forcibly thrown from the vehicle by
Casey, is very low from the effects of the shock. A late
report states that Bill Christian has been surrounded by a
posse and shot to pieces several miles southwest of the city
but this report lacks confirmation."

On July 23rd, 1895, both Bob and Bill Christian were seen near South McAlister in company of another man. They were all heavily armed and appeared to be confident of their safety.

It was reported upon good authority that the Christian Brothers stole a goodly sized herd of cattle from J. J. McAllister who lived near the town of McAllister during the spring of 1895, and that they made a clean get-away with them too.

On July 26th, 1895, the two Christian Brothers and another man held up and robbed the Wewoka Trading Company's store at Wewoka, I. T., at about 7 o'clock in the evening. They did not succeed in getting the safe open but took $37 in cash from the cash drawer, two Winchester rifles, three belts of cartridges and clothing for the gang to the amount of $200. Their gang consisted of six men at that time, but only three engaged in this holdup, all being old bandits and having their headquarters about 60 miles west of Eufalia, I. T.

On July 27th, 1885, the Christian Brothers with their entire gang were in Milburton, I. T., all heavily armed and evidently intending to hold up the M. K. & T. Express, but the United States Marshal for that district chanced to be on the ground with a large force of deputies and their plans were frustrated.

On August 2nd, 1885, the Christian Gang, consisting of eight men, held up and robbed a store at Lumpee, I. T., which is 7 miles north of Calvin.

On August 5th, 1895, the gang held up another store near Calvin, I. T.

On August 8th, officers arrested Doc Williams near Purcell, Okla., on a charge of harboring outlaws and obstructing the action of Federal Officers.

On August 9th, 1895, United States Marshals Springfield and Stockton had a 30 minute interview with the Gang at a point five miles south of Milburton, I. T., about sundown of that date and it was reported that one of the outlaws was killed in the fight which ensued and that the rest left that vicinity very hurriedly when they did get started.

On August 12th, 1895, at about midnight, the Christian Gang rode through the town of South McAllister, I. T., and were not molested.

On August 17th, 1895, Deputy United States Marshal Charles Baird arrested Foster Holbrook, one of the Christian Gang, also one of their most trusted lieutenants, and filed him in the South McAllister jail for future reference. Holbrook was credited with having six murder charges hanging over his head.

On August 21st, 1895, United States marshals arrested Irene Champion, Bob Christian's sweetheart, W. H. Mickle, E. Mickle, George and Lee Noland on a charge of harboring outlaws, they having been apprehended in the act of carrying sacks full of provisions to the outlaw camp in the wee small hours of the night.

On August 22nd, 1895, United States marshal arrested Jack Reeves, another member of the Christian Gang and placed him in the Oklahoma City jail. On the same day, the officers arrested Old Man Christian, Jesse D. Finley and Tullis Welsh on a charge of harboring outlaws.

On August 24th, 1895, United States marshals jumped the Christian Gang near Rush Springs, Cheyenne County, and in the fight which followed one of the Christian Boys was badly wounded. Following this fight it appears as though Oklahoma knew the Christian Brothers no more and it is believed that Bob died of his wounds, but this is not authentic.

When not touring the eastern part of Arizona and Western New Mexico Black Jack Christian could usually be found at or near the Williams Goat Ranch by his friends. His long suit was the robbing of isolated stores in the outlying districts. When at the Williams' Ranch he never slept in the cabin but bedded down in a cave at some distance from the cabin, going to the cabin only for his meals.

There is no question but what Black Jack Christian was 100 per cent outlaw and he and his able assistants never overlooked any proposition whereby their efforts might be rewarded by any class of loot possessing a pecuniary value, including cattle and horse rustling, and never permitting a human life to interfere with any of their arrangements.

While it has been stated that John Sontag, the noted California outlaw, came to Arizona and joined Black Jack in one or two of his ventures in outlawry, this report is much doubted by old time peace officers of Arizona. Although it is a well known fact that Sontag and his partner, Chris Evans, did quite frequently disappear from their regular range in California for weeks at a time, there is no authentic record that they operated either independently or in co-operation with Black Jack Christian or any other Arizona outlaw.

At one time while in hiding on the Williams Ranch, Christian sent to town by Williams' partner for some 50-95 Winchester Express cartridges. When the partner reached town and made inquiries for the cartridges at the hardware store, a man named Shaw chanced to be in the store and, knowing that Black Jack Christian was the only man in that country owning such a calibered gun, immediately surmised that he was in hiding at or near the Williams Goat Ranch and inasmuch as there was a reward of $6,000 offered for the person of Black Jack Christian, defunct or otherwise, Shaw hurriedly took the matter up with Deputy Sheriff Ben Clark and for a goodly share of the $6,000 reward money, agreed to lead a posse to the cave on the Williams Ranch where he felt sure Black Jack was in hiding.

That night Shaw guided a posse consisting of Ben Clark, Charlie Paxton, Bill Hart and Fred Higgins to the immediate vicinity of the cave where it was thought that Christain was in hiding. Shaw explained to the men just how they could station themselves so as to prevent their quarry from leaving the cave without detection. Leaving Ben Clark in charge of the situation, Shaw went back to town.

In the morning, not having seen any signs of life around the cave, the posse started down to the Williams' cabin to get breakfast. Fred Higgins chanced to become separated from the other three men and crossed the creek in his wanderings to get his bearings and suddenly came face to face with Black Jack Christian and two companions.

Higgins dropped behind a boulder and fired one shot and then hurriedly re-crossed the creek and met the balance of the posse who, having heard his shot, turned back to investigate. The three outlaws disappeared into the brush along the creek and the posse fired a volley into the brush after them and, mounting their horses, rode back to town.

It appears as though Black Jack and his two companions had come out of the cave just after the posse had started down to the cabin for breakfast and, the outlaws being more familiar with the trail than were the possemen, overtook them through accident.

About twenty minutes after the posse had ridden away, Williams came that way, leading his horses to water and as the horses shied at something which they saw in the brush, he investigated and found Black Jack Christian lying there in a dying condition. He called for help and the dying man was carried to the cabin and made as comfortable as was possible, but he died in a very short time.

A man named Sam Jones chanced along about this time, rode into Clifton and told Ben Clark to go out and get the man whom they had killed. A Mormon freighter who chanced to pass the Williams Ranch a short time after the departure of Jones for town, loaded the body of Black Jack on top of his load of lumber and hauled it to town.

The posse, after having fired the volley into the brush, not knowing how many members of the Black Jack Gang might be present and fearing that their four men might be in the minority, decided to ride while the riding was not all taken up. Had they known that they had killed Black Jack, they surely would have remained long enough to have taken charge of the body out of respect for the $6,-000 due and payable upon satisfactory proof of his death.

The fact that they did not report their killing of Black Jack when they arrived in Clifton, is accepted as proof that they did not know that they had killed him. Jones was the first to report the death of Black Jack in Clifton.

The statements herein recorded concerning the passing of Black Jack Christian can be verified by William Sparks of Globe, Billy Birchfield, Charlie Paxton, who was a member of the posse and Charlie Williams who owned the goat ranch and who was an old time friend of Black Jack's. There have been repeated many versions of how Black Jack Christian met his death but this one can be proven by living witnesses.

At the time of the killing of Black Jack Christian it was reported that Black Jack Ketchum had been killed, but this report can be easily proven in error as Ketchum was operating along the New Mexico-Arizona line about this time and was an entirely different Black Jack, as subsequent chronicles will prove.

Tom and Sam were born in or near San Diego, Texas, and brought by their parents to New Mexico while they were quite young. They were raised in the mining town of Kingston, N. M., and, so far as is known, their boyhood days were no different from those of other boys reared in similar environments. They were notoriously lazy, as boys, but were not considered bad boys.

It is not known at this late day just when they broke out and joined the wild bunch. They operated in the Black Range and the Mogollon Mountains of New Mexico in a small way for some time and then came into the San Simon Valley of Cochise County, Ariz., where they worked at various ranches as able bodied cow hands until they had familiarized themselves with the lay of the land and get-a-way trails.

One day Tom Ketchum rode into the little mining town of Bisbee where he was at first believed to be Black Jack Christian who had been killed a short time before. These two men, in a general way, resembled each other very much, both men being quite large, dark complexioned, dark mustache and hair, quite similar features and both being engaged in the same occupation. After explanations had been offered and accepted, Tom Ketchum, in the Brewery Gulch Saloon, declared that from that day hence he would be known as Black Jack.

He quickly gathered together a band of outlaws and set forth on his tour of crime, consisting of the holding up of stages, trains, banks, post offices or any other institutions promising monetary loot.

Black Jack (Tom) Ketchum, his brother Sam, George Franks, alias Bill Carver, a man named Spindel, and Cole Young, rode into Nogales, Ariz., one day and held up the International Bank. One man who was an eye witness to the event, claimed that they obtained $16,000, but others have stated that they obtained nothing, and it is generally believed that this holdup netted them nothing but worry.

In the August 6th, 1896, issue of the Tucson Citizen, appears the following: "An unsuccessful attempt was made by five mounted Americans to rob the International Bank of Nogales at 12:30 p. m. today. The time was well selected, as but one man was on duty, John Dessart, the president, being the only person in the bank at that time. Two men went into the bank while the other bandits remained on duty on the outside. Mr. Dessart showed fight and succeeded in holding them at bay until assistance arrived. Several shots were fired and Mr. Dessart was hit once but not seriously wounded. The robbers made their escape, pursued by a posse of citizens. They went in the direction of Calabasas. There is great excitement in town and if the robbers are caught there is probability of a lynching bee."

Inasmuch as a cowboy named Bob Forest had recently arrived in Bisbee direct from Separ, where Black Jack and his gang were known to have held up a store and post office just before the Nogales episode, Sheriff Bob Leatherwood and Deputy Sheriff Johnson arrested him and held him for investigation but he was afterwards released as it was proven that he was not in any way connected with the Black Jack Gang.

The Nogales posse trailed the bandits from Nogales to Lochniel and from there across the international line into Mexico, and after following their trail for fifteen miles across the line they lost the trail and returned to Nogales.

On August 27th, it was reported that the Black Jack

BLACK JACK TOM KETCHUM

Gang had been crowded back into Skeleton Canon in the extreme eastern part of Cochise County by a posse of United States Marshals and their deputies, headed by United States Marshal Hall of the New Mexico District, with one troop of cavalry from Fort Bayard and one troop from Fort Grant.

On August 29th, it was reported that while Deputy Sheriff Burt Alvord was gathering up the worn out horses left at Mud Springs by the pursuing posse, he was surprised at seeing Black Jack and Jass Williams on an adjacent hill within easy rifle range of the officer, but as he had been busily engaged in his work, he had not noticed them until they hailed him and waved their rifles and six shooters at him in a defiant manner, with invitations embelished in words not to be found in the Good Book, to come over and fight them, but as Alvord was sadly in the minority and they were in a well protected location, he wisely declined their urgent invitation to participate in a friendly exchange of lead.

Alvord quickly gathered his bunch of horses and drove them back to Tombstone where he reported his findings to Sheriff Fly. The following morning Fly, with a posse, left Tombstone for Mud Springs to accept the fight challenge. They jumped the gang at Mud Springs, split them into two parties and followed the larger party across the Animas Valley into Chihuahua, Mexico, where, on account of heavy rains, they lost the trail and did not find it for several days.

They finally located the trail which led them into the Arjos Mountains. Here they found a regular fortification which had evidently been used for some time. The trail led from here back into the United States, where it was presumed that they were trying to rejoin Black Jack and Jess Williams, who constituted the portion of the gang which was left in the United States.

Evidently they succeeded in joining Black Jack, as it was reported on excellent authority that on September 17th five of the gang including Black Jack, had appeared at a ranch near Dos Cabezas, which is a few miles south of Wilcox, Ariz., and that here they killed a steer belonging to a rancher, who rode out to see who was doing the killing of his beef. When he had approached to within a short distance of the outlaws, they fired a shot in his direction and then waved him back.

After a short consultation among themselves, they beckoned him to come on up to them. When he reached them he recognized some of them. They made no secret of their identities and informed him that they would never be taken alive. They offered to pay him for the beef that they had killed.

The balance of the cattle in that vicinity were very much agitated by the smell of blood of the slaughtered animal so the outlaws assisted the rancher in rounding them up and driving them out on the range away from that vicinity. The outlaws were all mounted on horses bearing the "96" brand, showing that they had raided some ranch for the purpose of providing themselves with mounts. They were all heavily armed and provided with a supply of ammunition ample to last them for some time.

Under date of October 8th, the Arizona Citizen stated that a part of Black Jack's Gang headed by Cole Young, who had participated in the holding up of the International Bank of Nogales, had been trailed to Rio Puerco, New Mexico, a small town on the A. & P. Railroad about 35 miles west of Albuquerque, where they held up a passenger train.

Conductor Healey, who had charge of the train, stated that they had been bothered very much en route by a hot crank-pin and that they had made a stop at Rio Puerco, which is nothing more than a flag station, to administer first aid and that, while working with the refractory pin, Brakeman Stevens discovered the gang riding on the tender of the engine and, believing them to be hoboes, ordered them to unload. One of the outlaws took a shot at him and the bullet passed through the bail of his lantern, followed closely by another which passed through the top of the lantern, extinguishing it.

Deputy United States Marshal Loomis chanced to be riding the train and jumping to the ground, opened fire on them with a shot-gun and was heard to exclaim, "I got him." Chief Special Agent Cade Selvey of the A. & P. Railroad was also riding on the same train and the bandits evidently knew it as they demanded him to come out in the light where they could get a shot at him. There were believed to have been seven men in this gang, Black Jack and Jess Williams having remained behind in Arizona.

After the train had reached Albuquerque a message was received from the operator at Rio Puerco to the effect that Loomis, who had remained behind at Rio Puerco, had positively identified the slain bandit as Cole Young, for whom he had been searching for some time. There were rewards out for Cole Young, dead or alive, to the amount of $3,000.

Young was wearing a hat purchased of Soto Brothers, of Wilcox, Ariz., when shot. He also wore the official badge of the outlaw gang, a plain gold ring on the third finger of his left hand, the same having been placed there in connection with the oath of allegiance to their cause. After this unsuccessful attempt at holding up the train, the balance of the gang headed over the state line into central New Mexico.

Under date of October 28th, it was reported that the gang was trailed from Rio Puerco to a point not far from San Antonio, New Mexico, where they held up the White Oaks-San Antonio stage. The driver positively identified them as the men who had held up the stage a short time before. From that point they left a plain trail south to Separ, New Mexico, where they held up and robbed the store and post office at that place. They obtained $80. Black Jack Ketchum was positively identified with the gang at this place.

Under date of November 3rd, the robbery of the post office at San Simon, Arizona, was reported. There were four men implicated in this robbery and Black Jack Ketchum was positively identified as having been one of them. A posse was formed immediately and followed the robbers who headed for Sulphur Springs Valley and in the general direction of Tombstone.

On November 11th the bandits were in hiding in the Sulphur Springs Valley where they had plenty of friends as desperate as themselves. Two of the gang, Hayes and Davis, were in the second Separ post office robbery and were positively identified by those who knew them well.

Mr. Joseph Temple, agent for the New Mexico and

Arizona Railroad at Huachuca Siding, says: "I and another employe were in the office when suddenly two men entered and with much ado, ordered 'Hands up,' at the same time we found ourselves peering into the barrels of two ugly looking pistols, manufactured by Mr. Samuel Colt. It is needless to say that we both complied with the request with the utmost alacrity, whereupon the dark complexioned highwayman, presumable Black Jack, volunteered the following information, 'We are out for the stuff but we do not want to rob any individual person but are after the railroad and express companies. We do not want to kill any one, but if necessary it will not trouble us much to do it.' At the conclusion of this speech he ordered me to open the safe under penalty of death if I refused. He accompanied me to the safe to see that it was properly done.

"In the meantime, the other employe was being looked after by the other robber who, when looking through his clothing for a concealed weapon, found his purse containing some money. The robber pocketed the purse but when the old gray haired employe appealed to him, saying that was all the money he had, the heart of the robber was softened and he returned the purse without opening it.

"The money drawer of the safe was placed on the table and the robber, to make sure that nothing was held back, investigated the contents himself and then ordered everything in the safe, papers and all, to be placed on the table. He noticed my reluctance in bringing forth things promptly and I was advised in forcible language that they would stand no monkey business and by the way they flourished their guns, I knew that they meant it. I was then ordered to separate the checks from the cash and when this was done he placed the cash in his capacious pocket.

"After looking about and passing jocular remarks about things and persons in general, the robbers concluded that they had gotten everything of value. Before leaving however, Black Jack took another look into the safe and seeing some small packages which I had overlooked, put them in his shirt front and we were then marched out to where their horses were tied.

"The younger robber had me in tow and when about half way to their horses asked me if Tom Smith's saloon was open yet.   Tom had closed unusually early that evening and I told him so.   This robber, who was Jess Williams, declared that he had an elegant thirst and knowing that there was some wine in the freight house, told me to go back and get some.   We returned to the warehouse, Williams holding a lamp in one hand and his six shooter in the other. The wine was found and I was ordered to uncork a bottle and sample it first.   Williams then ordered me to take two bottles, uncork them and take them out to his partner.

"Black Jack and the aged employe were found patiently waiting.   Black Jack being employed in the pastime of tearing open the packages he had just taken from the safe a few minutes before, burning the wrappers and investigating the contents.   I explained that the jewelry belonged to private individuals who had left it in my care for safe keeping and asked that it be returned.   Both robbers looked at the jewelry by the light of the fire and concluded that it would be of no use to them and handed it back to me.

"Both bandits were very talkative and gave an account of their holdups at Separ and San Simon and stated that they might call there again.   They stated positively that a few officers would be killed if they continued to pursue them.

"Williams passed the bottle for a farewell drink and we were forced to take one each; then the robbers mounted their horses and rode away.

"These men were at my station for from 30 to 40 minutes and during the entire time each man had one hand on his gun.   Neither man was masked and the coolness, fearlessness and utter abandon with which they conducted their robbery impressed us with the full force of their remarks that they would not be troubled much at putting out a life with a leaden missile if necessary to further their ends.

"The Indian trailers, who came later, found where two

horses had been standing just beyond where Black Jack and
Williams had left their horses, showing that two men had
been watching and waiting in case of an emergency. The
four horsemen were traveling together when the trail was
lost in the mountains to the south."

Post Officer Inspector Waterbury, after having made
investigation of the Bowie Post Office robbery, under date of
November 19th, made the following report to the chief of
this division at Denver:

"This report covers depredations committed by Black
Jack and his gang, which includes postoffice robberies and
holdups of various kinds in New Mexico and Arizona since
July 20th, 1896, at which time the post office at Separ, N.
M., was held up and robbed. Since that time the gang has
held up the A. & P. mail train at Rio Puerco, N. M., a
Southern Pacific train at Deming, N. M., the post office at
Bowie and at Teviston also.

"These bandits have successfully held up and robbed
four stages on the San Antonio and White Oaks, N. M.,
Stage Line, cutting open the pouches and rifling the regis-
tered mail, robbed the Separ post office a second time, held
up the post master and robbed the post office at San Simon,
Cochise County, Arizona, 16 miles east of here, (Bowie),
made an attempt to rob a Nogales, Arizona, bank at mid-
day and robbed the railroad station at Huachuca Siding.

"They have killed three men, a Mr. Parker who lived
near White Oaks, N. M., and who had informed on them,
another cattleman on the Gila River in Arizona, whose
name I have not yet learned, and one of the United States
Customs officers who was in a sheriff's posse following them
above the Mexico Boundary line after the attempt on the
Nogales bank; his name was Robson.

"In their attempt to rob the post office at this place,
(Bowie), Postmaster Wickersham took a shot at one of
them, the bullet passing within a few inches of Black Jack's
head, since which time the gang has sent word to the postmaster that they would come back and kill him on sight.

"When robbing the post office at San Simon they brutally pounded the postmaster over the head with a revolver and, when done, kicked him into insensibility.

"When they robbed the Separ post office the second time they pounded the old postmaster, Colonel Milligan, over the head with a revolver in a shameful manner, practicing at him as a target with their revolvers.

"In the second Separ robbery, they first held up the Southern Pacific Railway agent and after taking all of the railway and express money, as well as his own personal money, they compelled him, at the point of a Winchester, to march in front of them, with a mask on, and go into the store and post office ahead of the outlaws and order the crowd to throw up their hands, so that if any one was shot, he would be the first one to be hit."

On October 15th, Sheriff Fly of Cochise County, Sheriff Bob Leatherwood of Pima County, Ariz., accompanied by Deputies Doyle, Johnson, Alvord, Hildreth and Line Rider Robson, picked up the trail of Black Jack and his gang about 12 or 14 miles south of Bisbee and followed it across the Sulphur Springs Valley, through the Swisshelm Mountains, through the San Simon Valley into Skeleton Canon.

The posse sighted one of the robbers in Skeleton Canon and Doyle started to take a short cut to head him off but his horse stepped into some sliding shale, his saddle turned and Doyle was badly hurt and his gunstock broken so that it was worthless. He was sent into San Simon with messages to the officers at Lordsburg and Deming that the robbers had turned in that direction.

Shortly after Doyle had left the posse, they overtook the bandits down in Skeleton Canon and a fight was quickly on. Line Rider Robson was killed by the first volley from the outlaws. Sheriff Leatherwod and Deputy Alvord dismounted quickly and their horses, taking fright at the shooting, broke loose and ran directly into the outlaw camp.

Black Jack's horse was dropped by the first fire of the posse and Black Jack, seeing Sheriff Leatherwood's horse coming his way, caught him, removed his saddle from the dead horse and, under a heavy fire, placed his saddle on Leatherwood's horse.

Hildreth, who had worked around to a point above the outlaws, was made a target of by the whole outlaw gang and his horse was shot from under him. As he struck the ground moving, he kept moving until he had reached cover behind a tree. Just as Black Jack had completed the transfer of his saddle from his dead horse to Leatherwood's horse, Hildreth shot the horse to keep Black Jack from escaping, the latter being protected by the horse so that Hildreth could not get him. In all probability this hostile act on the part of Hildreth peeved Black Jack considerably, so he took a shot at Hildreth which scratched his neck in passing, leaving Skeleton Canon in possession of the posse.

On account of the posse members having been in such an exposed position, they lost practically all of their horses and were unable to pursue the bandits until provided with mounts. It being impossible to get Robson's body out of the canon before decomposition set in, it was buried within a few feet of where he fell.

John Slaughter, sheriff of Cochise County, Burt Cogswell and Billy King then joined the posse and followed the gang toward the Mexico line. When the outlaws had reached a point near the line they divided, the larger bunch going into Mexico and the other two, who were later identified as Black Jack and Jess Williams, bearing away to the southwest and finally drifting back in New Mexico by way of Guadalupe Canon.

On October 27th, a posse in charge of Sheriff Shannon of Grant County, New Mexico, accompanied by Special Deputies Frank M. Galloway, Frank McClinchey and Steve Birchfield, took the trail of the robbers who had just held up the Separ store and post office and followed the trail into Arizona and out into the San Simon Valley. The robbers had been positively identified as Black Jack and his gang.

The officers found where the gang had made camp for one night on Squaw Mountain and from the sign, believed that they were on a hot trail and very close to the outlaws. The

posse decided to camp for the night and did so.   Just after
dark, two mounted men passed their camp but as the officers could not identify them, laid low and permitted them
to pass by unmolested.

Fearing that the outlaws might discover them and attack
them as they slept, they decided to keep one man on guard.
At 2:00 a.m. of November 1st, Galloway took second watch.
Birchfield was awakened by a noise and raised up from his
sleeping place and in so doing awakened Shannon and
McClinchey.   An object was seen coming directly towards
where they were camped and each man reached for his gun.
Shannon's gun got caught in his saddle and he was unable
at that instant to release it.

At a distance of fifty feet, McClinchey hailed the approaching object twice with,—"who's there? Who's there?"
There was no reply and Shannon ordered the men to fire.
McClinchey ad Birchfield both fired and the object dropped
to the ground in a heap.

Shannon, believing Galloway to be standing at his side,
called to him but received no answer. He immediately realized that a terrible mistake had been made and upon investigation learned that his fears were true.   The object
which they saw and challenged, was Galloway, and one of
the bullets had struck him squarely in the head, killing him
instantly.   Inasmuch as he had not answered the challenge
of his brother officers and under the existing circumstances,
there was no one to blame for this lamentable accident but
himself.   Had he replied to the challenge, all would have
been well.

On November 19th, Black Jack and some of his gang ate
dinner with a rancher in the San Simon Valley south of San
Simon.   They talked freely and recounted many of their
recent deeds, calling each other by their names and apparently enjoying themselves over these reminiscences.

As they were leaving, they informed the rancher that
they were, and had been, riding quite a number of horses
picked up on the range, but that they had no intention of
stealing them or riding them to death and that they would

all be left on their own home range when they were through
with them.

At Dos Cabezas, a few miles south of Willcox, they
stopped and left two horses which they had "borrowed"
a few days previously.   While there, Black Jack stated
to the owner of the horses that they had been in Willcox
on Nevember 13th and 15th and saw the United States
Army Paymaster who was bound for Ft. Grant to pay off
the troops, but that he had too strong a guard for them to
tackle.   When they left Dos Cabezas they went toward
Bowie.

On November 29th, Special Agent Breakenridge of the
Southern Pacific, reported that one of the posses had just
had a battle with Black Jack at the Diamond "A" Ranch
on Deer Creek, about 60 miles south of Separ, N. M., near
the Mexican Line, at about 8:00 a. m. of the day before.

It was reported that a posse in charge of Deputy United States Marshal McClinchey of the New Mexico District had met Black Jack and three of his gang at the
Diamond "A" Ranch and in the gun fight which ensued
Bob Hayes of the outlaw gang was killed and Jess Williams
wounded badly.   Black Jack and the fourth man made good
their escape and headed into Arizona, followed by the
posse.   None of the posse were wounded in this fight.

J. L. Dow, sheriff elect of Eddy County, New Mexico,
in telling of this event, says: "On the evening of Tuesday,
November 27th, we had been following the trail of Black
Jack and his gang of outlaws for several days when we
struck a place where they had recently broken camp, and
from there their trail led toward Deer Creek.   We were
satisfied that the robbers were out of provisions and concluded that they would go to the Diamond "A" Ranch
the next morning for supplies.

"In order to get there ahead of them we went around
the trail and by hard riding all night reached the Diamond
"A" Ranch at daylight.   After getting breakfast we did
not have long to wait.   Just as we expected, two of the
robber gang came riding into the ranch.   They were Bob

Hayes and a large dark complexioned man whom I knew to be Black Jack. I had only two men with me but I knew that they were dead game.

"When they arrived about 60 yards from the house I called out for them to throw up their hands. Both men snatched out their pistols, jerked their horses' heads up between us and themselves, leaning back in their saddles, and opened fire, which we returned. In pulling his horse back, Black Jack jerked his horse to his haunches and then set him wild by clinching him with his spurred heels to keep from falling off. The horses began plunging and, seeing Hayes fall from his horse, Black Jack headed for the brush. Seeing that he was about to get away, I shot his horse, killing it. The animal fell on Black Jack's rifle but Black Jack swiftly lifted the horse sufficiently to enable him to secure his gun and then disappeared in the bushes.

"Hayes, though mortally wounded, fought to a finish, firing two shots at us while lying on his back, dying. I do not think that any of us touched Black Jack on account of the way in which his horse was cavorting around. Black Jack ran back to his gang, mounted behind another man and rode away under our fire."

Bob Hayes was identified as Sam Hassells, a native of La Porte, Iowa, but for many years a resident of Gonzales County, Texas, from which county he was sentenced to five years in the penitentiary on a charge of horse stealing. As there was another charge awaiting his discharge from the penitentiary, he made his escape when he had only about four months to serve. He came to New Mexico and threw in with Black Jack. There was $6,000 reward on him at the time he was killed.

On January 17th, 1897, a reward notice was printed in the Arizona Citizen to the effect that the Government would pay for the apprehension of the three men who held up the White Oaks-San Antonio stage four times, $500 per man for each offense, making a total of $6,000 for the three men on this one charge.

They were described as follows: "Black Jack, 38 years

of age, about six feet in height, weight about 200 pounds, black hair, black mustache and beard, very muscular and strong, broad shouldered and very dark complexion. George Musgrave, alias Jeff Davis, alias Jesse Williams, alias Jesse Johnson, six feet one inch in height, weight 200 pounds, 22 years of age, light complexion, round smooth face, brown hair, has had one leg broken—think it was the left one—has noticable bend in that leg.

"Tom Anderson, five feet nine inches in height, weigh one hundred and fifty pounds, 30 years of age, sandy complexion and sandy mustache."

On April 7th, 1897, Black Jack and ten men came up out of Sonora, Mexico, according to the Arizona Citizen, and camped near Humphries Ranch and on May 9th they were camped at Ruch's Spring in Cochise County, and their gang consisted of 18 men.

In the fall of 1897, the exact date not now available, Black Jack and his gang held up and robbed a Southern Pacific train between Willcox and Cochise and made their get away, going south toward the Mexico Line. This event is vouched for by old time peace officers but the details of this holdup are rather vague.

A well known prospector stated that on October 3rd, 1897, he saw and talked to Black Jack in the Sierra Madre Mountains in Sonora, Mexico, a short distance south of the Arizona Line. That he was well acquainted with Black Jack, that he had seven men with him and that they were pleasantly located in a good house, had plenty of provisions and money and were slipping across the line into Arizona frequently and raiding stores for supplies which they packed back to their camp below the line.

The Arizona Citizen of December 2nd, 1897, states that Black Jack and 12 of his gang crossed the line into Sonora, Mexico, at the customs house of La Morita, due south of Bisbee, a few days before and that on Thanksgiving Day he, his cousins Jess Williams and Tom Anderson had ridden into Frontieras, Sonora, and proceeded to get drunk and shoot up the town. They were arrested and fined for being drunk and then released. They had $9,-000 in their possession at the time of their arrest.

On December 8th, 1897, Black Jack, his brother Sam Ketchum, Dave Atkins, Ed Cullen, Leonard Alverson and Ed Bullion held up a Southern Pacific train at Steins but they met a streak of hard luck in the person of Wells-Fargo Messenger Jennings, who was well supplied with artillery and ammunition and the nerve to use same and he used both with such good effect that Ed Bullion, at the scene of the holdup, was forever cured of his vicious habits.

A posse was organized in Lordsburg and hurried to the scene of the holdup where the trail was picked up easily and followed into Texas Canon in the Chiricahua Mountains, where Atkins, Cullen and Alverson were captured and taken to Silver City, New Mexico, where they were charged with train robbery, found guilty and sentenced to ten years in the penitentiary at Santa Fe.

On December 29th, it was reported that Black Jack and his gang had crossed back into the United States from Mexico and were headed for Silver City with intent to release Atkins, Cullen and Alverson from the hands of the law but if this was their intention they never carried out the intent.

On January 17th, 1898, the Arizona Citizen reports Black Jack and gang surrounded in the mountains near the international line and in the fight which ensued one outlaw had been killed and four captured and that later two more were captured and shot while trying to make their escape but the particulars of this fight were never published that there is any record of.

It is believed that Black Jack's Arizona Gang was broken up about this time and that he, his brother Sam and Spindel headed back into New Mexico and that, after crossing the Rio Grande River, they separated. Black Jack stopped in Sierra County to rest up and Sam and Spindel went up the river together as far as San Antonio, Sam turning northeast and Spindel going on up the river until just below Socorro he met Sheriff Bursum who was looking for him. Socorro County paid the burial expenses. This story has been confirmed by some and denied by others and is here given for whatever it is worth.

Sam Ketchum drifted back into central New Mexico and gathered himself a gang of soldiers of fortune and they held up a Colorado Southern passenger train on Twin Mountain Curve near Des Moines, New Mexico, where he and his brother Black Jack had held up the same train on a previous occasion. They robbed the express car and the passengers and made a temporary get away. A posse took their trail and overtook them near the head of Ute Creek in Colfax County and in the running fight which followed, Sam was wounded. He made the gang go on without him and he made his way to a ranch house where the posse of officers found him.

He was suffering from a badly wounded arm which was sadly in need of attention but he forbade the doctor dressing it, saying: "I am not going to let you cure me up and then break my neck." A few days later he died from the effects of infection.

When Black Jack parted from his brother Sam and Spindel he rode to a ranch near Engle, New Mexico, saying that he wanted a place to work and rest his horse for a few days. The rancher put him to work digging a well and as the ranch was quite a distance from town and several miles off the main traveled road Black Jack was safe, for a while at least.

His horse which was a well bred one, judging from his muscular development and chest dimensions, was his first care. This fine animal was fed with clock-like regularity and rubbed down twice daily. His saddle gun was his next care and at lunch time each day he would take it from its scabbard and take two shots at a target of some kind, carefully wipe it out and return it to the scabbard.

Black Jack's work was entirely satisfactory but one day a cowboy from an adjoining ranch had been to town and as he passed the place where Black Jack was helping to dig the well, he stopped to gossip. During his pause he chanced to mention that an outlaw named Sam Ketchum and his gang had made an attempt to hold up a Colorado Southern passenger train and that Sam had been badly wounded and was not expected to live. The cowboy rode on and at quitting time Black Jack called for his time and, eating a hasty lunch, saddled his horse, mounted him and rode away into the darkness of the oncoming night.

It was afterwards learned that in the fight with Sam Ketchum and his gang that Sheriff Farr of Albuquerque was killed by Bill McGuiness who was later apprehended and sentenced to life imprisonment in the State Penitentiary at Santa Fe. One deputy sheriff was killed and one wounded in this fight.

The day before Sam died Black Jack was laying plans to rob another train. He staked out two horses at Twin Mountain Curve and then went into Folsom, New Mexico where he boarded the blind baggage of Conductor Frank Harrington's train which left Folsom at 10:30 p. m. and rode it to the curve, which was where he and Sam had held up the same train once before.

Upon the arrival of the train at Twin Mountain Curve Black Jack climbed over the engine tender and covered Engineer Kirchgrabber and his fireman with a gun and ordered them to stop the train. Kirchgrabber had no stop order from the train dispatcher but Black Jack held a stop order in each hand and the train was quickly stopped.

Kirchgrabber and his fireman were ordered down to cut off the express car. As soon as the train came to a stop, Express Messenger Fred Bartlett opened the express car door to investigate the stopping of the train at this point and Black Jack shot him in the jaw as a reward for his curiosity.

Conductor Harrington, hearing the shot, had a hunch that all was not well, so he opened the little trap door between the smoking compartment and the mail car and crawled through, accompanied by his double barreled shot gun of the sawed off variety. He put out the light in the mail car, opened the end door about two inches and when he saw Kirchgrabber and his fireman trying to cut off the express car and a man with six-gun in each hand superintending the operation, he knew just exactly what was happening as though some one had told him. The gent with the two six-guns discovered him about the same time and flipped a leaden pellet in his direction which ruined a perfectly good sleeve to his uniform coat. This peeved Harrington considerably and he loosened a handful of No. 7 buckshot out of that sawed off shot gun and the man behind the pair of sixes caught the most of it in his right arm.

Black Jack lost all interest in subsequent events and disappeared into the brush, having decided that he did not care to hold up this particular train any longer. Conductor Harrington, not knowing just how many more outlaws might be in this immediate vicinity, lost no time in playing hookey from that particular location.

The following morning another train crew saw Black Jack wandering around in the vicinity of the railroad track, not far from where he had staged his lone handed holdup of the night before and they reported the matter at their first stop to Sheriff Rinard. The sheriff went out and found Black Jack wandering around in a half crazed condition.

He was taken into Trinidad, where his right arm was amputated at the elbow. He was then taken to Santa Fe for safe keeping and later to Clayton, New Mexico, for trial and execution.

While awaiting his sentence of execution to be carried out he wrote the following letter to President McKinley:

"Three men now confined at Santa Fe for rail robbery at Steins Pass in 1897 are innocent. They are Leonard Alverson, Dave Atkins and Edward Cullen. William Carver, Sam Ketchum, Broncho Bill and I did the job. I have given my attorney these names and a list of what was taken and where same can be found. I make this statement, realizing that my end is fast approaching and I must very soon meet my maker.   T. E. KETCHUM."

Black Jack Ketchum is credited with 15 murders. He was executed at Clayton, New Mexico, at about 1:15 p. m.

of April 26th, 1901. While the officers were adjusting the noose he asked the time and upon being told, said: "You'd better hurry up a little for I am due in hell for dinner."

A few minutes later Black Jack Ketchum went to his death as gamely as he had lived. He was a heavy man and his head was cleanly severed from its body by the drop.

George Musgrove, alias Jeff Davis, alias Jess Williams, alias Jess Johnson was a cousin to Black Jack Ketchum and was at one time a duly accredited member of the Sam Bass Gang of Texas. He was also a member of Billy the Kid's gang in Northern New Mexico during the Lincoln County Cattlemen's War and then came down and joined Black Jack and stayed with him until the gang went to pieces. Then, deciding that a life of outlawry was not altogether a bed of roses he reformed and went back into Texas, changed his name, married, raised a family and became a good citizen, well thought of by all who knew him.

In some manner or another the Cochise County authorities located him and he was brought back to stand trial on a murder charge. Inasmuch as all of the material witnesses were either dead or were scattered, there was not enough evidence at hand to warrant a conviction and as he introduced witnesses to prove that he had for many years lived the life of a law abiding citizen, the presiding judge informed him that he took pleasure in being able to permit him to go back to his home and family with a clear record to compensate him for the noble effort he had made to live down his unenviable past.

BILLY GROUNDS AND ZWING HUNT

A RTHUR BURCHER, Alias Billy Grounds, alias Billy the Kid, it is stated was a native of San Antonio, Texas. His right name was unknown in the southwest and he, having worked for a man named Grounds at some time in his hectic career and also on account of his extreme youth having been called Billy the Kid, a combination of the two names was formed and every one knew him as Billy Grounds.

Richard Hunt, alias Zwing Hunt, was a native of Bosque County, Texas, and his parents lived at Kopperl in that county. He was known only by the name of Zwing Hunt in the southwest and if any of his friends knew his right name they never advertised it to the public as he lived in Arizona and New Mexico under it, operated under it and was buried under it.

These two boys formed a partnership which lasted until death parted them. Hunt furnished the oxen and Grounds freighted lumber from Morse's Sawmill. But this work became irksome and he and Hunt drifted into the wild bunch and during the last months of their lives shared equally the ups and downs of life's rough road which they had chosen.

At the time of Billy's death he was credited with having killed twenty-one men during the 19 years of his checkered career. Zwing Hunt, although only twenty-four years of age at the termination of his Arizona career, was credited with having killed his share of men, both good and bad, but there appears to be no record left of just how many he did have on the credit side of his Life's Ledger

No matter what Billy's faults may have been, there is no question of his love for his mother, as he wrote letters to her with almost clock-like regularity, telling her in detail of his daily life and work.

On one occasion, Grounds, Hunt and twenty-seven others of the outlaw type, recruited from the rank and file of that order, made a trip down into Mexico taking up their temporary residence at, some say Matamoras whilst others say it was at Monterey, but be that as it may, they patiently waited for months until such time as the bank was reported plentifully supplied with funds and they then raided it, securing a large amount of money and a cigar box full of diamonds.   They also looted the Catholic Church in their raid and secured a solid gold image of the Virgin Mary and Child Jesus.

In their get away they were pursued by Mexican soldiers, or Rurales, to the International Line and in the run· ning fight which ensued it is reported that they had only one man wounded while the Mexicans lost several of their men who fell before the superior marksmanship of the Americans.

After crossing the International Line the gang broke up and in pairs and small squads they went their various ways.   Grounds and Hunt took the wounded man to their camp where he afterwards died, probably from lack of medical attention and infection of his wound.   It has been stated by some that for some reason, either sentimental or otherwise, they buried his share of the loot which has been stated to have been about $8,000 but said by others to have been nearer $800, in the head of his grave and, so far as is known, it still keeps him company in his last long sleep.

Upon another occasion Grounds and Hunt waylaid a bunch of 19 Mexican smugglers over in Skeleton Canon where they had stopped for lunch and to rest.   They had quite a herd of laden mules with them.   In those days Mexican smugglers coming into the United States usually came up through Guadalupe Canon and down through Skeleton Canon and then out across the little hills and arroyas to Tombstone, Willcox, Benson, Tucson, Prescott and points north, where they would exchange their goods for guns, ammunition and whiskey which would be smuggled back across the line into Mexico and disposed of at a price many times the amount of the purchase price or its actual worth.

When the smuggler gang had settled down to their lunch, the most of them having removed their side arms and belts of ammunition in order to make themselves comfortable, Grounds and Hunt opened up on them, Billy from behind a rock and Hunt from behind a tree, with such telling effect that before the Mexicans realized an attack the majority of their number was either dead or wounded.

After the shock of the attack, the balance of the smuggler gang rallied, connected themselves with their artillery and put up a wicked fight for a few minutes. But they had very little chance against the superior arms and marksmanship of Grounds and Hunt and quite soon the Mexican population in Skeleton Canon was reduced to the minimum, or less.

It appears as though after the Mexicans did get into action, they must have concentrated the most of their fire on Hunt who was behind an oak tree, as, after a lapse of nearly fifty years time, the bullet marks can be plainly seen today. It is possible that Grounds may have also received an equal share of attention but as he was ensconsed behind a large rock the marks of battle have no doubt been long since removed by erosion.

It has been stated that Hunt received a painful, though not dangerous wound in this fight but this has been denied by those who claim to know positively, but this is of small consequence as he and Grounds made a real fight against great odds. A well known rancher over in that locality, in telling of this event, says that Hunt was wounded and that after Grounds had placed him under what is now known as "The Outlaw Oak" and made his as comfortable as possible under the circumstances, he started out to attend to the financial end of the deal. During the fight the pack mules had become scattered and Billy mounted his horse and began rounding them up. When he found one which was too wild to approach he would shoot him to gentle him. After having rounded up the treasury department of the smuggler gang, the boys found that they were possessed of about 40 bars of gold, 90,000 Mexican silver dollars and 19 dead Mexicans.

One mule is reported as having escaped and it is presumed that he was packed with gold bullion on one side and silver on the other for the reason that several years later some cowboys working cattle on the flat about a mile to the west of the battle ground, picked up 80 or 90 Mexican silver dollars which they found scattered over the ground. Quite a quantity of these silver dollars were also found in the hollow of the Outlaw Oak and many others were picked up from time to time in the immediate vicinity of this fight.

About ten years later a well known government official, in company of a cowboy friend, while riding up through Skeleton Canon chanced upon one of these old rawhide "kiacks" or rawhide carriers, and the cowboy dismounted and after looking at it gave it an energetic kick, breaking his foot. Investigation showed that the supposedly empty "kiack" contained six or eight thousand dollars in gold bullion.

Grounds and Hunt stayed in that vicinity until a Mexican with a yoke of oxen and a wagon chanced to come their way. They took him in on the deal with the promise of one-tenth if he would haul this loot to their camp. The bargain was closed and the gold was hauled to their camp, the Mexican killed and the wagon burned.

It is stated that they took the 90,000 Mexican dollars up the canon a short distance and buried them between two large oak trees but they were evidently dug up and spent by someone else as a later investigation showed a hole about four feet deep between the two oaks in question, empty, and can be seen today by any one caring to pass that way.

In those days it was not uncommon for outlaws to openly boast of their deeds especially when spending their ill gotten gains over the bars of the many saloons which at that time were very much in evidence while Volstead was still attending St. Olaf's College away up in Minnesota and having no thought of the 18th Amendment. Some one had evidently listened in on their conversation and learned of the silver cache, resurrected it and put it into circulation. Probably some advocate of free silver. They left the hole anyway. Mexican silver dollars at that time had the same purchasing power as did the American dollar.

It is also stated that Grounds and Hunt were implicated in another wholesale slaughter of Mexican smugglers which netted them another one hundred thousand dollars in gold bullion and nearly a quart of diamonds, all of which was taken to their camp and buried, but as the particulars of this deal were never set forth it is possible that this may be only a dream, a pipe dream; but, there is no question but what Grounds and Hunt were implicated in many adventures which netted them immense pecuniary profits.

They at last decided that they had sufficient of the world's goods to last them for the balance of their natural lives and started to leave the country. They were in the vicinity of Charleston on the night of March 25th, 1882, and at 8:30 p. m. of that date four employes of the Tombstone Mining and Milling Company, named Austin, Cheenery, Hunt and Peel, were in the office of the company's building, just across the river from Charleston, when there came a knocking at the door as though made by the butt of a gun and some one called, "Come in." The door was thrown open and two masked men armed with rifles, entered. As the first man entered the room he fired a shot at Mr. Peel who chanced to be on the outside of the counter, and he fell with a bullet near his heart. The second bandit pointed his rifle at Mr. Austin and pulled the trigger but Mr. Austin dropped behind the counter just the fractional portion of a second before the trigger pull and the bullet went wild. Both men backed out and disappeared, one of them losing his hat in his haste.

The murdered man was the son of Judge B. L. Peel. The following paragraph appeared in the April 3rd, 1882, issue of the Tombstone Epitaph, "Perhaps I am not in a condition to express a clear, deliberate opinion, but I would say to the good citizens of Cochise County that there is one of three things you have to do, there is a class of cut-throats among you and you can never convict them in court. You must combine and protect yourselves and wipe them out, or you must give up the county to them, or you will be murdered one at a time as my son has been.

(Signed) B. L. PEEL."

In checking up on location, boot prints, horse-shoe prints, hat and other data, it appeared as though Grounds and Hunt had committed this crime. It was later proven that early the following morning they were at Lewis Springs, a short distance east of Charleston, and that they were very nervous and very carefully keeping out of sight of strangers, that a detachment of soldiers rode up and they kept out of sight until after their departure. Inasmuch as there were already warrants out for their arrest on other charges, they became more wanted than ever.

At 7:00 p. m. of March 28th, 1882, Deputy Sheriff E. A. Healey, who was in charge of the Sheriff's office during the temporary absence of Sheriff Johnnie Behan, received word that two notorious characters, for whom warrants were laying in the sheriff's office, named Billy Grounds alias Billy the Kid, and Zwing Hunt, would be within eight or ten miles of town during the night or the early morning of the 29th.

The message received at about 7:00 a. m. of March 29th, reads as follows: "Healey, send coroner out to Jack Chandler's Ranch; one of our men dead, Billy Grounds dying, also Hunt. Jack Young shot through thigh. I got creased in the neck. E. H. Allen."

In the April 3rd, 1882, issue of the Tombstone Epitaph, appears the following: "The parties whom Breakenridge was sent out to arrest were notoriously hard cases—the worst of the type of cowboy rustlers. For this reason Mr. Harley very wisely decided to send out what he considered a sufficiently large force to insure their arrest without resistance; but, careful as he was, and as well as he thought he knew the desperate men he had to deal with, he was mistaken as the sequel shows.

"The man, Zwing Hunt, was a young man, tall and slim, quite sandy complexioned, sandy mustache, and his face, neck and hands badly freckled. It is said that there had been a warrant for his arrest for nearly, if not quite a year, but he had never been captured. The last Grand Jury brought in three or four indictments against him, it is reported, for cattle stealing.

"The Kid, or Grounds, is said to be quite a young man, with a round red face and of shorter stature than his companion, Hunt. He is also under indictment for cattle stealing, having been engaged in the same thefts with Hunt."

A. Lewis testified that he was at the Chandler Ranch on the morning of March 29th, 1882, that some one came to the door and called him by name, and then said: "Come out, I want to see you." Lewis claims that he got up and went to the east door of the house where he found a man with a gun in his hand, who instructed him to go around the corner of the house. He did so, and met Breakenridge, who said to him: "You know me now?" Lewis replied that he did. Just then the firing commenced and he stepped behind a tree and Breakenridge behind another.

Then someone opened the west door, fired a shot and Breakenridge fired a return shot into the door. Something dropped and about the same time, a man whom he afterwards learned was Allen, ran a few steps and fell into a small arroya about two rods distant. As he left his tree to run down into the arroya, some one took a shot at him. He thought that Gillespie was the man whom he met when he came out of the east door of the house.

Lewis further stated that the parties in the house that night were Billy Grounds, Zwing Hunt, Elliott, Caldwell and himself. That Grounds and Hunt were not in the habit of stopping there as he had never seen them there before. He also stated that when Grounds and Hunt came to the ranch they told him that they had some business with Elliott. But Elliott was not there, so they went on to "Soldiers' Hole" and returned the next day and stayed there at the ranch the balance of that day and that night.

Lewis also stated that Grounds and Hunt were very watchful and went out with field glasses and took observations. From their conversation he received the impression that they were looking for officers to drop in on them at any time. He said he heard them tell of writs out for them and Hunt said that he "Would just as soon see his grave as to see the inside of Yuma prison." They said that on certain charges they would surrender themselves but on others they would not. They had mentioned coming up the San Pedro River a few days previously, but did not mention Charleston.

Lewis also testified that as he passed out of the house on the morning of March 29th, 1882, Billy Grounds said to him, "If they ask you, tell them that we are not here." Then Lewis added, "I think that Grounds took the west door and Hunt the east door. Grounds was shot down in the west door and Hunt must have been at the other door; when Gillespie was killed, I suppose that it was Hunt who killed him."

Billy Breakenridge stated that Lewis did not come out of the house until the shooting was over and that he never took a stand behind any tree near him as there was only one tree there. Breakenridge said he was behind that tree and that it was not near large enough either. Lewis went on to a place of safety and made it snappy.

John H. Elliott, who was living at the Chandler Ranch at that time, states in part: "Grounds and Hunt came to the ranch Tuesday morning when I saw them first; Hunt, when he came, asked me to take a message to town for him; he sent a note which I delivered to Chandler. Hunt seemed anxious that Chandler should come out. Grounds and Hunt were watchful and excited as though they apprehended something, but I heard them say nothing. Grounds, after being shot, was found in the west door on his back. Hunt was found some 500 yards from the house. It was nearly an hour before we found the body of Gillespie. Hunt was close to the east door when I left the house."

Those who are familiar with the details of this spirited encounter cannot understand why Elliott should say that it was nearly an hour before the body of Gillespie was found, when he was shot through the head and died instantly, falling directly in front of the east door of the house.

Deputy Sheriff Billy Breakenridge's testimony as to what took place at Chandler's Ranch just at the first break of day on March 29th, 1882, and which he corroborates 46 years later, is that when he and his posse arrived at Chandler Ranch that morning, he stationed Gillespie and Young behind the woodpile at the east end of the house, with instructions to wait there until such time as either Grounds or Hunt should come out to look after their horses or to get wood with which to prepare breakfast. They were then to cover them quickly and order them to "Put 'em high and keep 'em high," as it was more than likely that neither one of them would be armed at that early hour and under the conditions, not to shoot unless absolutely necessary.

After stationing Gillespie and Young behind the woodpile, he took Allen and started around to take station in the small arroya which passed about 30 feet from the house on the west side. Just as they had reached the corner of the house, he heard Gillespie shout to those inside to open the door and when some one inside asked who it was, Gillespie replied, "It's the sheriff." The door flew open and Gillespie fell with a bullet through his head. Another shot, and Young fell with a bullet in one thigh.

The west door flew open and bullets came out. Allen fell and Breakenridge took cover quickly behind an oak tree which stood nearly in front of the house and getting a line on the man who was in the west door, fired at him. He heard the man drop onto the floor and saw his feet sticking out of the door. Allen had been creased along the side of the neck and was soon able to be up. Just at this stage of the game the east door flew open and a man ran out and started to the top of the ridge back of the house. Breakenridge picked up Allen's Winchester and sky-lighted the man as he reached the ridge, then pulled the trigger. The man fell, but quickly got up and disappeared over the top of the ridge.

Just then a man named Lewis, also known as Bull Lewis because he was a bull-team freighter, came out of the house with his hands in the air and saying "Don't shoot, Billy, I'm neutral, I was here when they came but I could not refuse to let them camp here because it is not my house and I am just camping here too." Lewis went down to the other house.

Deputy Sheriff Billy Breakenridge then took the trail of the wounded man over the ridge and found him in a bunch of bear grass over the ridge a short distance. He called to him to "throw up his hands" and Allen, who by this time was once more taking an interest in matters mundane, heard the challenge and hurried up the ridge to where Breakenridge was.

Hunt called out, "I'm done for; come and get me Billy." Breakenridge did not know but that this might be some trap, so he called to Hunt to get up and come to him. Hunt replied that he was shot through, so Breakenridge gave him instructions to turn over on his face and spread out his arms and while Billy covered him, Allen went to Hunt and relieved him of his guns. Zwing was found to have been shot through both lungs.

A wagon was secured and the dead, dying and wounded were loaded into it and taken in to Tombstone. Billy Grounds passed out shortly after midnight, having received two buck-shot wounds through his head and one through his body. Of the six men who were engaged in this early morning's gun battle at Chandler Ranch, in less than two minutes after Gillespie had been dropped in front of the east door by the first shot, Deputy Sheriff Billy Breakenridge was the only one on his feet and unwounded.

Findings of the Coroner's Jury: "We, the undersigned, a jury impaneled by the Coroner of said county, (Cochise), on the 31st day of March, 1882, * * * * after viewing the body and hearing such testimony as has been brought before us, find that his name was William Grounds, age—, a native of—, and that he came to his death on the 30th day of March, 1882, from the effects of a gun-shot wound, received on the morning of March 29th, 1882, at the hands of Deputy Sheriff Breakenridge, of Cochise County, while resisting arrest by said deputy, * * * * and consider his act justifiable. (Signed)

"Fred Dodge, A. H. Emanuel, Alf Tregido, Thomas Mugane, H. Baron, John Cody, G. W. Atkins, H. H. Tuttle."

In the April 17th, 1882, issue of the "Tombstone Epitaph" appears the following open letter, "Editor Epitaph, Don't you think it would be a very politic thing to do, viz: remove the cowboy, Hunt, from the hospital to the County Jail? It appears to my mind that he is liable to leave his present quarters at any moment and I feel sure that every justice-loving, law-abiding citizen and resident of this county would be glad to hear of his incarceration in the public prison where he will at least be in secure hands for the time being. Let the proper officials see to it that the miscreant shall not escape from Justice. By publishing this in the first issue of your valuable journal, you will greatly oblige, truly yours, ARGUS."

From the editorial column of the Epitaph under date of April 28th, 1882, is quoted as follows, "Zwing Hunt took leave of his friends in Tombstone most unceremoniously last evening, not even paying his doctor's bill; this shows base ingratitude on his part.

Then followed the following local news item, "The noted cowboy, Zwing Hunt, whose capture cost the life of one good man and the wounding of another, and who has been lying in the County Hospital, suffering from a wound through the lungs, received in the fight at the time of his capture, was quietly taken out last night between the hours of 8 and 9 o'clock and put into some kind of a conveyance and driven away, whence or where, no one knows. On Sunday last a brother of Hunt arrived in this city from Texas; since his arrival, Hunt has been rapidly convalescing and in better spirits than at any time since his confinement."

In the June 10th, issue of the "Tombstone Epitaph" appears the following: "DEATH OF ZWING HUNT. The restless character who so often faced death unflinchingly has at last 'crossed the divide' into the great unknown valley of the future. Whatever else can be laid to his charge, the fact of his bravery all will admit. It is hardly necessary to admit that he was not a saint, but whether he was a mortal or a venal sinner, those who knew him best, must determine.

"From all accounts, Zwing Hunt was the child of circumstances and a creature of excitement. Generous to a fault, rash to the extremity of foolishness and as brave as an Arabian fire-worshipper, Zwing would do to go tiger hunting with; but he is dead. The same deadly aim, impelled by the same insatiable thirst for the blood of white men, that has caused many a brave man, tender women and innocent babe to seek the presence of the Creator unushered, sent Zwing Hunt to the bosom of his Father and his God.

"Yesterday afternoon, Hugh Hunt, brother of the deceased, reached here, and states that after escaping from the hospital, they struck out for the Dragoons on horseback and reached there well into the night. Zwing was very weak and sick and vomited several times during the journey and when they got into the Dragoons, declined to go any further in consequence of his disability.

"The original plan was to keep going until they reached the fastness of the Chiricahua Mountains where they could dodge the officers of the law with more celerity than in the exposed plains of timberless foot-hills. They lay all of the following day in the Dragoons and then went toward Morse's saw-mill.

"During the entire month of May they wandered through the strongholds of the Chiracahuas, Zwing recovering with remarkable rapidity. On May the 30th they removed from the Sweetwater, near the end of the Swisshelm Mountains into Russell Canon, enroute to Morse's Mill.

"On the morning of May 31st Zwing baked bread while Hugh made coffee and broiled the meat. Just as they sat down to eat, a volley was fired at them. Hugh thought that the officers had located them, but, when he saw that they had been attacked by Indians and that they were in the act of shooting again, Zwing pulled his gun, and exclaimed, 'Dammit, go to shooting.' It was the last sentence he ever spoke as he fell with a bullet through his left hip, one through his abdomen and two through his head, dying almost instantly.

"Zwing had fired twice and Hugh five times. Seeing that Zwing was dead, Hugh ran and jumped onto a hobbled horse and rode the fettered animal for nearly half a mile, headed for Camp Price.

"The Indians, who were on foot, followed him for about three miles, firing continuously but he escaped injury. Arriving at the camp, he reported the affair to the Commanding Officer. Lieutenant Clark and ten men accompanied him to the camp. The Indians had cut off the middle finger of Zwing's right hand. At the scene of the killing were three large juniper trees and under the middle one a shallow grave was scooped out and the mortal remains of Zwing Hunt laid to rest therein, and on the trunk of the middle tree, were carved these words, 'Z. Hunt, May 31st, 1882.

"He was 24 years of age the day he was shot at Chandler's Ranch. He stated that he thought that Breakenridge's posse was the Earps or he never would have fired into them."

Intimate friends of the Hunt family state that Hugh Hunt was Zwing's uncle and not his brother as was stated at the time. They say that Hugh made arrangements for a team and wagon to be brought to a point near the hospital and that Zwing was loaded into it and taken high up into the Chiracahuas to recuperate from the effects of his wound. That a few weeks later Hugh Hunt made his way down to a soldier camp and notified the officer in charge that he and his brother had been jumped by Apaches that morning and that his brother, Zwing Hunt, had been killed and, as no one of them knew Zwing, that they accepted Hugh's statement as correct and final and the body was buried.

His friends further state that this was a frame up to get Zwing out of the country; that the finding of a dead man who had been very recently killed by Indians suggested an idea to them which was carried out. It is said that a couple of shots were fired into the face of the corpse to mutilate it so that identification might not be positive should any of the impromptu Coroner's Jury chance to have ever seen him before.

As soon as the news of Zwing's death had been circulated around over the country and no one was looking for him, he and Hugh made their way out of the country back to Texas where he died some time later, in the home of friends.

The source of this information is considered reliable, or at least it should be, as it comes from Zwing Hunt's most intimate friends. This being the case, who then is the unknown who was buried over in Hunt's Canon under the juniper tree? Quien sabe?

ROBBERY OF THE G. & C. STORE

AT 7:30 p. m. on December 6th, 1883, five men rode into Bisbee from toward Tombstone, dismounted about 100 yards from the store of Goldwater and Castenada, tied their horses to the ground and proceeded to mask themselves, all but one man who was afterwards identified as Tex Howard, alias Tex Willis. All wore blanket lined canvas overcoats and each man was armed with a Winchester saddle gun and two six-shooters.

After having made their hasty preparations, they walked briskly toward the Goldwater-Castanada store. W. E. Delaney and Dan Dowd, alias Big Dan, took position just outside of the front door to act as guards, while O. W. Sample, alias Big Red, John Kelly, alias Yorkey, and Tex Howard entered the store.

The following day being pay-day at the Copper Queen Mine the payroll was supposed to have been in possession of Goldwater-Castanada, but it chanced that the money in question did not arrive, it having missed stage connections enroute. They looted the safe and obtained money and jewelry, variously estimated at from $900 to $1000, the exact amount never having been published.

In the meantime, the outside guards were also busy. Every person appearing upon the scene of action being ordered inside of the store. John Tappinier refused to enter the store and turned to run, but two bullets cut him down and he died instantly. The sounds of these two shots caused others to investigate and Delaney and Dowd shot at every man whom they saw and D. T. Smith and J. R. Nolley were quickly added to their list of dead.

Mrs. R. H. Roberts, hearing the shooting, stepped to a window facing the street and looked out. As she stood, partly concealed by the window curtains, she was seen by Delaney and Dowd and they, believing that she was a man waiting for a good shooting chance, shot her dead.

As the outlaws were working their way toward their

horses, Deputy Sheriff William Daniels opened fire on them and wounded Big Red Sample, but all of the outlaws managed to get to their horses and they quickly mounted and were away. Sheriff Ward of Cochise County wired from Tombstone that a reward of $1500 would be paid for the apprehension of each man. A posse was quickly formed and in pursuit.

John Heith, the owner of a saloon in Brewery Gulch, took a very active part in the organization of this posse and at times virtually took charge of it in his efforts to lead them away from a plain trail left by the outlaws. He acted in a very suspicious manner, always calculated to favor the outlaws, and the other members of the posse became suspicious of him.

When camp was made at dark that night, Heith was detailed to guard the horses and while he was engaged in that duty, the other members of the posse held a business meeting with him as their subject. In piecing the evidence covering the events of the few days previous to the hold up, it was learned that Heith had been very friendly with this bunch of men and that they had been making his saloon their headquarters.

It was decided to arrest him and send him to Tombstone where he could be safely held for investigation. The men drew lots for the arresting honor and Ed Barker, assayer for the Copper Queen Mining Company, and Stewart Hunt, afterwards sheriff of Cochise County, were the lucky ones. They rode out to the herd, made the arrest quickly and effectively, not giving Heith any chance whatever to use his gun. They then took him to Tombstone where he was placed in jail to await further investigation.

Sample and Howard went to Clifton where they met an acquaintance named W. W. Bush, and to him they related what they had done also displaying a gold watch, naming it as a part of the loot. They talked freely to him and told him of their plans and what directions had been taken by the other three men. As soon as he could make a quiet get away from them, he went to Deputy Sheriff Hill and disclosed all of the information which he had received from Sample and Howard. Hill immediately took up the matter with the Cochise County authorities with the result that Sheriff Ward did not leave a stone unturned, working night and day until all of the gang were landed in jail. In forty-five days from the date of the commission of the crime, all six men were in jail and not a shot had been fired in their apprehension.

Sample and Howard were arrested at Clifton. Kelley, masquerading as an east bound hobo, was arrested at Deming. Dowd and Delaney crossed the line into Mexico but Ward followed them and arrested Dowd at Coralitos in the State of Chihuahua and Delaney at Minas Prietos in the State of Sonora.

A special term of court was convened on February 4th, 1884. These men were arraigned on the 8th and all pleaded "Not Guilty" to the crime of murder. Their case was set for the 9th and on the 11th they were found "Guilty" as charged and on the 19th death sentence was pronounced, to be carried out on March 6th.

Inasmuch as Heith had staged an afternoon dance at his saloon on the day of the crime, it was presumed that this was done with the intent of getting as many people away from the vicinity of the proposed crime as possible. It was proven that the crime was planned in his saloon and that he received a portion of the loot, the same having been found in his possession.

Heith demanded a separate hearing which was set for February 16th and was completed on the 20th. The evidence brought in at the trial was mostly circumstantial but he was found "Guilty of having been an accessory before the crime" and was sentenced to a life term of imprisonment in the state penitentiary at Yuma.

The people did not take kindly to the decision of the jury in the Heith case and at about 8:00 a. m. of February 22nd, 1884, a bunch of Bisbee and Tombstone miners went to the Cochise County Jail, where there had been twelve men on guard day and night. However, at this hour in the morning, with the night force off duty, and the day guard partaking of their morning's meal, Sheriff J. L. Ward chanced to be the only man on guard and, being but one man against at least 100 drink infuriated miners, he could do nothing but let them have their way and take Heith out.

They took Heith west on Toughnut Street until the railroad crossing was reached and here they swung him up to the cross arm of a telegraph pole. His body hung there nearly all day and was viewed by thousands of men, women and children.

Some enterprising citizen went to the Cochise County Commissioners and obtained a permit to build a tier of seats around the scaffold upon which the other five men were to be hung, expecting to charge fifty cents admission, but the night before the date set for the execution a mob went to the court house and demolished the seats. It is understood that the majority of the members of this mob consisted of well known and prominent women of Tombstone.

A few days before the execution of these five men, John L. Sullivan, then heavyweight champion of the world, chanced to be in Tombstone and these men, learning of his presence in town, sent for him to come and visit them in the county jail. John, being a good old scout, went.

Dan Dowd said to him, "John Sullivan, you think you are a great man because you can knock out any man in the world in five rounds but the sheriff of this county, who is a much smaller man than you, can knock out five men in one round."

At 1:10 p. m. of March 8th, 1884, the funeral procession started, headed by Sheriff J. L. Ward, Frs. Callagher and Jovenciau; next Omar W. Sample alias Big Red, accompanied by Sheriff Robert Paul of Pima County; then came James Howard alias Tex Howard alias Tex Willis, accompanied by Wallace Corbett; next came Daniel Dowd alias Big Dan, accompanied by Deputy Sheriff Hatch; next in the procession came W. E. Delaney, accompanied by Deputy Sheriff Crowley of Willcox and last in line came Daniel Kelley alias Yorkey, accompanied by Deputy Sheriff Fred Ward.

All of the prisoners marched to their doom with pleasant smiles on their faces and Delaney, Sample and Kelley recognizing familiar faces in the crowd, shouted their last good byes to them in a cheery manner. All shook hands with the officers and priests and denied their guilt.

As the condemned men stood on the scaffold, taking their last good-bye look at the world, Sheriff Ward asked them if they had anything to say. Dan Dowd said "It's getting pretty hot, so you might as well go ahead with the hanging." Tex Howard said, "Dan, it's liable to be a whole lot hotter where we are going." When the black caps had been adjusted, Kelley shouted, "Let 'er go," and they "Let 'er go."

MAX STEIN, TOM CAPEHURST, BILL CARVER AND FRANK LAUGHLIN

ONE APRIL day in 1900 Max Stein, Tom Capehart, George Frank alias Bill Carver and Frank Laughlin, holdup men and all around crooks, departed from Tombstone in a hurry; possibly it might have been in the night time but, anyway they left. Their first stop of any note was over in the San Simon Country near the New Mexico-Arizona Line.

Feeling the need of refreshments in favor of the inner man after their long, hurried journey, they made camp. In checking up on their commissary department they noted with deep regret that they had neglected bringing along any fresh beef but this deficiency did not delay their meal very long as they shot a beef and supplied themselves with fresh beef enough to last them for some time.

State Ranger George Scarborough and Deputy Sheriff Walter Birchfield chanced to ride up to this locality quite soon after the gang had departed and, finding the remains of the beef, hit the fresh trail and followed it. They had no idea that they were following a tough bunch of out-laws but thought they were on the trail of a bunch of Mexicans who might have rounded up and killed a beef, just to provide themselves with some fresh meat.

About 30 miles south of San Simon they overtook the gang, who had undoubtedly decided to go south and cross into Mexico. Scarborough and Birchfield both recognized their men and knew that they were up against a bad gang with odds in favor of the bad ones but they did not allow that fact to interfere in the least with the festivities and the ball opened by an overture of lead in this all star performance. Scarborough was badly wounded in one leg and while Birchfield was attempting to staunch the flow of blood the gang traveled on believing from the silence on the other side that both of their pursuers were either mortally wounded or dead. Birchfield received a wound of minor importance.

Birchfield made Scarborough as comfortable as possible and then, taking the better horse of their two, started to San Simon to get a wagon. There was a cold rain falling and as it takes considerable time to ride 30 miles through mesquite and grease wood thickets and over ridges and through arroyas and get a wagon back, Scarborough only lived a short time after reaching San Simon, having died from loss of blood and exposure.

"THE WILD BUNCH IN 1901"

When leaving Tombstone this gang evidently intended going to Clifton but while killing beef and preparing their meal they apparently changed their minds and headed for Mexico, and were traveling down the San Simon Valley a few miles to the east and almost parallel with their trail out from Tombstone, when overtaken by Scarborough and Birchfield.

After the fight over in the San Simon Valley, it was proven by subsequent investigation that this bunch split up and scattered and not one of the four was ever seen in that vicinity again.

Mac Stein immediately left Cochise County and a short time afterward was killed in Utah while assisting in a train robbery out there. He learned, when it was too late, that holding up trains, even in Utah, is a prohibited outdoor sport.

Frank Laughlin went to Wyoming and, instead of changing his ways and starting life anew, started right in where he left off down in Cochise County, Ariz., and killed himself another man, which resulted in a hard hearted jury voting him a life sentence in the state institution for the wayward.

Tom Capehart went to Colorado where he was fortunate enough to draw a life sentence on a murder charge and from that day forward Tom never knew what it meant to miss a meal or a suit of clothes. Colorado is a good state in this respect.

Bill Carver alias G. W. Franks was at one time a leading member of Black Jack Ketchum's gang and after he assisted in the Nogales, Ariz., bank holdup and the Black Jack gang was split up, he went north and was in Sam Ketchum's gang in the fight between that gang and peace officers on July 16th, 1899, near Cimmaron, N. M., in which Sam Ketchum was mortally wounded.

Carver then went north and joined Butch Cassiday's gang and participated in the Winnemucca, Nevada, bank robbery on September 19th, 1900, which netted them $32,-640 in gold. He went then over into Concho County, Texas, where he became involved in some argument with Oliver M. Thornton whom he shot and killed. A short time later he turned up at Sonora, Texas, and was killed on April 2nd, 1901, by Sheriff Briant of Sutton County.

APACHE KID

THE APACHE KID was another well known outlaw who ranged over Southern Arizona, dealing misery and desolation enroute. He made it a point to kill any one who opposed him or his wishes and he was actually more feared by his own people than Geronimo because Geronimo had responded at times to kind treatment and had great respect for certain army officers who had given him a square deal. The Kid took special delight in killing his enemies and he was never punished for any of his crimes. He was only apprehended once, and then escaped.

The Apache Kid was a son of Toga de Chuz, a San Carlos Apache chief who was Geronimo's brother. The Kid was raised by Al Sieber who was at that time chief scout at San Carlos, and who taught him to speak English and write a little. Some authorities have stated that Apache Kid was a Carlisle Indian School graduate but this is entirely in error as he never went to school a day in his life. Robert Geronimo, son of Chief Geronimo, now living on the Mescalero Reservation, who is the Kid's cousin, recently made this statement.

It is thought that the Kid's identity had been twisted in some manner with the identity of the Carlisle Kid who was a Carlisle Indian School graduate. Upon the event of his graduation, some silly, sentimental, but well meaning woman told him that now his education was completed, and as he was a smart boy, that he must now go back to his tribe and make a special effort to see that his people were not imposed upon by the white men.

Soon after his return to his tribe he became angered at an army lieutenant and, obtaining a gun, shot the lieutenant. He was promptly apprehended and placed on trial in a military court and sentenced to hang. Sentence was effectively carried out at Ft. Grand, and another blood-thirsty career was nipped in the bud.

Toga de Chuz had, away back about 1848, had some trouble over an Apache maiden with another Indian named Rip. They were only about twenty years of age at that time and in the encounter following are argument Toga de Chuz was awarded the decision by a large and admir-

DEPUTY SHERIFF HUNKY DORY HOLMES

ing audience. He was awarded the maiden too.

Rip never forgave Toga de Chuz, neither was he willing to forget and one morning 40 years later Toga de Chuz awoke in the Happy Hunting Grounds, with his heart split in two. Investigation quite plainly showed that Rip had revenged himself for the forty-year-old insult.

Apache Kid, who had been a model Apache up to that

date and also being first sergeant of the scouts, was looked upon as a man of much importance. Also he was the eldest son of Toga de Chuz and as such was expected to avenge his father's death. Taking five of his scouts he went up to where Old Rip lived and shot him. He then, instead of returning to his troop of scouts, went back above the fort to where his own people lived.

When Al Sieber, who was absent at the time of the killing of Old Rip, returned and learned what had taken place he sent word up to the Kid to come down to the post. The Kid came, and with him were ten Apache bucks, all fully armed. Sieber stepped back into his tent and brought out his rifle, seeing all of the Indians prepared to shoot, he fired one shot and killed one Indian. All of the rest of them fired at him, but only one bullet struck him, and this one shattered his shin bone in a frightful manner. Seeing Sieber drop, they all ran away, each one confident that his bullet had done the work.

A few miles from the fort they encountered a man named Bill Dihl and killed him; then striking over into the San Pedro River Country, they followed it up for some distance and from there worked over onto the head of the Sonoita and killed Mike Grace. They were apprehended in the Rincon Mountains by Lieutenant Johnson and in the fight which ensued two of their number were killed and all their horses shot, this putting them on foot. This is how the Apache Kid came to break out.

He later returned to Ft. Grant and surrendered and was tried on a desertion charge and sentenced to a term in the military prison but President Cleveland pardoned him after he had served a few months of his time.

Kid was later arrested again on a charge of having killed a whiskey peddler and he and six others were sentenced to life terms in the state penitentiary at Yuma. Sheriff Glen Reynolds and "Hunky Dory" Holmes, one of his deputies, started from Globe to Casa Grande where they were to take the train, with six Indians and one Mexican. At the Gila Crossing the Indians were taken out to walk up a long sandy stretch from the river and this gave them the chance that they had been waiting for and each officer was grappled by three Indians and their arms taken from them.   Both officers were dead in less time than it takes to tell about the instance.   Eugene Livingston, who was driving the stage, hearing an unusual noise, looked back and received a bullet just over one eye but as it was only a glancing shot Gene is still living although he was down and out for some time.   The Kid obtained the keys to the handcuffs from Reynolds' pocket and released everybody. The Mexican was also released and instead of making his escape he went to Florence and notified the authorities.

Holmes' body when examined showed no bullet hole or any other injury which would cause death.   He had died of heart failure due to the excitement.

The Apache Kid was never apprehended and died of tuberculosis in the Sierra Madre Mountains of Sonora, Mexico, in 1900.   His squaw came out of the mountains and back to her people and she told the story.

MEYERS, SMITH AND GREEN HOLDUP

D URING the spring of 1887 a Southern Pacific passenger train was held up and robbed at Vail, a small station about 20 miles east of Tucson, Ariz. The holdup men, of whom there were three, after robbing the Wells-Fargo Express car and the passengers, cut off the engine and boarding it, went west toward Tucson.

The lone engine was located at Polvo Siding, about four miles east of Tucson. Sheriff M. F. Shaw was notified and, organizing a posse which included some first class Papago trailers, lost no time in getting to Polvo where they expected to locate the trail of the holdups. Investigation at Polvo was vigorously pursued but there was absolutely no trace or signs of the robbers having left the railroad right of way on either side at this point.

Some time later another train was held up at Vail, this being in August of the same year. Engineer Jim Guthrie was at the throttle and Bob Bradford was on the opposite side of the engine. When Guthrie saw the stop signal he sensed a holdup and disregarded it. As they passed it, a bullet from the south side of the track cut the left half of his mustache off as cleanly as though cut with a pair of scissors.

Guthrie was just congratulating himself that he had outwitted the holdups when he plunged into an open switch and his engine was grounded. He and Bradford both jumped off the engine and struck the ground running. As they were carrying no "stop orders" they did not even slow down until they reached a dense mesquite thicket at a perfectly safe distance, and here they remained until the outlaws had departed from that immediate vicinity.

After the train had come to such an unceremonious stop one of the bandits placed a charge of dynamite against the door of the Wells-Fargo car and thus ruined a perfectly good door. There were only two bandits involved in this transaction. After shooting the express car door one of the bandits entered the car, lighted a lamp, found the express messenger and, after trying to bend his six shooter barrel over his head, threw him out of the car.

While bandit number one was busy looting the express car bandit number two was busy with his rifle persuading

M. F. SHAW, EARLY DAY SHERIFF OF PIMA COUNTY

the train crew and passengers that it was very dangerous for trespassers up around the head end of that particular train.

After cleaning house in the express car both bandits turned their attention to the passengers and announced that the usual collection would be taken up, requesting all

present to respond liberally as their donations would be
applied to a worthy cause.   Needless to say the entire
outdoor congregation contributed bountifully and when the
painful ceremony had been concluded the robbers, not having any engine to ride as they had on the previous occasion,
left the right of way and disappeared to the north.

Once more Sheriff Shaw gathered together his faithful
posse and rushed to the scene of action.   This time they
found a clearly defined trail of the two train robbers which
led them directly to the Colossal Cave which is about five
miles north of Vail.   The posse had no trouble in locating the loot which had been hidden in the cave, all of which
was recovered.

The outlaws had not tarried at the cave very long and
once more the posse took their trail.   This time it led
straight to Pantano, where it was learned that they boarded
an east bound train and rode into El Paso.

In October, 1887, a west bound Southern Pacific passenger train was held up by two men on the steep grade
about four miles west of El Paso.   One of the bandits
took charge of the engineer and fireman while the other one
attended to the financial end of the deal which involved
the Wells-Fargo Express car.

Wells-Fargo Messenger Smith was armed with a
double barreled shot gun, a six-shooter and plenty of ammunition for both, but as soon as he realized that he was
right up against an honest to goodness holdup, he blew out
the light, opened the door and informed the man in charge
that he would surrender the car to him in the interests of
safety first.

Smith started to climb down with his guns but after laying them on the floor right at the door, he forgot all about
them.   After informing the bandit in charge, loudly and
plainly, that he was neutral and not searching for trouble,
the bandit, using scandalous language, ordered Smith to
get back up in the car and light the lamp.   Just as he had
stepped up on the first round of the ladder, the bandit
kicked him and the momentum of the kick raised him
enough that his hand closed right on the handle of his six

shooter which he had forgotten all about. Now Smith was a reasonable man and did not mind a little thing like being held up, but did object to being kicked after having been so kind to the bold, bad man, so he took a good firm hold of the handle of that six shooter, swung it over his left arm and pulled the trigger. He scored a bulls eye. Dropping the six shooter and picking up the shot gun he then took a snap shot at the other outlaw who was covering the engineer and he fell dead with a handful of buck shot across the groin.

The mortal remains of the two dead outlaws were loaded into the baggage car and the train backed into El Paso. There was much excitement around the station and a great crowd gathered to view the remains. No one appeared to know them until a Mrs. Green identified them as two men who had roomed with her for several months. She stated that they were both railroad men from Chicago, one named Meyers, an engineer and the other a trainman called Smith. She also said that they and her son were great friends and that he had taken a trip or two with them to Tucson. When asked where her son was, she said that he had gone to Fort Worth a few months before, and was working on a farm near there.

Young Green was brought back to El Paso where he made a full confession, stating that he was only with them one time and that, becoming scared, he had taken his share of the loot and departed for Fort Worth. He was tried, found guilty and sentenced to a five-year term in the penitentiary.

Green stated that on two occasions, after trains had been robbed at Vail, the engine would be cut off and Meyers would run it on into Millville, a suburb of eastern Tucson. He said that they would then take off their loot and Meyers would reverse the engine, open the throttle just enough to allow sufficient steam to escape to move it slowly backward to Polvo Siding when the engine would strike a slight grade on the east side of the siding and stop. This explained the mystery of why no trace could ever be obtained of any one leaving the engine at Polvo.

Meyers, Green and Smith came to Tucson from El Paso and took lodging at the Belmont Hotel. They mixed freely with the Southern Pacific trainmen and became quite intimate with a conductor named Gillespie, who carried them between Tucson and El Paso between holdups. Green only took part in one holdup.

After the first holdup by the three men, they buried their loot in the dense mesquite brush just east of town and later Meyers and Smith showed up at the yard office of the Southern Pacific and visited for some time with the trainmen and other employes whom they met there. They went down into town and picked up Green and they all went to supper together and then to their room at the Belmont.

The following day they dug up their loot and transferred it to their room. A Tucson policeman, named McLeady, became suspicious of these three men and followed them to their room and stationed himself in the hall just outside of their door where he was found by the landlady who bawled him out in the latest approved style and compelled him to leave there without getting any information as to what was going on inside of the room. It was an actual fact that they were even then, as the irate landlady was delivering her caustic oration to McLeady, dividing the loot.

Upon the testimony of Green, Gillespie was arrested and charged with having been an accessory to the holdups on account of their having always ridden with him between Tucson and El Paso but it was proven in court that it was the custom of railroad men to carry each other on their trains, and he was acquitted.

Had Gillespie kept his mouth shut to any reasonable extent, he would have gotten off clean, but, wishing to make himself solid with the railroad company, he testified at his trial that a man named Doc Smart was evidently one of the gang as he had carried him every time that he had carried the rest of the bunch on their trips back and forth.

An intelligent Arizona jury found Smart guilty of being an accessory and he was sentenced to five years servitude in the State penitentiary at Yuma.

One day, while awaiting his transfer to Yuma, Smart was visited by Gillespie. It is not known for sure just what passed between them, but it is presumed that Gillespie gave Smart a gun with which to shoot his way out of jail should the opportunity offer. Shortly after Gillespie's departure from the jail, three shots were heard back in the cell house and investigation showed that Smart had shot himself three times in the head. The gun with which he had inflicted these wounds upon himself was of small caliber and of the brand known as a suicide gun. But in this case it had failed to live up to its reputation, all three bullets having struck the skull at an angle, passing between the skull and scalp, from where they were later extracted and he soon recovered and was none the worse on account of the self-inflicted wounds.

Smart was shortly afterwards taken to Yuma but he was not there very long until some state official interested himself in his behalf and he was pardoned out after about four months servitude.

Just on account of one man receiving a kick, two men were killed and two more received a five year sentence. Moral: "Don't kick."

SHEHAN, HART AND JOHNSON HOLDUP

BACK in 1887, when Southern Pacific trains were held up with alarming frequency by the outlaws infesting Cochise County, a train was held up just west of Steins near the New Mexico-Arizona state line. United States Marshal W. K. Meade and Sheriff John Slaughter of Cochise County, arrested Larry Shehan and a man named Johnson on suspicion of their having been implicated in this hold up. They were brought to Tucson and turned over to Sheriff M. F. Shaw of Pima County for safe keeping.

In due time they were tried before the federal judge and acquitted on the grounds of insufficient evidence. As they passed out of the county courthouse, Johnson tarried long enough to inform Sheriff Shaw that they never had robbed any trains but, as long as they had been accused of it, they were going to get busy and rob one.

They went from Tucson to Willcox where they went to work for about a month, during which time they were joined by Dick Hart. They then took their saddles and bridles and other horse furniture and boarded the train for El Paso. From there they went to Chihuahua City, Mexico, where they purchased horses and returned to the United States via Casa Grande, Mexico. They entered the United States at Lang's Ranch, Cochise County, southeast of Tombstone, and from there went on toward the north.

They struck the Southern Pacific track about half way between San Simon and Steins, made camp in a dense mesquite thicket about half a mile south of the track and when the time was ripe, held up a Southern Pacific passenger train. This venture was a financial success but the Wells-Fargo Express Company refused to make public the extent of their success.

United States Marshal W. K. Meade, Deputy United States Marshal Billy Smith, Sheriff M. F. Shaw of Pima County and his under sheriff, Charlie Shibbell and special

Agent Lem Harris of the Southern Pacific Company, with three Papago trailers, lost no time in getting onto the ground.

A special train was ordered and horses, provision and bedding hastily loaded and gotten on the way. Upon arrival at the scene of the holdup the horses were jumped out of the cars, quickly saddled and the officers started cutting for signs.

The officers, believing that this holdup was pulled by some one from Lordsburg and that they would circle around for a while and then go back there, instructed the conductor in charge of their special to pull on into Lordsburg, where they would meet the train later.

The trail, instead of leading them to Lordsburg as they had expected it would, took them south through the San Simon Valley, taking them further and further from their bed and board every minute. But as the train robbers had 12 hours start of them and the trail was a plain one, they did not wish to take time to go to Lordsburg for bedding and provisions which were at that time 22 miles to the east of them, instead they hurried ahead on the trail.

Judging from the signs, the robbers took every advantage of their 12 hour lead over the posse. Some distance down the San Simon Valley the officers found $200,000 in railroad bonds which the robbers had thrown away as useless, and to lighten the loads that their horses were carrying. These bonds were registered and thus not negotiable.

The posse followed the trail for four days and ate only one meal during that time. On the morning of the fifth day they rode into Gray's Ranch where they fed their horses and themselves. At this point, on account of a high wind and much dust, the trail was lost. This being the only watering place for miles range cattle coming in for water had entirely obliterated the robbers' trail, but the Papago trailers, by taking wide circles around the ranch finally picked up the trail once more, away to the south, and further trailing showed that the outlaws had crossed the line into Chihuahua, Mexico. At that time officers in pursuit of outlaws never paid any attention to the international line, but went right ahead and got their man, if they could.

On the night of the fifth day they found where the robbers had made their first stop since the holdup. The possemen were very much tired out and used up for the want of sleep, so they made camp on the ground as had the outlaws. The following morning the posse came to a ranch and found that the outlaws had stopped there as they went through the country a couple of days before.

While stopping at this ranch, Larry Shehan had accidentally shot himself, but not seriously. The outlaws had talked freely in the presence of the inmates of this ranch and the officers learned that the outlaws had entered the United States by way of this ranch and that they had bargained for a certain ranch near Casa Grande, a little village a few miles below Janos. They told the owner that they were going up into the United States and that they would return in a few days and pay him cash for his ranch.

Knowing now just where to look for their game, they lost no more time in following trails, but made direct for Janos, where there was a Mexican Customs office. It might be well to state right here that the Papago trailers who accompanied the posse were not mounted, but trotted right along with the mounted officers and often, when circling for signs, covered much more ground than the mounted men did. Sheriff Shaw states that their power of endurance was nothing short of marvelous, especially when taking into consideration the fact that they only had one meal each during the first four days out.

Upon arrival at Janos, the posse rode right up to the Mexican Customs House and introduced themselves and informed the officer in charge what their business was and asked for food for themselves and their horses. They were instructed to take their horses around to the rear of the building and turn them into the feed corral and then come back into the house and get food for themselves. As they had been riding all day in a drizzling rain, they left their saddle guns in the Customs Office.

While they were busily engaged in divesting their weary horses of riding equipment their attention was suddenly arrested by a suspicious clicking sound which had but one interpretation to them and upon looking further into this matter they discovered about thirty Rurales circling the corral, each one standing behind a business looking piece of artillery, each said piece of artillery having its hammer pulled back to zero.

Those five men were not the least bit cold any more. They accumulated considerable heat immediately and it was not artificial either. They could not put up much of a fight with their six shooters against thirty carbines or rifles and as they were a long distance from home, they accepted the position with as good grace as was possible under the circumstances. After they had been divested of their side arms, they were taken into the large detention room of the customs house. This particular room was protected by heavy iron bars and they felt quite secure in it.

United States Marshal Meade, being in charge of the party, made a pathetic appeal to the officer, but it availed him nothing. He was informed that they were charged with "armed invasion," "bringing savage and hostile Indians into Mexico," "smuggling arms and ammunition into Mexico," being "undesirables" and "cattle rustlers." That they could not be released without authority from the City of Chihuahua.

There was nothing to be done but for them to take their medicine and like it and wait for the wheels of Mexican justice to make another revolution. Meade tried to get the officer in charge to permit him to go to Casa Grande under guard for the purpose of apprehending the outlaws, because if the latter learned of the presence of officers from the United States in that vicinity, they would lose no time in getting away from there, but all to no purpose.

While they were cursing and discussing the situation, Sheriff Shaw chanced to look out of the window and saw a cowboy passing whom he had known back up in the United States. He called him over to the window and explained

the situation.   The cowboy told him that he was working for Lieutenant Britton Davis who owned a ranch a
short distance from Janos.   Shaw asked the cowboy to have
Davis to come to the customs house the following morning.

The next morning Davis came to the customs house and
took the matter in question up with the officer in charge but
the official was exceedingly obdurate and Davis accomplished nothing.   He then asked if he might talk to the men and
his request was granted him.   The officers gave him an accurate description of the outlaws and where they were. After they had proven to Davis who they were, he once more
took the matter up with the officer in charge and offered to
make a bond of any size for their release but the officer again
refused to accede to his request.

Davis lost no time in getting to the railroad and into El
Paso where he took the matter up with railroad officials
and, as the Mexican Central Railway was a heavy loser on
money shipments, they got in touch at once with the Governor of Chihuahua and were quickly furnished with authority
to act at once and act quickly.

A high Mexican official, accompanied by Wells-Fargo
Messenger Bob Paul, lost no time in getting to Janos with
instructions for the officers in charge to make thorough investigation of the men whom he was holding and if they
appeared to be what they claimed to be to release them at
once and offer them every assistance possible in the apprehension of the outlaws.

The officer in charge, instead of releasing the officers as
instructed, left them in charge of a guard and, taking every
available rurale, set out for Casa Grande.

Upon arrival of the Mexican officers at Casa Grande, they
investigated and found that their men were there; that they
had purchased a ranch and that the Mexican from whom they
had purchased it was still living there while looking around
for another location.

The officers easily located the house and gave the grand
hailing sign.   One of the outlaws came to the door to investigate the pass word and he was instructed in choice Span-

ish to come out and tell his two partners to come out also. The outlaw consigned them to a hotter place than Yuma and informed them that if they would permit the Mexican ranchman, his wife and children to pass out to a place of safety, that they would fight the entire Mexican Army. This man was evidently a Texan and actually believed that they could do it.

Permission was given and the Mexican, his wife and children came out and hastened away. A big Mexican Sergeant of the Rurals then made a run and landed against the door, hoping to tear it from its hinges, but he never had a chance to realize what a grand mistake he had made, as he had scarcely struck the door when a bullet came through to meet him and some corporal was promoted to his rank the following day.

The outlaws were doing wonderful execution among the Mexican Rurales until one of the Mexican supporters of Porfirio Diaz was struck by a brilliant idea, and lived long enough to carry it out. He slipped to the back of the house and, piling some brush against the wall, set fire to it. The outlaws were soon forced out into the open and quickly fell under the short range fire of the Rurales. They took heavy toll of the Rurales though and, while it is not known with any degree of certainty just how many were killed, the number is estimated to have been between fifteen and twenty. The Mexicans kept all of the recovered money but very generously returned the jewelry which they recovered to the two officers who accompanied them.

After the fight at Casa Grande the Mexican Customs Officers informed Meade and Shaw that their reputation for honesty and integrity had been firmly established and that, after 12 days confinement, they were permitted to leave that place. In fact they left everything they took there with them except the clothing they wore and their reputations.

Their horses, saddles, rifles, revolvers, ammunition and all other equipment were retained.

Upon their release they made their way to the Davis

Ranch where they were provided with mounts with which to ride to Lang's Ranch, which was just over the line. Here they obtained remounts and lost no time in getting back to Tucson.

Shaw stated that he did not mind the misfortunes of the five days' travel or the twelve days' confinement, but to think that Bob Paul should come along after they had located the outlaws for him, and get into the fight and then worst of all collect the reward for the killing of the gang was a little too much.

But such is life.

BURT ALVORD, BILLY STILES, BILL DOWNING, OWENS BROTHERS, MATT BURTS AND BRAVO JUAN HOLD UP

A SOUTHERN Pacific passenger train was held up near Cochise, about midnight of September 9th, 1899. The baggage and express cars were cut off and taken west to a point just east of Dragoon by four of the gang, while the others remained with the train to prevent news of the holdup being wired out of Cochise. Upon arrival of the baggage and express cars in Dragoon Pass, the strong box was dynamited and robbed of a heavy shipment of money.

The Wells Fargo Express Company was quite reticent about stating just how much money was in the strong box upon this occasion, but it has been reported by the wise ones that this holdup netted the wild gang in the neighborhood of $100,000; regardless of the amount stolen, in an incredibly short time the country was flooded by paper bills having corners torn off or being otherwise mutilated, but their mutilation did not interfere in the least with their purchasing powers and, so far as is related, no one ever turned them down on that account.

Burt Alvord was constable at Willcox at that time and Bill Downing, who was his deputy, was the only officer in Willcox at the time of the holdup. When the news was received of the holdup, Downing made a pretense of getting together a posse for the pursuit of the train robbers, but the only men he asked to accompany him were Perry Smith and Al Wien.

Downing, with his posse of two, rode to Cochise and not being able to obtain any positive evidence regarding the identities of the holdups, they rode west toward Dragoon Pass, after obtaining all available details of the holdup.

They had not ridden very far when Wien heard a noise off to one side of the road, as though horses were walking, and called Downing's attention to it. Downing deliberately

drew a match from his pocket, lighted it and applied it to
a cigar which he had been carrying unlighted in his mouth,
then informed Wien and Smith that nothing more could
be done until daylight, when he would get a larger posse
and follow the trail of the holdup gang. They then rode
back to Willcox and when daylight had arrived, a larger
posse went out, headed by Sheriff Scott White and George
Scarborough.

Constable Burt Grover of Pearce and Deputy Sheriff
Page of Johnson held a consultation and decided that Al-

BURT ALVORD

vord and Stiles, with their gang, had staged this train holdup. Grover also knew that Matt Burts had been traveling
with this gang for some time and was probably implicated
so he hunted Burts up and took him to Pearce where he
made him a deputy.

One day Grover staged a big drunken blowout and worked himself into a frenzy over the fact that the gang had
pulled off this holdup without having given him a chance
to help. He became so rabid that he shot up the town and
got Burts so drunk that the latter told about the holdup in

detail, even to the pre-arranged signal which Downing had used when danger had threatened, that of lighting a dead cigar which he had been carrying in his mouth. He said the holdups had seen the light and stopped until Downing and his posse of two had turned back.

Burts related the story in all its sordid details, about how they had met in a deserted house about two miles west of

BILL DOWNING

Willcox, all of the gang being present except Downing who, being a deputy constable, stayed in town to organize a posse when the news of the holdup reached him. They talked the matter all over and laid their plans and just as they were ready to start their eight mile ride to Cochise, some one of their number discovered a hobo asleep in a back room of the house.

Not knowing how much, if anything, he had heard, they called a short business meeting and it was decided that hè must not leave there alive. They drew straws to determine who should act as his executioner. Burt Alvord drew the short straw. He quietly stepped into the back room. A shot; the deed was done and Burt Alvord had added the crime of murder to his account.

Two Wells Fargo Officers whose names are not now remembered came to Willcox to investigate this holdup as well as several others which had been staged in the same vicinity from time to time during the year. Each man would look up Downing who as deputy constable would be very much interested in the apprehension of the outlaws, and introduce himself. In both instances after the man had introduced himself to Downing and explained his business, Downing would suggest some kind of an investigation and they would ride away together. Downing would return alone and the man would never be seen in Willcox again.

One day Wells-Fargo Officer Billy King came to Willcox to make further investigation and while loafing around in the Bucket of Blood Saloon Burt Alvord came in. When he saw Billy King, he spoke pleasantly to him and asked him to step outside with him. King, undoubtedly thinking that Alvord desired to give him some dope on the holdup situation, walked out into the yard back of the saloon with Alvord. They had no sooner closed the door of the saloon when a shot was heard and Alvord came back into the saloon and informed all present that he and King had just had an argument in which King had reached for his gun and that he had been forced to shoot him in self defense. Alvord, being constable, told his story to the Coroner's Jury and was, in the absence of evidence to the contrary, exonerated on the grounds of self defense.

It was following the killing of Billy King that Burt Grover and Page appeared on the scene with their evidence and, with the assistance of a few determined deputies sworn in for the occasion, quickly and quietly arrested the entire gang including Constable Burt Alvord and his deputy, Bill Downing. So sure were the latter of their alibis that they made no resistance.

Alvord and his gang were rudely disillusioned after their arrest, when they learned the evidence which had been stacked up against them, and they quickly realized that they had been caught with the goods on them. Although Downing was not with them when they held up the train, it was proven that Downing had received his share of the loot. Wien and Smith testified that on the night of the holdup, when they accompanied Downing on his search for the robbers, that he had never made any investigation of the riders whom Wien had heard off to one side of the road and that he had deliberately lighted a match and applied it to his cigar and then turned back toward Willcox, so his guilty connection with the gang was established.

The entire gang was taken to Tombstone under heavy guard. Upon arrival there Billy Stiles asked to be accorded an interview with the district attorney and a meeting was quickly arranged. Stiles turned state's evidence and made a full confession which corroborated the evidence already in hand.

Following the confession of Stiles, the balance of the gang spent the most part of their time calling down vitriolic maledictions upon the head of the double crosser. In fact, their obnoxious remarks hung so heavily over his head that Stiles asked to be quartered elsewhere, out of hearing of their malodorous blessings.

In view of the fact that Stiles had come clean in his confession and signified his intention of serving his time and then becoming a good citizen, at the same time stating that he was anxious for the case to come to trial so that he could testify against the balance of the gang who had subjected him to such vile allusions in connection with his family history, he was permitted to come and go as he pleased as long as he came to the jail every night to sleep. In fact, he was accorded all the priviledges of a trusty in and around the jail.

At about noon of one day in April, 1900, while there was no one in the jail but Jailor George Braven, Stiles slipped

in and invited him to inspect the business end of a large calibered six-shooter. Braven started for his gun and Stiles shot
him in the leg. Braven dropped and Stiles obtained the keys
to the cells and released all of his gang, locked Braven in
a cell, joined his gang and they all disappeared. The time
was well chosen as it was during the noon hour and no one
in the building except Braven and the county prisoners.

Bill Trainor was another member of the Alvord Gang
but he reformed and left the gang a short time before the
Cochise holdup. He was credited with being one of the
fastest and most deadly two gun men in the southwest, using either hand with equal dexterity. After his reformation he entered the service of the Arizona Cattlemens' Association as an under cover man. His wide knowledge of
cattle rustler habits, and the identities of many of them, en-
abled him to deliver the goods to those higher up and the
ranks of the rustler element were being thinned out to a
noticeable extent.

Trainor and Bill Downing met one day in Willcox, bitter words and lurid threats passed between them, Downing
accused Trainor of being a snitcher and they parted with
the understanding that there would be a six-shooter broadcasting upon the occasion of their next meeting.

A few days later, Downing was standing at the bar in
the Bucket of Blood Saloon when Trainor and Al Wien
entered. As they lined up to the bar, Trainor saw Downing's reflection in the mirror and turned to face him but
Downing, who had already drawn his six shooter as Train-
or entered the saloon, shot him dead. Trainor did not have
any show at all. Inasmuch as Downing had plenty of
friends to testify that Trainor had threatened to kill him
the first time they met, he was exonerated on grounds of
self defense.

Then came the Cochise holdup, the arrest of the gang
and their subsequent escape. Downing did not remain in
hiding very long until he appeared upon the streets of Willcox and paraded up and down in open defiance of the law.

One night he imbided of the cup which is cheerful and then made his way to a hotel and went to bed.

Late the next day which was in August, 1908, he awoke with a dark blue taste in his mouth and the first thought which entered his head was to get out and fill his radiator. He did not hesitate long enough to buckle on his gun or put on his coat. As he walked down the street enroute to the nearest drink emporium in town, he met Deputy Sheriff Billy Speed who covered him with his artillery and ordered him to "Stick 'em up and make it high;" Downing put 'em high and then dropped his right hand slightly. Speed played safety first and dropped him with a well planted bullet. Had Downing been armed there would have been more to tell.

Downing, whose right name was said to be Jackson, claimed that he was the original Sam Bass of Texas fame and song and many of his friends also insisted that he was the one and only Sam Bass, but history does not substantiate his claims. There was no question but what he had been a member of the Sam Bass gang before he came to Arizona. It was claimed that Downing had killed more than thirty men in his life. There was a standing reward of $5000 on his head at the time of his death.

Alvord, after his escape from the Tombstone jail, gathered unto himself another gang of outlaws and made an attempt to hold up an El Paso and Southwestern passenger train at Fairbanks one day and bumped into Sheriff Del Lewis who chanced to be in the right place at the right time. He discouraged their efforts along the holdup line and they made themselves plenty scarce around that vicinity, but not until Lewis had shot up one of their gang, who managed to make his get away into the thick mesquite brush. It was noticed a few days later that the buzzards were holding some kind of a convention in the brush a few hundred yards from town and investigation showed that the wounded man had crawled out there and died.

The buzzards had rendered positive identification impossible but, after inspecting filled teeth and some old bullet wounds, it was decided almost positively that the body was that of Burt Alvord as he was so well known around over Cochise County, he having been a deputy sheriff under Sheriff Slaughter and later, constable at Willcox.

The identification of the body of the dead outlaw was evidently in error as later information was received which stated positively that Alvord had gone to Jamaica where he died a few years later.

Billy Stiles and his brother Bud, who was also an outlaw, were born and raised near Casa Grande, Ariz. When these boys were twelve and ten years of age, respectively, their father punished them for some boyish prank and it weighed on their infantile minds until they imagined that they had a real man's grievance. They went into the house, obtained the family shotgun and ambushed the old man as he came around the corner of the house and Billy, so it is stated, decapitated the old man with a load of bird shot at close range.

Billy made himself scarce in Arizona after his escape in the Tombstone jail, and the next that was heard of him was that he was killed in a gun fight out in Nevada, the particulars of which never reached Tombstone. There was a standing reward of $5000 on his head at time of his departure from Cochise County.

Bud Stiles decided that the climate around Tombstone was not beneficial to his health and that a quick move might prolong his life to a noticable extent so he departed Tombstone just a few jumps ahead of the sheriff and landed in Deming, N. M., where he died from an attack of small pox soon afterwards.

Tom Yoes, alias Bravo Juan, another member of the Alvord-Stiles combination, or another auxiliary branch of the wild gang, was shot in the leg but made his get away into Mexico where he later married and raised a family and, so far as is known and hoped, his life since his hasty departure from the United States has been spent in the honest pursuit of maintenance for his family. It is related that he occasionally comes across the line to visit relatives who live

in Southern Arizona. While perhaps his past has not been entirely forgotten, it has been overlooked and it is believed that
Bravo Juan appreciates the fact to the limit.

John Patterson, alias Jess Dunlap, alias Three Fingered
Jack, Bob Brown and the two Owens Brothers attempted to
hold up an El Paso and Southwestern passenger train at
Fairbanks on February 20th, 1900, but their efforts netted them no pecuniary reward as they found Wells-Fargo
Shot-gun Messenger Jeff Milton right on top of the job
with both feet and a sawed off shot-gun which contained
more sleep producing pellets than a doctor's medicine case.

Milton was not the least bit stingy when it came to spray-
ing outlaws with Wells-Fargo buckshot and the holdup gang
soon decided that they had urgent business elsewhere and
immediately set about transacting it.   Jeff carelessly permitted his left arm to get in the way of a large calibered bullet
and it was found necessary, later, to remove about four
inches of shattered bone from his arm just above his elbow.

Milton had used his shot-gun with such good intent that
Three fingered Jack had received a mortal wound but his
companions loaded him onto a horse and carried him as far
as they could, but were forced to abandon him at a nearby
ranch where he was found by a Sheriff's posse. He was taken
back to Tombstone but died shortly after arrival there.   It
is stated that he gave a full statement of details surrounding the Cochise train holdup of September 9th, 1899, before he died but this has been denied by close friends of
the accused men.

The Owens Brothers were later apprehended and sentenced to a term of years in the State Penitentiary at Yuma
and when they were released they dropped down and out
of sight.

Bob Brown was apprehended and he too served a sentence and dropped out of sight.

Matt Burts, after having served his sentence in the Arizona State Pentientiary, went to California where he engaged in the cattle business and made good.

In November, 1825, in company of some friends he drove

up to a house where he had some business to transact. Shortly after entering the house four shots were heard and investigation showed Burts and another man lying on the floor
dead; investigation showed each man with two bullets in his
body. It is not known just exactly what lead up to this
double tragedy but presumed to have been the outcome of
some discussion over water or grazing rights.

GRANT WHEELER AND JOE GEORGE

GRANT WHEELER and Joe George alias Black George, rode into Willcox January 3, 1895, and made the purchase of a quantity of giant powder and a supply of ammunition, saying that they were intending a trip into the mountains on a prospecting tour.

They rode west out of town and tarried long enough between Willcox and Cochise to hold up an S. P. passenger train. In the express car they found among other valuables, 8,000 Mexican silver dollars in sacks of 1,000 each. They placed a charge of dynamite on top of the strong box and then stacked the eight sacks of Mexican silver dollars on top of the dynamite and touched it off.

With the explosion of the dynamite, silver went higher than ever before in the history of our country. It tore an extensive opening in the roof of the express car as it departed upon its aerial flight and favored the desert with a shower of silver dollars upon its return. This holdup was perpetrated in 1895 and frequently, even yet, Mexican silver dollars are to be found after having laid dormant for thirty years.

Wheeler and George made their get away for the time being. They went to California where they joined Sontag and Evans in some of their misdirected adventures and George was killed while being implicated in a train holdup out there.

Grant Wheeler came to Deming, N. M., where he spent the bulk of his ill gotten gains in riotous living and while sojourning in Deming became involved in a saloon fight in which he was badly wounded but recovered.

After recovering from his Deming wound, he decided that he might once more visit Arizona with safety, but when he reached Tombstone, he found that although he had been gone, he had not been forgotten. He found himself so popular in that vicinity that he headed quite a procession out of town, said procession consisting of the sheriff and his posse.

Wheeler managed to keep a few jumps ahead of his pursuers until he reached Mancos Cañon away to the north, and here it was that on April 25, 1895, not being acquainted with the country, he permitted himself to be trapped in a blind canon where he could see no possible escape from either death or a long term of imprisonment in the Yuma Penitentiary. He used the last cartridge in his six-shooter as the means of escaping a life worse than death, also saving the state the expense of his trial, as well as paying the penalty of his crimes by self-inflicted death.

LITTLE DAVE, BIG DAVE, DUTCH JOHN

O NE day in the early 80's a cowboy rode into Lordsburg and reported his finding of a dead man in Granite Gap, twenty miles to the southwest. A coroner's
jury was quickly impaneled, loaded into buckboards and on
horseback and was soon on its way to the Gap.

Upon arrival there the dead body was quickly identified
as that of a well known character known only as Dutch John,
who came to Arizona from Colorado with the Walker Expedition in 1861, posed around over the country as a cowboy or a prospector, but in reality was a member of the outlaw gang. He had apparently been sitting on the ground,
leaning against his saddle, and some one had struck him
with an axe from one side, as his face was sliced off and
hanging by shreds of flesh only.

The coroner's jury rendered a verdict that this man,
known only as Dutch John, had come to his death by having been struck with the sharp edge of the axe, wielded by
hands of party unknown. The axe being a mute witness
to the crime, the body was buried and the incident closed.

Many years later, a stranger appeared in Lordsburg and
asked to be directed to some old timer. He was referred to
B. B. Ownby who had lived in Lordsburg since about 1880
and who had been a peace officer nearly all of the time of
his residence there.

The man introduced himself to Mr. Ownby and informed
him that he was from Oklahoma and that years previous a
man known as Little Dave, with whom he had been acquainted since boyhood days, had come to his home in Oklahoma and taken up residence with him. Little Dave was
then suffering from the ravages of tuberculosis and not able
to do any hard work, so he did little jobs around the place
until he died several years later. Before he died he had
made a written and signed statement, which was handed
to Mr. Ownby by the stranger, to be read.

An abstract of the statement was to the effect that Little Dave, Dutch John and six more members of the outlaw gang not named in the statement, had held up and robbed the Tombstone-Benson stage of eight bars of gold. Each member of the gang, taking one bar of gold as his share, paired off, and each pair rode in a different direction.

Little Dave and Dutch John chanced to be paired together and started toward Lordsburg. They had been two days and nights without sleep and Dutch John repeatedly told Little Dave that the first man who fell asleep would lose his bar of gold and his life too. Little Dave stated that he was well enough acquainted with Dutch John to know that he was fully capable of carrying out this threat.

When they stopped at Granite Gap to make coffee and rest their horses, Dutch John removed the saddle from his horse, threw it on the ground and then sat down and leaned his back against it. Little Dave volunteered to rustle the wood, build a fire and get the coffee started, knowing that the activity would prevent him from going to sleep.

Dave obtained the axe from the pack and collected a lot of dry wood, which he threw down as close to Dutch as he could without exciting his suspicion, and then started cutting it up into suitable lengths for the camp fire. He worked around until he was within good striking distance of Dutch John and, noticing that John's eyes were closed, he struck him with all his strength and John settled down a little lower against his saddle and was dead instantly.

Dave then took both bars of gold and buried them in the middle of the road, at the highest point in the Gap. He then saddled up and rode around Lordsburg to Separ, 20 miles further on, took the train and went back to his old home in Oklahoma, which was then known as Indian Territory, and cast his lot with his old friend, remaining with him until he became a victim of the great white plague.

The old time friend, whose name cannot be given, asked Mr. Ownby if he would take him out to Granite Gap. They went there and made extensive search for the two bars of buried gold, but the roads through the gap had been washed out and changed in places and as their search was fruitless, they returned to Lordsburg. The friend declared that he knew the gold was there because Dave had told him it was. He purchased two burros, a camp outfit and a supply of provisions and, packing one burro and riding the other, he started back to Granite Gap.

He never returned by way of Lordsburg, so it is presumed that he actually found the gold bars and left that vicinity via some other route. He could have caught the train at Separ, 20 miles to the east of Lordsburg or at Steins 20 miles to the west.

Little Dave, whose family name was Davis, had a brother who was much larger than he, and in consequence of such a difference in their sizes, one was called Little Dave and the other one Big Dave. Big Dave was also a member of the wild bunch and kept his dues always paid up to date.

Curly Bill, Doc Holliday and Big Dave chanced to meet in Clifton one day and became involved in a friendly argument among themselves in which Big Dave found himself on one side all by his lonesome. As a result of this one sided affair Big Dave left Clifton in a hurry, not even stopping long enough to steal a horse but, walking out ten miles to the first stage station, he stole one of Old Man Pomeroy's stage horses which he rode bareback to Separ, a distance of 75 miles, arriving there the following morning.

Upon his arrival in Separ he was met by a representative of the law who took him to Lordsburg where he was accorded a hearing before the Law and Order League. His defense was that Doc Holliday and Curly Bill had both informed him plainly that if he was caught in Clifton after daylight the following morning that they would shoot him on sight.

He also stated that he was sufficiently acquainted with both of these men to know that they would do just exactly as they had promised him they would do and that he took great pleasure in getting just as far away from Clifton as possible. He had really borrowed Old Man Pomeroy's horse with intention of sending him back by some one from

Separ. As such practices were not uncommon among cowboys and his statement had all of the earmarks of truthfulness, he was told to go and never return. He took the first
train out of town and neglected to leave his forwarding
address.

JOHN SLAUGHTER

JOHN H. SLAUGHTER was born in Louisiana and, when a mere boy, came west and landed in Texas. During the Civil War he saw service with the Confederate Forces and after peace was declared, he entered the service of the Texas Rangers with an appointment as lieutenant. For many years he did his bit toward ridding Texas of undesirable citizens represented by the rustler and outlaw element.

In 1877 the Tombstone strike brought him to Arizona, where he arrived in the San Pedro Valley in due course of time, with his entire herd of cattle and all of his worldly possessions. He later purchased land about 20 miles east of where Douglas now stands, and established what is known as the San Bernardino Ranch and it was here that he lived until his death, which occurred in 1922.

While Mr. Slaughter and his cowboys were driving his immense herd of cattle from the Pecos Country into Arizona, he met a noted outlaw known as Bitter Creek Gallagher who had thirteen notches cut in the stock of his gun and still had room, and the desire for more. It was his announced intention of running off as many of Slaughter's cattle as he could handle and selling them across the line in Sonora, Mexico, where they would at that time have found a ready market.

Slaughter immediately recognized Gallagher, as he chanced to be an old acquaintance from the Pecos Country, and knowing that he was a man devoid of all manly instincts and one who would kill for the sake of killing, also that he would steal anything that was not red hot or nailed down, he ordered him to hit the trail.

The Bad Man from Bitter Creek went his way and lay in wait for John Slaughter at Ft. Sumner, where he boasted to his friends that he was going to kill Slaughter and confiscate his entire herd. A friendly cowboy, who had heard Gallagher's bombastic talk, rode out and met Slaughter and informed him that Bitter Creek Gallagher was intending to ambush him at the Chisum Ranch.

John Slaughter was an old hand at the ambushing game
and was on the lookout for Gallagher and when a short distance from Chisum's Ranch he located Gallagher waiting for him. He rode up to within good rifle range of him
and shot his horse, putting him afoot. Slaughter then dismounted from his own horse and shot it out on the ground
with Gallagher.

JOHN SLAUGHTER

When the smoke and dust of battle had subsided Bitter
Creek Gallagher was found to have made a futile attempt
at stopping one of Slaughter's rifle bullets and failed. He
lived for several hours and just before passing out he remarked, "I needed killing anyway."

Mr. Slaughter served one term as Sheriff of Cochise
County and served the known outlaws with the famous
ultimatum, "Outlaw, get out of Cochise County or get killed." Needless to say, many of them left and some of those
who stayed to argue the situation with him found themselves unable to leave by the time that they had changed
their minds.

BILL BRAZELTON

DURING the summer of 1883, the stage coming into
Tucson from the west was held up several times by
a lone highwayman near Silver Lake which was just
outside of the city limits. It seemed impossible to get any
tangible clew to the identity of the outlaw who had insti-
tuted this daily hold up service. The tracks of two horses
could be found going out from town but none away from
the scene of action. Sheriff Shibbell and his deputies spent
much time in attempting to solve the mystery but their efforts netted them no results.

A man named Elias, a first class trailer, got busy and,
going to the place where the stage was always held up, took
the back trail into town. The tracks led to the corral of
one of the many livery stables in town. Elias entered the corral, examined the feet of all of the horses therein and
finally pointed to one horse, with the remark, "There's the
horse which made those tracks."

This horse was the property of a man named Bill Brazelton, who had drifted into town some time before and obtained employment at the livery stable as corral man. Whenever he had any leisure time he would saddle his horse and
ride out of town for a short time and return in time to perform his evening's work of feeding and watering the horses.

Sheriff Shibbell placed a watch on Brazelton and the
next time that he saddled his horse for his late afternoon's
ride, the watcher hurried to Shibbell with the information
and Brazelton was followed at a safe distance by the sheriff
and some of his deputies. Brazelton turned into the mesquite brush and Shibbell and his men rode on and hid near
the spot where the stage had been regularly held up. Here
they awaited the arrival of the stage.

Sure enough, it was not long until Brazelton also walked
to the spot and hid in the thick mesquite brush on the opposite side of the road. When the stage came along he
held it up as per usual and robbed it. After he had com-

pleted the job, Sheriff Shibbell and his men stepped out
and called upon him to surrender but he knew full well
what his surrender would mean, so opened fire on the officers
and was shot and killed in the gun battle which followed.

When they had rounded up his horse the mystery was
solved. He would ride to the spot of his intended holdup
in time to reverse the shoes on his horse and then when he
had ridden back to town there were no tell-tale tracks with
their toes toward his destination. The trail of two horses
going but none returning. This set of shoes had apparently been made especially for this purpose as there were four
nail holes on each side of every shoe and so the holes were
accurately spaced, that when shoes were reversed nails could
be pushed through the already made holes in the horse's
hoof and all the hard work there was to do was for him to
turn the nails down and cut the clinchers off with a pair of
nippers which he carried in his saddle pockets. Upon arrival at the corral he would remove the tell tale shoes as
soon as possible and reverse them to their proper position.

Upon arrival in town, Sheriff Shibbell investigated every
man whom Brazelton had ever been seen associating with and
finally one man confessed that he and Brazelton had been
good friends and that Brazelton had told him what he had
been doing but that he had never been out on any holdup
trips with him, and as there was no evidence to show that he
ever had, he was not held. Brazelton had taken this man
into his confidence enough to inform him that he had pulled
three stage robberies near Silver City, New Mexico, two
in the northern part of Arizona and four almost within the
city limits of Tucson.

KID (JOHN) THOMPSON

A T ROSCO, California, a small station about 12 miles out of Los Angeles, in December, 1893, the north bound express of the Southern Pacific was held up and robbed by two men who were heavily masked. Posses scoured the country in that vicinity but no clew as to who the robbers were was ever unearthed at the time.

At the same place in February, 1895, this train was again held up. Two men signaled the engineer to stop and he, sensing a holdup, opened up the throttle and attempted to run their signal and in so doing ran into a siding which had a closed switch at the opposite end and the train was ditched, killing the fireman and a hobo who was riding the front end of the engine.

The express car was blown open and robbed and the robbers departed without leaving any trail which could be followed and there was no evidence as to who had committed the crime. The money taken consisted of about 1200 Mexican silver dollars.

In the fall of 1895 Kid Thompson and Charlie Etzler came to Phoenix and from there went to Tempe where they camped down on the Salt River for some time. Etzler hired out to a man named Baker who owned a ranch over on Tonto Creek and he told Baker of things Thompson had told him concerning the California holdups. Baker sent word to Special Agent William Breakenridge of the Southern Pacific who was located at Tucson and he went at once to Phoenix where he met Etzler.

Etzler told him that Thompson had told him that he and a man named Johnson had held up both trains at Roscoe and that they had taken the Mexican money to Johnson's Ranch where they buried it. Kid Thompson then went back to Dakota and visited his people for a while and then came back to California. While beating his way on trains back to Los Angeles he met Etzler to whom he confided and proposed that Etzler accompany him to Johnson's ranch and that they would dig up the money and take his share.

When they reached Johnson's ranch, Johnson refused to let Kid Thompson dig up the money, fearing that Thompson would take it to Los Angeles and peddle it to the Chinks

JOHN (KID) THOMPSON

and that the railroad officers would get wise.   But he later told Thompson to go on to Tempe, Ariz., and that he would ship his portion of the money to him by express.

Thompson and Etzler beat their way to Tempe where they made connections with the Kid's share of the Mexican silver dollars which Johnson had sent him.   Thompson took a few of them at a time into Phoenix and disposed of them to the Chinks there until it was nearly all disposed of.

Thompson had been proposing to Etzler that as soon as the Mexican money was disposed of that they would take the proceeds and leave that locality and hold up trains in some locality where they were unknown and where the loot promised well. One day when Kid Thompson was in a barber shop having his hair cut Etzler hunted up the city marshal and told him his story and informed him that the Kid had his pockets full of Mexican dollars then. The marshal evidently did not believe his story and went to his supper after informing Etzler that he would see him upon his return.

Etzler, fearing that Thompson would learn of his conversation with the marshal, decided to get away from him, so he hired out to Baker to drive some cattle to Tonto Creek and on the way he told Baker his story.

Breakenridge took Etzler to Los Angeles the same night that he told his story and turned him over to the officials there for safe keeping. In company of several more officers, Breakenridge went to the Johnson ranch and dug up the balance of the Mexican silver dollars, as Etzler had told him right where to find them.

Special Agent Will Smith of the Southern Pacific at Los Angeles returned with Mr. Breakenridge to Phoenix on the first train and upon their arrival there Special Agent Breakenridge learned that Thompson was stopping at a ranch near town and he and Smith went out to arrest him. When they reached there they found that Thompson was in town. Smith said to the ranchman, "Tell the Kid that Will Smith, the Southern Pacific detective wants to see him to get some information, and for him to call at the Commercial hotel."

As soon as they started upon their return trip Breakenridge told Smith that the deal was all off and that as soon as Thompson learned that they were looking for him that he would drift. Smith informed Breakenridge that he knew Thompson well and that he had paid him for both information and help on previous occasions and that he knew that he would hunt him up.

The following day they again visited the ranch, only to learn that their quarry had flown. When the rancher delivered Smith's message to him, he mounted his horse and said that he would ride into Phoenix and see Smith.

Before Thompson went to California he had worked on

a ranch near Agua Caliente on the Gila River and had many friends there. Mr. Breakenridge took the matter up with Deputy United States Marshal John Slankard who went to Agua Caliente to investigate. He found where the Kid had been camped but evidently the Kid saw Slankard first as all signs present showed that the Kid had left camp in a hurry and had taken nothing with him. Slankard tracked him up the river toward Phoenix and found that the Kid had circled town and gone east.

Special Agent Breakenridge met Billy Moore, a deputy sheriff of Maricopa County, in Phoenix, and gave him a description of Thompson and asked him to keep a look out for him while on his way home up Salt River. When Moore reached the Crab Tree Ranch, about 30 miles out of Phoenix, he learned that Thompson and another young man had passed there the day before.

Moore hurriedly organized a posse consisting of I. E. Crabtree, E. E. Watkins, John Kemp, E. G. Keith and himself and got busy. They overtook the two young men just at dark in the Four Peak Range and demanded of them to surrender but Thompson and his friend refused, conveying the information to the officers in most emphatic language and opening fire after taking refuge under an overhanging cliff. The posse returned their fire. As it was very cold up there, the outlaws, having no fire wood, froze out before morning and surrendered.

Thompson's companion gave his name as Colonel Tupper. Moore brought them to Phoenix. Thompson waived extradition and Mr. Breakenridge took him to Los Angeles. When they reached there they found that the officers had already arrested Johnson and that he had made a full confession and both he and Thompson were sentenced to long terms in the State Penitentiary.

BUCKSKIN FRANK LESLIE

BUCKSKIN FRANK LESLIE was for years employed by the government as a scout, but late in the summer of 1877, on account of the government appropriation for the payment of civilian employes being exhausted, he, with about 35 more were laid off and they came from Ft. Grant to Tucson, Chief Scout Al Sieber and Tom Horn being members of this party.

Leslie was christened "Buckskin Frank" on account of his fondness for buckskin garments which were invariably trimmed with heavy fringe. He permitted his hair to grow long and he was considered a handsome man, especially by the ladies. He was very vain of his personal appearance and was declared to have been quite a dandy among the ladies of Tombstone. He always wore a pair of silver mounted, engraved, ivory handled six shooters which he was not the least bit backward in using whenever he considered it necessary to do so.

It is not stated whether, after he went to Tombstone, he threw in with the Law and Order League or the wild bunch, but though he herded quite largely with the latter element it has never been stated that he took any active part in their operations.

Leslie claimed to have shot John Ringo, but this was never proven and the manner in which John Ringo actually met his death is shrouded more or less in mystery. It has been generally believed that he committed suicide.

In November, 1882, Billy Claibourne, also known as "Billy the Kid" on account of his youth, became angered at Leslie and went away and returned with a double barreled shot gun, declaring to all within hearing of his voice that he was, "Going to get Frank Leslie." Some friend informed Leslie that Billy Claiborne was at the front door of the saloon where Leslie was located, waiting to take a shot at him when he came out.

Leslie went out of the back door, slipped around the side

of the saloon to the front and located Billy Claibourne "on the spot." Leslie did not ask him any questions but shot him in the back. Claibourne lived long enough to declare that Leslie shot John Ringo by slipping up on him while he was in a drunken sleep, and that he (Claiborne) was with him and saw him do it.

Mike Killean was unfortunately possessed of a very attractive wife and Leslie considered her very attractive also, and paid her considerable attention. Killean warned Leslie to keep away from his wife, but Leslie persisted in meeting her at every available chance.

Killean and his wife were living at the Cosmopolitan Hotel and Leslie, believing that Killean was not at home, one day went to the hotel with the intention of seeing Mrs. Killean. As soon as Leslie stepped up onto the veranda, which was about eight or nine feet above the ground, Killean opened fire on him, but missed.

Leslie backed away and dropped over the veranda edge and, clutching the edge of the floor of the veranda in his hands, hung suspended. Before he dropped to the ground his friend, a man named Perrine, who had entered the hotel by a side door, appeared on the scene and shot Killean in the back. Both men fled but were later arrested and placed on trial. Leslie swore that he had shot Killean in defending himself from the attack of a jealous man. This cleared Perrine and Leslie was released on the grounds of having acted in self defense. This was in the early part of 1880 and about 18 months later Leslie married Killean's widow.

Leslie and his wife lived in Tombstone, but they did not appear to get along very well together and in a short time after their marriage Mrs. Leslie obtained a divorce and went California, where she married some one else, and was living in Los Angeles a few years ago.

Later, Leslie married again and obtained a position as manager of Mike E. Joyce's Ranch out in the edge of the San Simon Valley at the foot of the Swisshelm Mountains. Later, Leslie hired a young man, yet in his teens, to work on the ranch.

Without any cause whatever, Leslie became very jealous
of this boy and in his insane jealousy, believed the worst of
his wife just because his wife appeared to like the boy. One
day Leslie stepped into the house and took a shot at the boy,
who was not hit, but who fell down and played "possum" until Leslie had shot his wife as she came in from another
room to see what had been the occasion of the first shot.

Just as soon as Leslie had left the house, the boy slipped
out, secured a horse and rode quickly to Tombstone, where
he informed the sheriff of what had taken place.

A few hours later Leslie rode into Tombstone and reported to the sheriff that an Indian had gone to the ranch
house and murdered both the boy and his wife and that
when he came to the house he had found them both dead,
lying on the floor. When faced by the boy whom he had
thought dead, he admitted his guilt. He was sentenced to
a life term in the state penitentiary at Yuma.

While serving his sentence in the penitentiary Leslie became a sort of an evangelist and upon one occasion he frustrated a jail delivery by quick action and, after serving a few
years of his life sentence, was granted a full pardon.

While in the penitentiary he became acquainted with a
young lady who frequently visited the penitentiary, and they
fell in love with each other and upon his release from that
institution they were married. This woman was a woman
of considerable education and refinement and they lived
together for several years, but were finally divorced and
Leslie went into Mexico where he was interested in mines
and cleaned up quite a tidy sum.

In 1896 he returned to the United States and visited his
old friend Wyatt Earp in Oakland that year. He then
slipped out of sight and there is no more record obtainable
of him.

WILLIAM E. WALTERS ALIAS
BRONCHO BILL

WILLIAM E. WALTERS, alias William Anderson, alias Billy Brown, alias Broncho Bill, arrived in Arizona from the Land of Nobody Knows Where, threw in with the wild bunch and took part in several train holdups. He soon became a very much wanted man, so much so in fact that he decided that a change of climate was absolutely necessary to his existence, so he faded away, to appear later in New Mexico. He drifted into Albuquerque and obtained employment with the Santa Fe B. & B. Department and was assigned to the paint gang.

One day a guest at the Alvardo Hotel, which is operated by the Santa Fe, reported that he had occasion to transact some business in the office, that he had left his pocket book and watch on the dresser of his room, locked the door and gone down, that when he returned to his room he found the door still locked but his pocket book and watch were missing.

Investigation showed that a painter had been painting the window frames of that room from the outside by standing on a long ladder. The paint gang foreman informed the investigating officer that a kid by the name of Billy Walters had been working at that place at the time in question.

Bill was arrested and put through the third degree but never weakened and as nothing could be proven against him he was released. He immediately drew what money he had coming to him and quit town.

Shortly after Bill's hasty departure from Albuquerque, there arrived in that town an officer in search of one Broncho Bill and from the description furnished, it was decided that the youthful painter was the much wanted outlaw.

Broncho Bill was next heard of in Cochise County where he was supposed to have taken part in several Southern Pacific train holdups. This was in 1899 and during that year, train holdups were quite fashionable on the Southern Pacific road. As several men had been killed in these holdups, the perpetrators were doubly wanted. Deputy United States Marshal Jeff Milton of Fairbanks, Ariz., had been especially instructed to make every effort to effect the capture of Broncho Bill.

BRONCHO BILL

There was a good price on Bill's head and he slipped out and away from Cochise County and was not heard of for some time. In a spirit of bravado he sent word to Milton that he was in the White Mountains and that he wished he would come and get him, also to be sure and bring along plenty of warm blankets and good horses, as he was very much in need of both.

Milton states that he was determined to accept Bill's invitation and took the matter up with Colonel Epes Randolph who, at that time, was Division Superintendent of the Southern Pacific, with headquarters at Tucson. Inasmuch as Broncho Bill had very recently been quite active in helping in several holdups of Southern Pacific trains between Steins Pass and Cochise, Colonel Randolph instructed Milton to go ahead and get the outlaw at any cost and generously offered to back him with all that he needed to the extent of horses, equipment, provisions, money and a special train.

Milton took Eugene Thacker, Tom Scarborough, and a man named Martin in with him on this deal and they outfitted a special train and routed it via Deming, N. M., over the Santa Fe to a point near Holbrook, where they were informed that Bill and his gang were intending to hold up a Santa Fe train. They hung around that locality for several weeks but Bill had evidently changed his mind, for the holdup was never staged.

On the night of July 4th, Milton received a wire that Bill and his gang had held up a dance on the other side of the mountain. In order to reach that point it was necessary for them to come back into Arizona and out over the Arizona Eastern, nearly to Globe.

They loaded their horses and equipment as quickly as possible and lost no time in getting back to Bowie, Ariz., where they found an engine steamed up and ready to couple onto their special train to take them anywhere they wanted to go. That night they went on to Old Ft. Thomas, where they jumped their horses out of the stock car of their special, and made camp in the brush.

Milton sent to Ft. San Carlos for some Apache scouts but did not keep them very long as they did not appear able, or willing, to locate any definite trail, so he sent them back home.

Milton and his men scattered around and spent several days in cutting for signs which they finally discovered. They took up the trail which led them over the highest pass in the White Mountains and they had almost given up all hope of locating the outlaws when one day as they were winding through canons and climbing pinacles, they found a nice, bright, new tin can with a "Double Circle" scratched on it. Milton looked at it and exclaimed, "I'll bet that Bill did that, and I will bet that is right where he is hanging out right now."

JEFF D. MILTON

They rode on toward the "Double Circle" Ranch and as they neared that place they arrested every one whom they met and took them along with them for fear that some one of them might carry word to Bill that there were officers in that locality looking for him. Milton was playing foxy and taking no chances.

Upon arrival at the "Double Circle" Ranch they camped out in the brush, back of the corrals, and each man took turns at watching. Milton was on guard one morning when a man rode into the corral, watered his horse and, as he turned to ride away, looked squarely into Milton's eyes and Milton, feeling sure that he had been seen, raised up and covered him saying, "Hold on partner, I want to talk to you." This man soon proved to Milton that he was not in any way connected with Broncho Bill or his gang, but the officers could not afford to let him go. He really proved quite useful, as he told Milton of a cowboy at a nearby ranch whom he thought could be relied upon to tell the truth and whom he thought might be able to give Milton some information.

They rode to the ranch together and as they entered the house Milton covered everybody in sight, not knowing but what Broncho Bill might be there too. He soon found that Bill was not among those present and quickly got busy interviewing the supposed to be honest cowboy, who informed Milton that Bill had not been at that ranch for over a month. Milton later learned that Broncho Bill had been at that ranch less than two hours earlier.

Milton brought his men to this ranch and disarmed all of the men there and virtually made prisoners of all of them. He then pursued the policy of watchful waiting. They had been loafing there for several days and Milton, to relieve the intense monotony of the situation, decided to go fishing in the mountain stream which passed a short distance from the ranch house. Taking one of the men with him, they fished down the canon for about an hour when they heard shooting above them. Milton's companion grabbed him by the shoulder and shouted, "Let's go! let's go!! let's get out of here!!!" Milton grabbed him by the arm and said, "Stay where you are, you fool, they are not shooting at us, but if you start to run they'll get you sure."

After the shooting had subsided, they sauntered up toward the house as though they had not heard any disturbance. As they neared the house, they looked back and saw three men coming along the trail from the same direction from which they had come. Milton and his men placed their guns handy and, assuming an indifferent manner, waited.

Two of the riders stopped about a hundred yards in front of the house and the other one rode boldly up and was met by some of the cowboys who went out to meet him, Milton and his men included. They were so close to the cowboys that they did not have a chance to warn this man so they chatted some cowboy talk with him and as he turned to mount his horse, Milton stepped out and said, "Hold on partner, I want to see you." He mounted his horse, shooting, but while he was undoubtedly shooting to kill, in his excitement and due to the prancing of his horse, he was placing nearly all of his bullets between Milton's legs.

As this man rode away, the officers had shot at him several times when he suddenly straightened up in his saddle and then fell to the ground. The bullet had entered his right side, passed through both lungs and out through his left shoulder. They presumed that he was dead and turned their attention to the other two men who were riding toward them and shooting as they came.

They shot one man's horse from under him and he struck the ground running and treed quickly. The officers tried to get him as he pushed his gun around the side of his tree to shoot and finally, after many futile shots, one bullet grazed his face, which caused him to jump back a little too far and another bullet caught him through the hips. The third man decided to move and lost no time in carrying out his decision.

Milton questioned the men at the ranch regarding the identity of the two men whom they had shot and who were lying there on the ground and at first they denied all knowledge of their identity but, under Milton's direct accusation that they did know them and that he knew that they knew them, they weakened and told him that the man who was shot through the lungs was Broncho Bill and that the man who was shot through the hips was named Johnson, and he also was a desperate outlaw.

Milton, believing that Broncho Bill was dead, took him

by the feet and started to drag him to the house. Bill began to strangle and cough and the doctor afterwards told Milton that this act was what saved Bill's life, that upending him had caused the blood to flow out of his lungs into his throat.

Milton sent a cowboy to the fort for a doctor who at first refused to come, but the commanding officer ordered him to go out and attend to the wounded men. Johnson died before the doctor arrived. The doctor stayed only long enough to dress Bill's wound. Said that he was not going to risk his life in that place. As a matter of fact, none of them knew whether they were safe or not as they did not know what minute the escaped outlaw might arrive with reinforcements. Every cowboy who came into the ranch while they were there was placed under arrest and disarmed for fear that he might be Bill's friend.

Before Johnson died he and Bill made so much fuss that it grated on Milton's nerves and he said, "Bill, they tell me that you once laughed at a man you had shot, and called him a coward because he made a howl. Why don't you brace up and be a man?" Bill replied, "Oh! you don't know how it hurts, you don't know how it hurts."

As soon as Bill could travel they took him into Santa Fe where, as soon as he had sufficiently recovered, he was placed on trial on a charge of train robbery, found guilty and sentenced to a life term in the Federal Penitentiary. This was in November, 1899. In April, 1917, on account of poor health he was pardoned. He came back into Arizona and went to work for the Diamond "A" outfit near Hatchita, Grant County, New Mexico, almost within sight of where he had held up one or two trains. A few years later he fell off a windmill tower and was killed.

HALDERMAN BROTHERS

THE HALDERMAN BROTHERS, who owned a ranch in the Chiracahua Mountains in Cochise County in 1900, were not much more than mere boys, one being about 19 and the other one about 23 years of age. Although young in years, they were quite old in crime and were thoroughbred outlaws and cattle rustlers.

They stole some of Ted Moore's cattle and worked the brands over. Moore suspicioned them and got busy with the result that he obtained enough evidence against them to guarantee them a home in the state penal institution for an extended length of time. Moore rode into Tombstone and filed the information against them and a warrant was issued and Deputy Sheriff Ainsworth was sent back with Moore to make the arrest.

Upon arrival at the ranch the officers rode boldly up, dismounted and walked into the yard where they found the Halderman boys. The arrest was effected without any difficulty and as soon as the warrant was read to them, they asked permission to enter the house for the purpose of closing the doors and windows, saying that it might be a long time before their return.

Ainsworth told them to go ahead and make their house secure and they disappeared inside of the door, only to appear almost instantly with their Winchesters, which had been standing just inside of the door. One of the Halderman boys shot Ainsworth dead and as he slid from the saddle to the ground, Moore turned his horse to get away and the other Halderman boy fired at him, the bullet passing entirely through his body from the back, but he lived long enough to get to his home where he told his mother and sister that the Halderman boys had shot him.

The Halderman boys lost no time in getting away from that immediate locality. They got as far as Socorro, New Mexico, where they were apprehended and returned to Arizona. They were confined in the Cochise County jail at Tombstone while awaiting trial for. the crime of murder.

At the time of the Alvord-Stiles jail delivery, the Halderman boys refused to make their get-away and remained behind. They did not at that time know that Moore had lived long enough to make an ante-mortem statement and they believed that there was no evidence against them except circumstantial, but when they were arraigned for trial they learned differently, but it was then too late. They were found guilty of murder and sentenced to be hanged. The sentence was executed in the county jail yard at Tombstone.

AUGUSTINE CHACON, ALIAS PELUDO

AUGUSTINE CHACON was also called "Peludo" which means "hairy," this on account of the heavy beard which he always wore. No one appears to know just where Chacon came from into the Tombstone country. Some say that he was a California Mexican, while others insist that he was a native of Mexico. His first appearance in Tombstone dates back into 1893, when he and four others equally as villianous as he dropped into that locality and proceeded to look the situation over.

Evidently they decided that Tombstone was tough enough without their presence there, so they journeyed away to the northward and in the due course of time landed in Morenci where they celebrated their arrival by holding up and looting Paul Becker's store. Just because Becker objected to their taking such unwarranted liberties with his property, Chacon inserted the business end of a long bladed hunting knife into his side and left it there.

Pablo Salcido, one of Morenci's native sons, evinced too much curiosity regarding the rapid evolution of current events and Chacon branded him with a bullet hole between the eyes.

Chacon and his gang helped themselves to what they desired from the store and departed by way of the back door. As they passed out of the back door Becker managed to crawl out of the front door and into a nearby saloon where he found Constable Fred Davis, who removed the knife from his side and took him to a doctor to have his wound dressed.

Possibly it may be thought strange that the inmates of the saloon did not hear the shots fired and make investigation, but in those days it was by no means uncommon for drunken cowboys and others to ride into or out of town accompanied by salvos from their artillery and even the local officers paid little or no attention to such noisy events.

Constable Fred Davis, accompanied by a Mexican trailer,

and armed with only a six shooter, started in pursuit of the bandits. They located the five outlaws and Dave charged them alone and wounded Chacon in one shoulder and he surrendered. Davis took him back to town and placed him in charge of a doctor until his wound could be dressed and then lodged him in jail.

AUGUSTINE CHACON AND CHAVEZ

Bill Keppler, John Smith and a man known as Jack the Ripper, headed the other four outlaws off and in the fight which ensued, killed two of them. The outlaws were all armed with Winchesters, and the two who were killed died with their hands on the levers of their guns.

After Chacon had recovered from his wound he was

placed on trial, charged with the murder of Pablo Salcido, found guilty and sentenced to hang. Fearing that Chacon might escape the frail jail at Morenci, also that he might be the cause of a noctural neck-tie party, he was sent to Tucson and lodged in the Pima County Jail for safe keeping.

During Chacon's stay in the Pima County Jail two Mexicans made their escape by sawing the bars of their cell window. A thorough inspection of the jail showed that Chacon had also sawed the bars of his cell window but, for some reason unknown, he delayed his escape until it was too late.

A few days before the execution of his sentence of death he was taken back to Solomonville. He did not remain in the Solomonville jail but a very short time, making his escape, accompanied by another Mexican outlaw. They, being without funds, held up the Solomonville Stage and then headed for Old Mexico.

In passing through Cochise County they chanced to meet Sheriff Slaughter and when the festivities attending said meeting were over, Chacon once more turned his attention to making tracks with the heel prints pointing northward, but he was all by his lonesome. As the outlaw who was killed wore a heavy beard, it was thought for some time that Sheriff Slaughter had killed Chacon, but subsequent events proved that such thoughts were in error as Chacon was positively located across the International Line.

Burt Alvord, who at that time was a deputy sheriff of Cochise County, with residence at Willcox, was strongly suspected of having been implicated in a Southern Pacific passenger train holdup with Billy Stiles and others but these suspicions were backed up more or less only by circumstantial evidence, and as the material facts were in the minority, the case had been temporarily shelved awaiting further developments.

Alvord, being well acquainted with Chacon and knowing just where he was to be found, proposed to the Cochise County authorities that if the case against Billy Stiles and himself was dismissed he would agree to deliver Chacon to the authorities at Solomonville. After due consideration his proposal was accepted.

Burt Alvord and Billy Stiles rode down into Old Mexico and soon located Chacon. He knew these men as brother crooks and welcomed them as such. They were appropriately wined and dined by Chacon and they then unfolded their plan of action, in part only, to him. They told him that they knew where a bunch of fine horses was located just north of the line in the United States and that if he would help them run these horses across the line into Mexico and find them a market for the horses, they would split the velvet right through the center with him. Chacon, having been wounded by an American and having had three of his gang killed recently by Americans, was ripe for any description of revenge, and a few days later two Americans and one Mexican rode up Guadalupe Canon and crossed the line into the United States. As soon as the party was fairly across the International Line the Americans informed the Mexican, who was Chacon, that he had erred in his judgment and that he was headed toward Solomonville, which meant a long ride and a short rope awaiting him.

Upon arrival at Solomonville he was turned over to the authorities who lost no time in arraigning him for re-sentence and within a few days after his return in December, 1902, a small but select party was held in the court house yard and Chacon was the most important man present. Chacon gave an exhibition of tight rope work and, not being in practice, the exhibition resulted fatally for him. After 17 minutes, the attending medico rendered a verdict that Chacon's reformation had been entirely successful and permanent and that he would never more violate the laws of man.

JOHN BLAIR

JOHN BLAIR was a member in good standing of the "Double 'Dobe Gang." Blair took everything in sight and also took smallpox back to camp with him from one of his trips. As soon as it became apparent that this dreaded scourge had fastened upon him he was rushed out and isolated in a small shack at a safe distance from the main camp and an old Mexican woman, who had passed through the smallpox ordeal herself, was hired to take care of him. Along about the fifth or sixth day she appeared upon the horizon and radioed the message that, "Senor Juan es muy murio." (Mr. John is very dead.)

A "committee of ways and means" was immediately appointed with full authority to take whatever action they might deem necessary in disposing of the remains of the late Blair. The camp was divided into two sections. One section armed themselves with picks and shovels and, after journeying a safe distance from camp, proceeded to excavate an opening in the bosom of Mother Earth, of proper dimensions to properly accommodate the remains of their late companion.

While one faction was busily engaged in digging the grave, the other faction was in the house playing a game of progressive seven-up, the loser of which was penalized to act as mortician.

When the hole had been extended to the proper length, breadth and depth, the loser in the seven-up game saddled his horse, rode to the door of the death shack, stepped to the door, tossed the loop of his saddle rope over the feet and around the ankles of the defunct John Blair, once more mounted his horse and, having taken a dally with his rope around the saddle horn, the funeral procession started.

This was probably the fastest moving funeral procession that John Blair ever traveled in, as it is believed that the speed limit was fractured in various places. The mortal remains of the late John Blair were quickly catapulted into their last resting place and soon covered by several feet of Arizona rocks and soil and camp activities immediately resumed the normal.

It is a matter of some discussion as to just how the said John Blair will rid himself of his rope hobbles on resurrection day.

HARRY C. WHEELER

H ARRY C. WHEELER was born in Florida in 1875.
He served in the Spanish-American War, taking part
in several engagements, the most prominent of which
was the Battle of Manila. In 1900 he came to Arizona
and located at Tombstone where, shortly afterwards, he became a member of the Arizona State Rangers and remained
with this organization until it was disbanded, having been
promoted from time to time until, at the time of the abolish-
ment of the organization, he had reached the rank of captain.

In 1905, while a member of the State Rangers, Wheeler
came to Tucson one day and, stepping into the Palace Saloon, was just in time to bump into a holdup man who had
all of the inmates of the saloon lined up against the wall.
Wheeler and the holdup man exchanged shots, with fatal
results to the holdup man. The partner of the holdup
man, who had been acting as lookout, stepped to the saloon
door and fired two shots at Wheeler and then ran away.
Wheeler was not injured by any of the shots fired at him.

On February 28th, 1907, while a lieutenant of the Rangers, and in Benson, he was wounded twice by J. A. Vail
who was endeavoring to shoot D. W. Silverton and wife.
Tracy was following Silverton and wife down the street,
cursing them loudly and threatening to shoot both of them,
and at the same time pulling a six shooter as though to
make good his threat.

Wheeler appeared upon the scene and ordered Tracy to
drop his gun, but he turned the gun on Wheeler and fired
twice, one bullet striking Wheeler's foot and the second
one lodging in his thigh. Wheeler then fired four shots, all
of which took effect. As Tracy lay upon the ground he
attempted to fire a third shot at Wheeler but Wheeler grabbed the gun from him. Tracy was loaded into the baggage
car of a passenger train which chanced to pass just at the
right time, and started for the hospital in Tucson, but died

at Mescal about five miles west of Benson. As he died he said, "There is a woman in the case."

In the investigation which followed the death of Tracy, it was revealed that Tracy claimed Mrs. Silverton as his wife, stating that he married her in Nevada and that shortly after their marriage she informed him that their marriage

HARRY C. WHEELER

was illegal as she already had one husband. They parted, she going to Phoenix and he to Vail where he was working as shipping clerk for the Helvetia Mining Company.

The woman in the case, accompanied by another man, for some reason or another never explained, came to Benson and Tracy being in town also, he armed himself and hunted them up on the street with bad luck to himself. Mrs. Silver-

ton admitted that she had known Tracy but that he was nothing more than a mere acquaintance.

During the early part of 1917 agitators and German
sympathizers under the guise of the I. W. W. organization
invaded Bisbee and began to do all that they could to ob-
struct the draft law and the production of copper, which at
that time was in great demand for the manufacture of cartridges for use in the World War. On June 27th of that
year they succeeded in getting the Calumet and Arizona and
the Copper Queen miners to walk out on a strike. There
was much talk made by the I. W. W.'s that they were going
to blow up the mines in order to halt the production of
copper.

A deplorable state of affairs existed in and around Bisbee. The copper industry was at a standstill and business
interests were paralyzed. Sheriff Harry Wheeler immediately got busy and appointed 275 deputies and they worked night and day in their tireless efforts to locate the ones
responsible for the conditions of affairs existing in the
Bisbee Mining District.

As a result of their efforts, 1187 agitators were rounded
up and on July 12th, 1917, loaded into the empty stock
cars of a passing train and taken to Columbus, New Mexico,
where was located a large military camp. The Commanding officer at Columbus ordered Sheriff Wheeler to take his
human cargo back into Arizona. The train was backed into
Hermanes, a small border town just inside of the Arizona
state line and here they were unloaded.

The following day the commanding officer at Columbus had them all brought into Columbus, where they were
provided with camping quarters and food. These I. W.
W.'s were well satisfied for the first few days with their
good luck, as they were being fed and cared for by the government which they were fighting against, they being nearly
all foreign subjects.

They were not kept under close guard, only under a mild
supervision, and as the food supply was reduced they drifted out and away until none remained.

Kidnapping charges were preferred against Sheriff Harry Wheeler, but were held up pending his return from France. When it was learned that he intended taking all of the deportation responsibility upon his own shoulders, the district attorney decided that should Wheeler be permitted to assume all responsibility for the deportation of the 1187 "wobblies" that, in view of the fact that he was an exceedingly popular man in Cochise County, it would be next to impossible to get a conviction against him in the face of public opinion, and he decided to quash the indictment against him and use him as a witness against all of the other deputies who took part in the great deportation act.

Wheeler entered the World War while matters were pending in the deportation case and returned a captain of Aviation Service.

The district attorney drew up an indictment against Harry E. Wooten, charging him with complicity in the deportation case, and subpoenaed Capt. Harry Wheeler as a witness in behalf of the state, believing that he had a sure case against Wooten and that after his conviction he would follow up with indictments against all of the rest of those who took part.

Wheeler was on the stand for three days and in giving his testimony he stated that he and he alone was responsible for the deportation from Bisbee of the 1187 men who were banded together for the purpose of obstructing the draft law and the production of copper which the United States needed so badly just at that time. After a trial lasting 90 days the case went to the jury and a verdict of "Not guilty" was returned in less than five minutes.

Capt. Harry Wheeler died in Douglas in December, 1925, leaving a wife and young son, also a host of warm friends who will miss his presence in their midst. He was one of the "little big men" who has played a large part in shaping the destiny of the State of Arizona.

PEARL HART

PEARL TAYLOR was born in the little town of Lindsay, Province of Ontario, Canada, about 1871. She was placed in a boarding school and while there, and only in her 17th year, met a man named Hart whose personal appearance was pleasing to her and he easily persuaded her to elope with him. They were married and lived happily together for a short time and then he began to abuse her. Before long he drove her away from their home by his continued cruel and inhuman treatment and she went back to her old home with her mother, where she remained only a short time.

Her husband sent for her and, under promises of loving treatment in the future, she returned to him. For about two weeks he treated her with the utmost kindness and consideration and then began to abuse her, even resorting to beating her frequently. This was in the fall of 1893, and she left him once more and, wishing to get as far away from him as possible, and knowing that if she went home to her mother he would find her again, she went to Trinidad, Colo.

For many months she wrestled in a catch as catch can style, making only a scanty living for herself and baby boy, who was born while she was back in her home town with her mother. She went from one town to another and finally landed in Phoenix, where she met her husband face to face one day on the street. She still loved him and, in spite of knowing that if she went back to him she would not be happy, and fight as she would against the temptation, her love for him won out and she went back to live with him once more.

They lived happily together in Phoenix for about three years and during this time a baby girl was born to them. Her husband, after three years of very pleasant home life, began to abuse her again and she left him for the third time. She sent her children to her mother back in Canada and she went back east and obtained employment in a well to do family as a servant.

During her two years' stay in the east, she heard of her husband occasionally. She tried to forget him but her efforts along that line were unsuccessful. He was the father of her children and she still loved him. He finally found out where she was and went to her; with his bland and al-

PEARL HART, THE LADY BANDIT

Photo courtesy of Cosmopolitan

luring promises, he once more persuaded her to return to Arizona and live with him.

They came back to Arizona and located in Tucson but as he was absolutely worthless and did not make any attempt at making a living for them, the money which she had saved during her two years' servitude in the east was soon gone and he began abusing her and her life was a living hell until

in 1898 he joined McCord's Regiment of Rough Riders
and left town.

Pearl went back to Phoenix and managed to get along
after a manner. She tried three or four times to commit
suicide but was prevented by the interference of friends.
Finally she obtained employment as cook in a mining camp
at Mammoth and she worked there for several months but
as her living quarters consisted only of a tent, pitched on
the bank of the Gila River, her health began to suffer.

She loaded all of her worldly possessions into a freight
wagon one day and started for Globe, but the roads were so
muddy that the horses were unable to pull the wagon
through and they turned back and Pearl once more landed
in the mining camp at Mammoth.

A few days later a man named Joe Boot, wishing to go
to Globe, made arrangements with a couple of Mormon boys
to take himself and Pearl Hart to Globe and once more
Pearl was headed in the direction of Globe, this time in company of Joe Boot. The roads were so bad that they only
made three miles the first day and camped. The following
day they managed to get into Globe where Pearl soon obtained employment as cook in a miners' boarding house
where she made good until one of the big mines shut down
and she was once more left with nothing to do.

Pearl had saved some money from what she had received for her work but just about the time that she was
thrown out of work one of her brothers who had located
her wrote her that he was in trouble and for her to send him
all the money that she could, so she sent him all that she
could spare.

Before Pearl could locate another position her husband
once more appeared on the scene, having been mustered out
of the army at Tucson. He was too lazy to work and insisted that she support him but she refused to support him in
the manner which he suggested and they quarreled and he
left. She never saw him again.

Just after her husband had left Globe she, being broke
and having no job, received a letter from home that her

mother was very ill and not expected to live and that if she expected to see her alive, she must come at once. One thing which can be said in Pearl's favor is, that with all of her faults, she fairly idolized her mother and the knowledge that her mother was liable to die at any minute, and that she had no money with which to pay her railroad fare to her mother's bedside nearly drove her frantic. Pearl herself says that she believes that brooding over her misfortunes drove her temporarily insane.

Joe Boot located what he thought was a profitable mining claim and suggested to Pearl that they go out and dig out enough pay dirt to get her home. She donned men's clothing and they went out to the mine and they worked night and day, but it was useless. She wielded a pick and shovel and did a man's work on the claim until every vestige of color had faded away.

Joe Boot sympathized with her as a true friend should but he had no money and was powerless to render her any assistance as it was impossible for him to get enough money on such a short notice to pay her expenses home.

He finally proposed to her that they rob the Globe stage, but though she at first refused to take part in any such enterprise, after brooding over her troubles for a while she finally weakened and consented, after she had made Boot promise that no one would be hurt. Boot informed her that it was easy enough, all that was necessary was to put on a bold front and the rest was easy.

On the afternoon set for the holdup, they broke camp, mounted their horses and rode over the mountains until they reached the Globe road. They located a bend in the road where they knew that the stage would have to be slowed down to permit the horses to take the turn. Here they took their stand.

When they heard the stage coming toward them they started forward on a slow walk to meet it. They pulled out to one side of the road and when the stage reached them, Boot pulled his 45 Colt's six shooter and Pearl her 38, and covering the driver, they shouted to him to stop sudden and elevate. He acted as though he was pleased to accommodate and while Boot remained mounted, Pearl dismounted and ordered the occupants of the stage to "pile out." Her order was carried out with the utmost haste. Joe told her to search for guns. This she did but found none; but later when she looked into the stage to see that there was no stray passengers hiding therein, she found that two passengers had left their six shooters inside of the stage. She gave Joe one of them, a 44 Colt, and kept the other one, a 45 Colt, for herself.

Joe then told her to go ahead and search the passengers. The man who appeared the most scared, yielded three hundred and ninety dollars. He shook so badly that he would probably have shook it out of his pockets anyway, had he not been relieved of it. The next man, a dude with his hair parted in the middle, assayed thirty-six dollars, a dime and two nickels. The third passenger, a Chinaman, yielded only five dollars. The stage driver had only a few dollars and they did not take it. They gave each of the three victims a dollar and ordered them to climb aboard the stage and not to look back. Their instructions were carried out, insofar as they could see.

During the balance of the day they rode over the roughest trails that their horses could negotiate and at dark they arrived at Cane Springs but did not stop there to make camp. They passed right on and reached Riverside at about 10 o'clock. They made no stop here but passed quietly through and kept on the same road for about six miles and then turned south toward Benson, where they expected to catch an east bound train.

They camped that night on the east bank of the Gila River and remained there until the next night in order to give their horses a chance to rest up. That night they rode within six miles of Mammoth and as both were well known there, they had need to be careful, so they hid in the bushes. They saw several wagons pass and many men on horseback, so they decided to change their resting place. Leaving their horses in the brush, they climbed up the side of a big sandstone hill to where there were some small caves and entered one of them. After crawling back about twenty feet, Joe stopped and told Pearl that he could see two bright eyes shining just ahead of him and that he was going to take a shot at them.

Joe shot and then crawled in further and investigated and found that he had killed a wild hog which had taken refuge in the cave. The powder smoke made breathing so difficult in the little cave that they backed out nearly to the entrance and stayed there all that day.

As soon as it was dark they went back to their horses, saddled them and rode back toward Mammoth. Joe slipped into town and obtained some provisions and tobacco without any one learning his identity. They then passed Mammoth, crossed the river again and rode as far as the school house and then hid themselves in the brush at the far end of a large field. They secured feed for their horses here and, making a bed of straw and dry grass, they forgot their troubles and slept all night.

At daylight the next morning they started on their journey to the railroad. After riding about ten miles their horses began to show signs of extreme weariness on account of the very hard service to which they had been subjected and having had very little to eat, and Pearl suggested that they turn their horses into some one's pasture and provide themselves with fresh mounts, but Boot said that they would not do that, so they rode on. Shortly afterwards they reached a wide ditch, which was full of water, Pearl jumped her horse safely over but Joe's horse fell short and landed in the water and he nearly lost his life before he could get un- untangled from his saddle. Finally he got his horse righted and out of the water but as their horses were both worn out they decided to make camp in order to let them rest and graze while they themselves did some cooking and much needed eating. The rain fell all day and kept them soaking wet.

As soon as it was good and dark they again started on their journey toward the railroad and rode steadily until five o'clock in the morning and again made camp. They had slept about three hours when they were awakened by shouts and shots.   They jumped and grabbed their guns but found themselves looking into the muzzles of two unusually large calibered Winchesters which were backed up by two members of the sheriff's posse.

They were captured within 20 miles of Benson and the chances were largely in their favor that they would have made their get away out of the country had they reached the railroad, as they had plenty of money.

They were first taken to Benson and then to Casa Grande on the first west bound train. From there they were taken to Florence, which is the county seat of Pinal County and in the county where the holdup was staged. On account of the better accommodations for women in the Pima County jail at Tucson, Pearl was transferred to Tucson.

On the day of her transfer to Tucson, she tried to commit suicide but the guards prevented her from carrying out her rash attempt. Pearl stated later that she was sorry that she failed. She and Joe Boot had sworn never to serve a term in the penitentiary.

One evening when Pearl was served her supper she hid the knife and its absence was not noticed by the jailer. That night she loosened and removed sufficient bricks from the double wall of the jail to permit her to escape but she was soon missed and located walking around town and returned to the jail from which she had so recently made her escape.

In due time she and Joe Boot were arraigned for trial and found guilty of robbery by force of firearms and Boot was sentenced to serve thirty-five years in the state penitentiary at Yuma. Pearl drew a five year sentence and served perhaps about half of it, being pardoned out.

About three years later Pearl was arrested at Deming, New Mexico, by Sheriff George Scarborough, on a charge of having been implicated in a train holdup which was staged near the New Mexico-Arizona Line, but there was not sufficient evidence to convict her and she was released.

Nothing more was heard of either one of these unfortun-
ates until about twenty-five years later, when one day an
elderly lady walked into the Pima County Jail and asked
that she might look the jail over. As such a request was rather unusual, without some explanation, she was asked the
reason for her anxiety to look over the jail, she replied, "I
am Pearl Hart and spent some time here about twenty-five
years ago and I would like to see my old cell."   Needless
to say she was accorded the privilege of inspecting her old
quarters and, after thanking the officer in charge for his
courtesy departed, no one knowing where to or when.

RUSSIAN BILL AND SANDY KING

RUSSIAN BILL was another member of the outlaw gang who kept his dues fully paid up and was in good standing. He was a character worthy of more than passing attention. He was possessed of finely cut features, a long sandy mustache and curly blonde hair which hung to his shoulders. He was considered a very handsome man. He spoke four different languages and always, when possible, discussed literature, science and art.

Bill claimed to have killed several men, but there is no proof at hand at this late date with which to substantiate his claim. However, not wishing to cast any reflections on his honesty we will admit, for the sake of evading an argument, that he may have killed several men, because those who were well acquainted with him believed him capable of it had the necessity arisen.

Bill, being in Lordsburg one day and desirous of visiting Deming, boldly entered the corral of one of the local livery stables and dropped his loop over the head of a horse which met his approval, cinched on his saddle, mounted and was quickly on his way.

It was not long until that particular horse was missed and investigation revealed the fact that Russian Bill had been seen riding that horse toward Deming. An officer was soon in pursuit and Bill was overtaken before he had gotten fairly started on his sixty mile journey.

Just about the time that Russian Bill was outfitting himself for his journey, Sandy King came into Shakespeare, a small mining camp located three miles to the south of Lordsburg, and proceeded to make a manful effort toward drinking all the booze in camp, but as a new barrel had just been brought in from the railroad Sandy made a dismal failure just as many a better man than he had done. Anyway, Sandy accumulated quite a liquor tonnage and proceeded to amalgamate with the natives, and declared that he was a bull rattler and that it was his day to rattle.

He entered a store and made some trivial purchase and started out without going through the formality of tendering a pecuniary remuneration for the aforesaid goods, whereupon the clerk, evidently fresh from the east and unaccustomed to the harsh, abrupt manners of the western bad man had the temerity to request payment for the purchase. Sandy, with the very best of intentions, took a shot at the clerk, which inflicted only a slight flesh wound in one arm. ·

The Law and Order League, which at that time was in perpetual session in and around Shakespeare and Lordsburg, gathered Sandy in for a hearing. Just at this stage of the game the deputy arrived with Russian Bill and it was decided to give them both a hearing at the same session of court.

The dining room of the hotel was the only room of sufficient dimensions to serve as a court room, so the tables were pushed back against the wall and the prisoners were accorded a trial, by a jury composed of miners and other known-to-be law-abiding citizens. Russian Bill admitted his guilt and he was sentenced to hang. They found Sandy King guilty of being "a damned nuisance" and he too was sentenced to hang.

There being no suitable tree nearer than several miles, in the execution of the two sentences the Law and Order League decided that there was no reason for any unnecessary delay and two rafters of the dining room served the purpose admirably and Russian Bill and Sandy King passed out via the rope route as scheduled. When they were pronounced dead beyond recall their bodies were cut down and buried by the side of the road, just outside of the camp. Their graves are still visible. The dining room furniture was re-arranged and the evening meal served without a hitch.

A short time after this event the sheriff at Tombstone received a letter from the American Consul at St. Petersburg, Russia, saying that Countess Telfrin was very desirous of locating her son William, who had been banished from that country to the United States for political reasons and that the last record she had of him, he was receiving his mail at Tombstone.

A picture of William Telfrin was enclosed and it proved to be an excellent one of Russian Bill. The sheriff, being a kind hearted man and wishing to save the Countess as much pain as possible, wrote the American Consul that the Countess Telfrin's son had committed suicide by hanging, and the incident was closed.

JOHN P. CLUM

JOHN P. CLUM was the first Indian agent at the Ft. San Carlos Agency, having been appointed to that position in the year 1874. One of Clum's first duties was that of rounding up Geronimo and his band and gathering them into the governmental fold at San Carlos.

Geronimo had lived for years in the Chiricahua Mountains down in Cochise County and did not wish to be moved away from there, but Uncle Samuel had issued the edict and had furnished Clum with authority and soldiers enough to enforce the order and finally Geronimo and his gang were rounded up at Apache Pass, near Old Ft. Bowie, and transferred to San Carlos. Geronimo could not submit to the jurisdiction of white men and in June, 1876, he went on the warpath in good faith.

On July 1st, 1877, Clum resigned the office as Indian Agent at San Carlos and the following year he was admitted to the bar in Pinal County. In 1879 he purchased the Tucson Weekly Citizen and transformed it into a daily, which was the first daily paper published in the Territory of Arizona.

In 1880 he went to Tombstone and founded the Tombstone Epitaph. He was also appointed first postmaster of Tombstone and when Tombstone was pronounced a full fledged city, Clum was elected mayor and served one term.

While it is not known for a certainty, it is believed that he remained in Tombstone until the slump in silver in 1889, and then went to California. He was heard of in Los Angeles a short time ago.

THE WHAM ROBBERY

O N THE morning of May 11th, 1889, U. S. A. Paymaster Major Joseph W. Wham, accompanied by an
escort of two noncommissioned officers and nine pri-
vates from the 10th U. S. Cavalry and the 24th U. S. Infantry, departed Ft. Grant enroute to Ft. Thomas, a distance of 46 miles, wtih the intention of paying off the troops
there on the following day. In addition to the military
escort, there was Major Wham's clerk, W. J. Gibbon, and
the drivers of the two ambulances in the party.

A stop was made at Cedar Springs, 25 miles from Ft.
Grant, to change mules, which had been sent on ahead the
day before. When about six miles from Cedar Springs and
fifteen from Ft. Thomas, at a point where the road wound
around down a long hill, an immense boulder was encountered, squarely placed in the middle of the road at a
sharp turn in such a manner that its several tons weight
entirely blocked the road.

There was no passage around it for the wagons and of
course transportation came to a sudden stop and the soldiers, rifles in hand, were hurrying to roll the geological
impediment from the passage way when a volley of shots
were fired at them from behind a rock wall, not more than
35 or 40 yards distant. Later investigation developed the
fact that this rock wall had been built as a breast-work.

Those of the paymaster's party who were not wounded
by the first volley, took their dead and wounded and sought
refuge behind a small ledge of rock on the opposite side
of the road and returned the fire of the attackers. The
man in command of the robber party sent men to take position on ridges to the right and the left of the ambushed
party, and it was only a matter of a few minutes until the
guard was harrassed by a sharp fire from both sides as well
as from in front.

The Paymaster's party, finding that it was impossible to
hold their position behind the ledge of rock with a deadly
hail of lead sweeping them from three directions, made a
break for the arroya which was about 300 yards distant and

five men were wounded while making this hurried trip.
Major Wham, his clerk and a corporal were the only ones
who were not wounded while changing position. The corporal was afterwards wounded.

The robbers, after having chased the soldiers away from
the immediate vicinity of the wagons, secured the strong

MEN CHARGED WITH WHAM ROBBERY AND LEGAL ADVISORS

box and broke it open with an axe. The $28,345.10 which
it contained was quickly divided up among the looters and
carried to a place of safety. After about 30 minutes of
fighting every one of the paymaster's escort was wounded,
but the robbers kept up their bombardment for about 30
minutes longer before taking their departure from that vicinity.

Some of the robbers, of whom 12 were counted, were
badly wounded. One of the robbers was so badly wounded
that his companions tied him on a mule and packed him
away. One wounded holdup man ordered another one to
shoot him and he did. Major Wham and his clerk were
the only ones of his party who were not wounded.

The robbers cut a lot of mescal stalks and dug the pith out of one end of each one and then stuck them into the rock walls of their breast works in such a manner that they appeared at a short distance to have been rifle barrels, all pointing directly at the point occupied by the wagons.

Over 200 empty shells were picked up behind the breast works, to say nothing of the large quantities found on spots occupied by the right and left flankers.

The following is a list of the wounded escort:
Sgt. Brown, shot through bowels and one arm.
Private Burge, shot through one leg and both hands.
Private Ham, shot in arm.
Private Wheeler, shot in arm.
Private Arlington, shot in shoulder.
Private Harrison, shot through ear.
Private Williams, shot through both legs.
Private Hamilton, shot in side.
Corporal Isaih Mayes, who accompanied the escort, was also wounded but the extent of his wounds is not now known.

The first two men arrested in connection with this robbery were M. E. Cunningham and William Ellison Beck, alias Cyclone Bill, a man answering the description of Cyclone Bill having been seen on the scene of battle. Bill was possessed of a long narrow face which was ornamented by long whiskers. He was six feet two in height on one side and only six feet on the other and this condition of affairs caused him a noticeable limp and it was by this peculiarity that one or more of the colored soldiers of the escort party identified him. It later developed that two deputy sheriffs had seen Bill on Eagle Creek, many miles from the scene of the holdup at a time when it would have been a physical impossibility for him to have been implicated in this act.

United States Marshal W. K. Meade immediately offered a reward of $500 each for the apprehension of each man involved in this robbery and there were scores of men riding the country looking for clues. In addition to thes: there were several troops of cavalry out, scouring the hills and mountains for the robbers, but as they were believed to have been local parties and had immediately gotten under cover, the soldiery did not accomplish any thing.

Will Webb, Lyman Follett, Ed Follett and Dan Rogers were arrested next. It was known that one of the robbers had a finger shot off in the fight and Lyman Follett was short one of his fingers. Tom Lamb was next arrested and then S. B. Henderson, but Henderson was released after the preliminary hearing.

On June 3d, 1889, upon arrival of the prisoners in Tucson, Gilbert Webb, father of the Webb boys, was also arrested on a charge of tampering with witnesses. Ed Follett was also released after the preliminary.

Private Burg of Co. "E" of the 24th Infantry, identified Cunningham, Will Follett and Will Webb as being members of the robbery party.

Sergeant Ben Brown, in charge of the escort, identified Will Webb and Gilbert Webb as having been members of the gang.

Frankie Lewis, a colored woman who chanced to be riding at this particular place at the time of the holdup and who hid in the brush, testified that she had seen Gilbert Webb and Tom Lamb engaged in shooting at the paymaster's escort. She also testified that she saw Tom Lamb at Ft. Grant on Thursday before the robbery.

William Haynes testified that he also saw Tom Lamb in Ft. Grant on both Thursday and Friday before the robbery and that he heard Lamb asking questions about what date they expected the paymaster, how long he would probably remain in Ft. Grant and when he would leave there for Ft. Thomas. The testimony of Haynes was corroborated by that of Harry Bobbenhausen, Private Flemming and Sergeant Purcell, who also saw Lamb at Ft. Grant on the same dates.

J. G. Holland, Charles Williams, Bishop Layton, S. C. Heaton, A. T. Posey and D. W. Wickersham testified that they had received money in various amounts, but amounting to quite a sum, from Gilbert Webb since the robbery.

On June 11th, 1889, Gilbert Webb, Will Webb, M. E.

Cunningham, Lyman Rogers, Will Follett and Tom Lamb were adjudged guilty as charged, and were admitted to $10,-000 bail each for appearance for trial in the fall term of court.

Members of what was known as the "Wham Jury" were David Allen, A. J. Stockton, John W. Kelso, W. H. Barnett, J. H. Hart, Heil Hale, Geo. Cooler, Adam Saunders, C. F. Gooding, C. C. Wheeler, Joseph Hoefler and M. W. Hammerstand.

The wounded men had so far recovered as to be able to testify at the regular trial and Sergeant Brown testified that after he was wounded in the body he got hold of a shotgun and fired three or four shots when a bullet struck him in the left arm, totally disabling him. In addition to his wounds, he had his clothing torn by two more bullets. He identified Gilbert and Will Webb and M. F. Cunningham as being members of the holdup party.

George Short identified Will Webb and M. E. Cunningham; J. E. Young identified Will Webb: George Arrington identified Gilbert Webb; Corporal Isaih Mays identified Warren Follett, Lyman Follett and Will Webb; Private Burg identified M. E. Cunningham, Will Webb, Will Follett and Dan Rogers and Julius Harrison identified Will Webb.

Henry Fowler testified that he found the money buried in his haystack and that Gilbert Webb came and got it.

After this trial had dragged along for about thirty days and nearly a hundred witnesses had been introduced to prove that none of the men charged with this robbery had been anywhere near the place on that date, they were released. The fact that after witnesses for the prosecution had sworn that they saw Cyclone Bill taking an active part in the robbery and two deputy sheriffs testified that they had seen Bill over on Eagle Creek at a time which would preclude all possibility of his being able to have taken part in the holdup festivities, the evidence for the prosecution was very much weakened and the air tight alibis of the defendants did the rest.

CLEVELAND, TAGGART, LEE AND JOY

FRANK TAGGART, Mitch Lee, Kit Joy and a Negro named George Cleveland, in December, 1883, held up a Southern Pacific Express train at Gage, New Mexico, about forty miles east of the Arizona line. Eugene Webster, the engineer, was killed. All of these men were speedily apprehended and placed in the Grant County jail at Silver City.

On the morning of March 10th, 1884, Taggart, Lee and Joy were taking exercise in the jail yard when the opportune moment arrived; they quietly overpowered the inside guard and locked him in their cell. Taking his gun, they slipped up on the two outside guards and held them up, relieved them of their weapons and placed them in their cell to keep the inside guard company. The night guard was asleep, but they brought him out and placed him with the rest and then rounded up the Chinese cook and threw him in for good measure. They also released Chavez, a murderer and a bad man named Spencer.

Having the arms of the guards, which consisted of three six shooters and two shot-guns, they were prepared for any emergency which might arise. They released the Negro, Cleveland, and then went to the Elephant Corral where they ordered Mr. Chapman, the proprietor, to saddle six horses. As the orders were backed up with six shooters and shot-guns, they were speedily carried out. While the saddling process was going on, friends supplied them with a Winchester each and two belts of cartridges.

The Negro caught a "bronc" and was thrown off, but he jumped on behind one of the other men and all rode off together. Frank Jackson mounted his horse and followed them, firing frequently, hoping to get some of them, also to let the posse, which was to follow, know where they were.

The posse overtook the men about 8 miles from Silver City. Chavez was the first one of the outlaws to be killed and Mike Lee received a wound which was considered fatal, presumably by Andrews and Parks of the posse. George Cleveland, the Negro, was killed by Ned Mayer. Joe Laffere chanced to walk directly toward the hiding place of Kit Joy and, seeing him, turned to jump to a place of safety and just as he turned, Joy shot him in the back with a load of buck-shot. Parks fired two shots at Joy and was positive that he wounded him, but Joy made his escape.

The posse intended hanging both Lee and Spencer at once, but Spencer talked them out of it for the time being and the posse started back to Silver City with the intention of turning them over to the authorities. Although suffering from a mortal wound Mich Lee would not admit anything, but Taggart confessed that he, Lee, Cleveland and Joy were the ones who held up the Southern Pacific Express at Gage in December, '83. They had all agreed that no killing was to be done, but that Lee was in the lead and that in the excitement of the moment he fired the shot which deprived Webster of his life.

The posse then placed Lee and Taggart in a wagon and backed the wagon under a small tree, adjusted ropes and pulled the wagon away. Although they had only one foot to drop, the execution was just as much of a success as though it had been official, with six feet of drop.

The bodies were then taken into Silver City for inquest. The usual verdict was rendered that Mitch Lee and Frank Taggart had come to their death at the hands of parties unknown and the incident was closed.

Kit Joy made his get away and returned to Tombstone country where he, single handed, was credited with holding up the Tombstone-Benson stage. A posse was soon in pursuit and Joy was located. In the fight which ensued he was wounded in the leg by a large-calibre bullet.

The wounded leg was amputated and after Kit had recovered he stood trial on the holdup charge and found guilty. He was sentenced to a term of ten years in the State Penitentiary at Yuma. He served his time and when released, returned to Cochise County, where he is still living.

Under his handicap of old age and only one leg, of late

years Kit has found it practically impossible to earn a comfortable living, so he went into the liquor business over in the Huachuca Mountains and soon ran afoul of the federal officers who arrested him with the goods right on him. He was brought to Tucson for trial.

In his plea to the judge for clemency, he said, "Judge, God worked six days and rested on the seventh. I worked that still just six days and was arrested on the seventh day and I guess that I am in now for a good long rest."

HENRY BROWN AND FRED WAITE

HENRY BROWN and Fred Waite were both members of Billy the Kid's gang until shortly before Billy's death. Believing that if they did not sever their connections with this gang they would surely be shot sooner or later, they decided to jump the game for good before they were snuffed out via the gun or rope route.

They both quit at the same time and rode together up into Indian Territory, which is now known as Oklahoma. Waite settled down, married, raised a family and became a good citizen.

Brown soon drifted across the Territory line into Kansas and dropped into Caldwell, a small border town about 20 miles west of Wellington. In the early days this place was one of the shipping points for cattle, which were driven up from Texas, and was considered a very noisy little town at that time.

Brown was soon apointed city marshal and, so as far as is related, made good for a while. His close association with the rough element, while acting in the capacity of city marshal, prevented him from forgetting his Arizona and New Mexico days and he soon threw in with the wild element completely.

He and three more men who were possessed of the same moral inclinations as he, rode over to Medicine Lodge one day and held up the only bank in town. They met with spirited resistance and in the fight which took place within the walls of the bank, they killed two of the bank employes who attempted to protect the interests of the bank. The robbers departed very suddenly, with a posse in close pursuit.

They were overtaken in the bad lands off to the south of Medicine Lodge and in the gun fight which took place, two of the outlaws were killed and Brown and one more were captured and brought back to town.

Inasmuch as these outlaws had been caught red-handed in

their crime it was not necessary for the state to go to the expense of prosecuting them, so the posse tarried just long enough on the edge of town to suspend Brown and his partner from the convenient limb of a huge cottonwood tree which chanced to be located in the right place at the right time.

JOEL FOWLER AND JOHN BURNS, BUTCHER KNIFE BILL AND PONY DIEHL

JOEL FOWLER was credited with being a member in good standing of the outlaw gang and entitled to the twenty notches showing in his gun stock. John Burns, while only a 19 year old boy, had several men to his credit and had considerable reputation as a bad man.

Fowler and Burns decided that life around Tombstone was entirely too tame for them so they traveled over Clifton way and organized a holdup on the Clifton Stage, which was a financial success.

It seems as though Pony Diehl and Butcher Knife Bill had also planned on holding up this same stage on the same day on which Fowler and Burns held it up but they ran in second place only. Each pair declared war on the other.

They met at a later date and as Fowler and Burns were both armed with double barreled shot guns, loaded with buckshot, they did some first class broadcasting and Butcher Knife Bill and Pony Diehl had no trouble on the pick up. In fact, Butcher Knife Bill picked up so much lead that he took absolutely no further interest in subsequent proceedings whatsoever. Pony Diehl, although badly wounded, managed to make his getaway by crawling into the brush and hiding. He finally regained enough strength to crawl to a house owned by a man named McGee, who was not at home at the time of Diehl's arrival.

Fowler and Burns trailed Diehl to McGee's house and, being afraid to enter the house, believing that possibly Diehl might have found friends and that they were quietly waiting to ambush them, they camped outside with intention of picking off any one coming out of that particular house.

After a wait of some time, McGee appeared upon the scene and Fowler stopped him and explained the situation, offering him $500 if he would go in and throw Diehl out so that they could get him in the open. McGee found the door fastened on the inside and broke it down and Diehl shot him dead before he could get clear of the wreckage of the broken door.

Fowler and Burns then slipped up and set fire to the house and it was soon burned to the ground. The following day the charred remains of Diehl's body were found in the ruins. Burns made his get away. Fowler was apprehended a short time later by officers from New Mexico, where he was wanted on seven murder charges.

While working near Socorro, New Mexico, for some cattle outfit, he went into town one day and proceeded to get drunk. The ranch foreman, who was a good friend of his, tried to get him to go home and Fowler shot him dead.

Fowler was taken back to Socorro and placed in the county jail. Inasmuch as there was absolutely no doubt as to his guilt and a conviction on any one of the seven charges would be the result of a trial, about 100 of the good citizens of Socorro entered the jail one night and hung him to the ceiling of his cell, thus making sure that he did not escape justice, and saving the state the expense of a trial.

CHEROKEE BOB AND BILL

CHEROKEE BOB and Cherokee Bill were a pair of misguided youths from the Cherokee Country back in Indian Territory who came to the great southwest on account of the possibilities of getting something for nothing. The first notable event of their young lives, after arriving here, was to hold up a Southern Pacific passenger train at Steins Pass, which is three miles east of the Arizona State Line in New Mexico.

On account of the reticence of the Wells-Fargo Express Company in stating how much money these two obtained, the full extent of their success is not known, but it is known that they tied the legs of a pair of overalls at their bottom and stuffed the money inside and that said pair of overalls was well filled, so we are forced to believe that their venture was a financial success.

They buried their monetary loot about three hundred yards from the scene of action and about 100 yards from the old turntable at the end of the spur track just west of town. They went into Lordsburg to wait until the dust settled, because it might have been embassassing for them to have been caught with so much money so soon after the holdup.

While there, Bob killed Bill, that he might have all of the money for himself. Bob confided his act to a woman and, as is usually the case, she spilled the beans to another man and this man chanced to be Dick Hart, who was the brains of a bunch of crooks who spent the most of their time and ill gotten gains in Lordsburg, and consequently, Cherokee Bob was mysteriously killed one night and Dick Hart and his gang disappeared.

The woman in the case waited for several days and then informed the local peace officers that she was afraid that Dick Hart and his gang had killed Cherokee Bob so that they could get clear title to the loot.

She told him that the money was buried about 100 yards

from the spur turntable and for him to go up the little arroya, keeping a sharp lookout for a piece of coarse wrapping twine which would be tied around the limb of a mesquite bush, to go ten feet beyond this marker and dig.

At the last moment she decided to go with him and they drove to Steins to investigate. They found everything just as represented, except the money. They found where it had been buried but it had been dug up and carried away.

It later transpired that Dick Hart and his gang had traveled toward Mexico by the shortest known route and that they were absent from Lordsburg thereafter.

GEORGE AND VIRGIL GATES

GEORGE GATES held up a store in California and came out of it with his hind legs full of bird shot. Soon after this painful experience he and his brother, Virgil, held up a passenger train at Copely Junction, killed the express messenger, looted the express car and made their get away.

They landed in Tucson but did not tarry long. Then they tried Tombstone and that town did not suit them so they went to Lordsburg. Craving a little excitement, they staged a saloon holdup which netted them about $1500 and two or three large sized diamonds which they removed from the persons of as many gentlemen of fortune as chanced to be pursuing their nefarious callings in the emporium.

It goes without saying that they made a quick get away and continued the motion until they reached Separ where they applied for and obtained lodging at a farm house nearby. Deputy Sheriff Herb McGrath and Joe Olney followed their trail and located them and when the officers walked in on them they found the Gates Boys sleeping with their guns at their sides.

When they were awakened from their sleep by the officers, they attempted to get action on their artillery but they were too slow by the fractional part of a second and both were instantly killed. All of the stolen property was recovered from their bodies.

George Gates was very romantic and a great reader of Sir Walter Scott's works and usually carried a copy of some one of these interesting books around with him and would drop down and read a few lines whenever the opportunity offered.

At one time he conceived the idea of holding up ocean steamers but as he could not find any one else who was as visionary as himself to assist him, he was forced to abandon this idea in favor of dry land amusements so common in the southwest in early days.

TIM HURLEY

TIM HURLEY killed Old Man Roberts at Salero Mining Camp and made his escape across the line into Mexico with Sheriff Bob Paul only a very few jumps behind him. Just as soon as he crossed the line, he imagined he was safe and that Paul would turn back, but apparently he was unfamiliar with the customs of the day for Paul slipped up on him and informed him that he could· have his choice of staying in Mexico as a corpse or returning to Arizona to take a chance of a jury of men, good and true, (?), turning him loose. Hurley decided that if he returned to Arizona with Sheriff Paul that he would stand a chance of dodging the issue in some manner at that time unknown to him.

All went well until Paul and his prisoner had reached Tubac, where they were met by a bunch of infuriated miner friends of Old Man Roberts, who fully intended taking Hurley away from Paul, and lynching him. Paul managed to slip away from them and landed his prisoner in the Pima County Jail at Tucson.

A few days later, Hurley; Jim Morton, under life sentence on a murder charge; Moyer and Gibson, awaiting trial on a murder charge; Jim Casey and Pat Mahoney, charged with highway robbery and Charlie French, charged with robbery of the United States Mail, made their escape.

Hurley was afterwards apprehended at Ft. Worth, Texas, and returned to Tucson where he stood trial on the murder charge and was sentenced to a life term in the state penitentiary. Morton was killed in Northern New Mexico while resisting arrest. Moyer was apprehended in Denver, Colo., and returned to Tucson where he stood trial on a charge of the murder of Joe Levy, jointly with Dave Gibson and John Murphy, who were gamblers, rustlers and all around bad men. Gibson had become starved and froze out while hiding out in the mountains and had come in and surrendered.

BOB PAUL

At the trial which followed, it was decided that Moyer fired the shot which passed through Levy's heart and that he was dead before the bullets shot by Gibson and Murphy reached him. Moyer drew a life sentence in the state penitentiary and Gibson and Murphy were released.

In the Tucson jail break, Jim Casey killed Jailer Holbrook. He was apprehended and returned to Tucson where he stood trial on the murder charge and was found guilty. He was sentenced to be hanged. Sentence was carried out in the court house yard in Tucson. When all was ready, he shouted, "Good bye, turn 'er lose." They turned 'er lose and Jim Casey passed on to his reward.

JOHN WYETH

JOHN WYETH, whose home was in the far east, decided to take Horace Greeley's advice and "go west," with the avowed intention of growing up with the country. He came as far west as Tombstone and decided that he had reached "the west," so he dropped off the stage and proceeded to get acquainted with his environment.

John decided that clothes make the man, so he decked himself out in such gaudy array that he soon earned the title of "Dude Rustler." He threw in with the wild bunch, paid his initiation fee and was soon considered as one of them.

One day he chanced to ride into a small mining camp about five miles north of Steins, where he absorbed quite a quantity of that liquid damnation known as "jig juice" and which would cause a jack rabbit to chase a mountain lion. With an alcoholic locomotion of his pedal extremeties, John started down the one little crooked street of said mining camp, shooting various and sundry holes through the perfectly good atmosphere of the camp.

The miners objected to an outsider taking such liberties in their midst and when the Dude Rustler emerged from the festivities he had as a souvenir of the occasion, one large calibered bullet lodged in his anatomy.

John was brought to Lordsburg, where Doc Simpson performed an assessment on his person and removed the mineral deposit. During his convalescence he decided that he did not desire to be a bad man at all, and being afraid that he might not live long enough to enjoy a wild life, also being some frightened that he might get a puncture which would render him unfit to hold whiskey, just as soon as he was able to travel he visited the Southern Pacific ticket office at Lordsburg, purchased the longest coupon ticket on sale therein and rode it to death.

———o———

Johnnie Behind the Gun held up the El Paso and Southwestern agent at Fairbanks and was apprehended, found guilty of the crime and sentenced to a term of ten years in the state institution at Yuma. He served the sentence, less good time, came back into Cochise County, settled down and became a good citizen. Unfortunately, a few years ago his mind failed him and he was adjudged insane and was sent to the asylum at Phoenix.

Johnnie always stripped his six shooters of their handles so that he could see the mainspring and know that it was in working order. He was possessed of a deep seated fear that he might get up against the real thing some day and that, with a broken mainspring, his artillery would be just about as useful as a stone in hand.

TOM KERR, MATT BLEDSOE AND BILLY ANTRIM

T OM KERR was a member of the famous Plumer Gang of Montana. In consequence of some of his evil deeds, Kerr decided to indulge himself in a safety first vacation and in consequence of such a brilliant decision he went A. W. O. L. and landed in Tucson, Arizona, where he entered into a partnership with some other kindred spirit, whose name is not now available, and together they meandered over to Pioneer Camp, near Globe, and installed a saloon.

Matt Bledsoe was another bad, bad man who had incurred the displeasure of the commonwealth of the State of Oregon to such an extent that he had been sentenced to a long term in the state institution for the detention of bad men, but Governor Slater, feeling sorry for him, pardoned him with the understanding that he should leave the state; this last condition was a wise forethought on the part of the Governor Slater as he probably was well acquainted with Bledsoe and knew that he would take the state with him if it was not tied down or red hot.

Bledsoe landed in Tucson and soon became intoxicated from the inhalation of the rarefied Arizona atmosphere and red liquor and just as he had decided that he was the adjutant general of the universe, Tom Kerr arrived from Pioneer Camp on a shopping tour and he and Bledsoe met. No one seems at that late date to know just what they agreed to disagree about, but one thing was certain and that was, that Kerr was quicker on the draw than Bledsoe, and as Bledsoe slumped to the ground with an expression of surprise and bewilderment on his face, he realized that his earthly woes had ended right suddenly, and must have sensed the futility of playing a red liquor flush to beat a pair of sixes. Kerr was exonerated on the grounds of self defense.

One day, shortly after the Bledsoe episode, Kerr entered

the partnership saloon at Pioneer Camp and, finding his partner asleep and the cash drawer empty, placed the muzzle of his six shooter in close proximity to his partner's head, pulled the trigger, and the cash drawed was squared. Kerr testified at the inquest that his partner resented his accusation that he had gone to sleep and permitted the cash drawer to be robbed and had gone for his gun and he was forced to kill him. He was exonerated by the coroner's jury because he was the only witness available, but he afterwards told the true story while drunk.

Kerr had employed Billy Antrim to team for him and one day, his liquor evidently not setting well on his stomach, became peeved at something which Antrim had, or had not done, drew his six shooter and deliberately shot him.

The people, believing that such ingrowing tendencies should be corrected, took Kerr out and suspended him from the limb of a conveniently located cottonwood tree and permanently broke him of the habit of killing people promiscuously.

GREEK GEORGE

GREEK GEORGE was another well known character about Tombstone, who, while not a member of any regular band of outlaws, eventually drifted into evil ways which caused his sudden demise.

In 1859, while Jefferson Davis was our Secretary of War, he authorized the purchase of a herd of camels, believing that they would prove to be better beasts of burden in the desert country than the pack mules commonly used by the quartermaster department of the regular army. The number of camels thus purchased has been variously stated to have been from 59 to 60 head.

These animals were considered a success as pack animals insofar as negotiating the desert sand was concerned, but were found to be useless among the sharp rocks which abound in various parts of the southwest in connection with the desert sand, especially the sharp edges and corners of the malapai rock which cut their feet badly.

A portion of the herd of camels were left at some fort in Texas, and they too were soon relegated to the discard. At the time these camels were purchased in Alexandria, Egypt, it was found necessary to employ some one familiar with the handling of camels. At that time it was difficult to find an Egyptian who cared to leave his country and come to the United States. Finally a couple of youths of immature age were hired for the trip, but as they appeared to be able to deliver the goods, their ages were not questioned.

Hi Jolly, one of the camel boys was left with the bunch of camels which was assigned to duty in Texas. The other boy, whom was known as Greek George came on to Arizona and remained with the camels until they were turned out on the desert to shift for themselves. Hi Jolly later came to Arizona.

Some Indians rounded up nine head and sold them to a circus for $500 per head and the balance went the way or all good camels. Inasmuch as there is not an animal in Arizona but what is afraid of a camel, their repeated stampeeding of burros, cattle and saddle horses caused them to be looked upon as a niusance and open season was declared on camels the year around and it is presumed that cowboys shot nearly all of them at one time and another. Frequently, however, small bunches were seen on the desert for years after the government abandoned them.

After Greek George's camel days went into the discard, he drifted around from one place to another, going from Yuma to Tucson and then from Tucson to Tombstone. He associated with the wild bunch, and, while never having been known to aid them in any of their evil deeds, he associated with them in preference.

He finally got his man, whether by fair or foul means is not at this late date known, and in his frantic efforts to elude the pursuing posse, worked his way into a blind canyon where it was impossible for him to escape. Knowing that if captured, he stood a good chance of being lynched, and if he escaped the violence of the posse it meant a life term in the penitentiary at Yuma anyway, he used his last cartridge upon himself and died in a few minutes from his self-inflicted wound.

TEXAS JACK

ABOUT the time Sheriff Slaughter took charge of Cochise County and issued his ultimatum of: "Outlaw, get out of Cochise County or get killed," Texas Jack and four more of his kind, who have never been named, left Tombstone, bound for Colorado. They were beating their way on freight trains and bumming their eats and drinks between relays.

A short distance south of Las Vegas, New Mexico, Texas Jack either fell off the train or was killed and thrown off. If was believed that the five of them became involved in some kind of an argument among themselves and that Jack found himself on one side of the argument all by his lonesome and that they had murdered him and thrown him off the train.

The train crew stated that all five men had ridden in the same car all the way from Albuquerque. The Las Vegas officers, who were Mexicans, questioned the four survivors closely and they told that Jack had been standing close to the door of the car and that a sudden lurch threw him out of the door to the ground. The gang all adhered to the same story and there being no evidence to the contrary, they were released.

No sooner were they released than they began to make themselves obnoxious about town to such an extent that the Mexican officers rounded them up once more and decided that inasmuch as they were all from Tombstone that they needed killing, so they set about their execution in a very effective although crude manner.

There being no trees convenient, they were taken into an old blacksmith shop, bound hand and foot, a loop of rope passed through a knot hole in the board wall of the shop, which chanced to have been located at the proper height, and slipped over the head of one victim at a time, a stout stick placed in the end of the loop on the outside and twisted as tight as possible. All four men were thus strangled to death.

TOM HARPER

TOM HARPER was born in Missouri and raised in Texas. While he was yet a young man, he came to Tombstone and threw in with the wild bunch. One day he stated to some of his friends that he was going over to Huachuca and a man named John Tolliday asked him to collect a bill from a man over there who owed him some money. Harper collected the money and also spent it and when Tolliday asked him for it, became very indignant and shot Tolliday.

Harper was arrested and tried on a charge of murder, found guilty and sentenced to hang on July 8th, 1881. On the day before his execution he wrote Curly Bill as follows:

"Tucson, July 7th, 1881.

"Friend Curly:—

"By the time you receive this I will, in all likelihood, be past seeing or writing you; as you well know, I am under sentence of death. I am to be hanged tomorrow, but at what hour I do not as yet know.

"Some unknown friend is in town and has interested himself in my behalf and petitioned the governor but, as yet, there has been no answer from him. I have made up my mind for the worst and I think I will face death like a man. I must go some time. When I have found all chance of a reprieve or commutation of sentence lost, I am prepared to meet it in its worst form.

"Curly, you are aware that I am not in the habit of lecturing any man, but in this case you may remember the words of a dying man, for I am to all intents and purposes such, and perhaps give heed to them. When I killed that man I believed that I was acting in self defense. I thought my life was in danger from him and, acting under the influence of that feeling, I shot. A jury has found me guilty of murder, a judge has sentenced me and by this time tomorrow (2 p. m.) I shall have ceased to exist.

"Curly, I want you to take warning by me. Do not be too handy with a pistol. Keep cool and never fire at a man

unless in actual defense of your life.   You must stand a
heap from a man before you kill him.   Words, do not hurt,
so you must never mind what is said to aggravate you.   As
I said before, don't try to hurt a man until he actually assaults you, and above all things never hunt a man.

"Give my kind regards to any of my old friends whom
you may chance to meet and tell them to take warning from
me.   I bear no man ill will and think I am going to die in
peace.   Hoping that you will take heed of what I write, I
am as ever your unfortunate friend,

"To William Broscius,   TOM HARPER.

"C/O George Turner, San Simon."

On the morning of his execution, Harper asked to be
permitted to look at the scaffold on which he was to meet
his death.   This request was granted and Harper, apparently satisfied, walked steadily back to his cell.   He met his
doom bravely and paid the penalty of his evil act.

WILLIS

A CERTAIN bad man named Willis, the balance of his name having been lost in obscurity, came to Tucson away back in 1873 and tarried a short time. He went over into New Mexico and killed a man at Deming. He landed next at Prescott, Ariz., where he killed a man. From there he went to Florence, where he killed a man. From Florence he went to Wickenburg and while there chanced to have business in some other part of town and, taking the shortest route to his destination, which took him across a man's garden, the man remonstrated with him and Willis added another victim to his list. Willis was known to have killed at least eight men. He came to Tucson and was arrested, tried, found guilty of murder and sentenced to hang.

While Willis was sojourning in the Pima County jail, Jesus Saguaripa, Clemente Lopez and Loccardo Lopez, rustlers and all around crooks, went to the home of Vicente Hernandes, who had a small store on what is now known as South Meyer Street, beat Hernandes and his wife to death, backed a wagon up to the store door and loaded it full and hauled it away.

At the investigation it was noted that one of the murderers had been barefooted and that he had tracked blood over the floor. A Mexican named Cordova was arrested and blood was found between the toes of one of his feet, he having only washed one foot after the crime.

Cordova was given the third degree and confessed that, while he had nothing to do with the actual murder, he was present and helped carry the goods out of the house and conceal them. He told who the real murders were and they were arrested. They confessed and exonerated Cordova.

On August 8th, 1873, the American population insisted upon taking justice in their own hands and lynching these three Mexicans. The Mexican people arose, armed themselves and declared that if their countrymen were hung that Willis should be hung too as they had reason for believing that his friends would cause his release before the date of his execution.

There was considerable heated argument regarding the situation but border diplomacy saved the day. The American element announced in a loud tone of voice that they might just as well lynch all four and call it a day.

The Americans and Mexicans entered into the spirit of the occasion with vim and while one party went down on the Santa Cruz River to cut cottonwood forks to set in the ground, others were busy digging holes in the ground for the reception of these forks.

When the two heavy forks were brought up from the river bottom, they were planted firmly in the holes which had been prepared. A long pine log was laid on the two forks and the gallows was ready. The four men were brought out and placed in two wagons which were backed under the gallows log. When the ropes had been adjusted, the wagons were hauled from under by willing hands and gravity did the rest.

This is the only lynching known to have been carried out in Tucson. The gallows was placed in the southwest corner of what is now the Pima Court House Yard and was then the corner of Leatherwood's Feed Corral.

GRIMES AND HAWLEY

CURT HAWLEY and a man named Grimes, decided to levy an assessment upon the Wells-Fargo Express Company. In the execution of their crime they killed Andy Hall and Dr. Vail.

Deputy United States Marshal Gabriel investigated and the evidence pointed toward Grimes, who did not come and view the dead bodies when brought into town. When Grimes was looked for, it was learned that he had suddenly taken his departure for Wheatfields to work on the railroad grade.

Gabriel sent two men, Lindsay and Lewis, to Wheatfields to get Grimes and bring him back for investigation. While they were gone, he was busy digging up further evidence, but with poor results. He followed Lindsay and Lewis to Wheatfields.

Upon arrival at Wheatfields, Lindsay and Lewis took up the matter with Capt. D. B. Lacy and they arrested Grimes and brought him in for questioning. They questioned him closely regarding his movements of the past few days but could get no admission of guilt from him. Gabriel arrived on the scene just as Grimes was about to be released.

Gabriel stepped up to Grimes and said: "That's the man! Put your handcuffs on him! I was on the hill and saw him shoot Hall three times." This sudden charge broke down Grimes' defense, and be exclaimed,—"No I didn't, I only shot him twice." Seeing that he had involuntarily confessed to his share of the crime, he admitted that a man named Hawley had been his partner. When asked what part his brother Cicero played in the game he said that he had not been present at the killing at all.

Gabriel, Lacy and Lewis then took their prisoner back to Globe where they left Lewis to guard him while the other two went out to look for Hawley. They found Cicero Grimes and when they told him that they had his elder brother arrested and that he had told the story of the holdup and the killing, he admitted that his elder brother and Hawley had planned it, but that he was not present at the robbery or the killing.

Before Gabriel could get started for Florence, an officer arrived from Globe with a warrant and demanded the prisoners. Gabriel, being a federal officer, refused to give them up as he had arrested them for murder and for the robbery of the United States mail, but said if they would go back to Globe and get an order from United States Attorney McKnabe for the prisoners, that he would turn them over to him.

Grimes made a confession in full, saying that Hawley was armed with a .44 caliber rim fire rifle and that he was armed with a .50 caliber Springfield single shot rifle. He said that they went out about four and one-half miles from Globe, where the road makes a sudden turn around a reef of rocks, and hid, while Cicero went on to the station where the pack train meets the buckboard stage.

As Cicero was well acquainted with Hall and Porter, he assisted them in transferring the express which was to be packed up to the mining camps by pack train. When all was complete, the pack train started and Cicero Grimes was several yards in the lead. As he passed the spot where his elder brother and Curt Hawley were concealed, he did not stop, but kept right on, calling out in a low tone of voice, "The treasure box feels heavy; the packer has no arms and Hall has an old gun with no cartridges, and has a pistol," he kept right on going and did not stop until he reached Globe.

When the pack train had reached the ambush, the mule carrying the treasure was momentarily out of sight of both the packer and Hall. The robbers opened fire, dropping the treasure-laden mule at first shot, and then began shooting at the men.

Porter, the packer, exclaimed,—"Andy, some one is shooting at us!" Hall replied,—"No, I guess not." Just then the bullets began to whizz around close to them and Andy Hall shouted,—"Indians," and, turning his mule down an arroya out of the trail and drew his six shooter and held it in readiness.

Seeing that Hall intended making a fight, Porter said,—"I will go to the ranch and get a gun and return," as he started for the ranch, which was about two miles distant, the robbers sent several bullets after him but none of them connected with him or the mule which he was riding.

Grimes then left cover and cut the treasure box off the dead mule, pried the staple off the box with a hatchet which they had brought along for that purpose, emptied the gold into a pair of saddle bags and then, he and Hawley started a retreat to the northwest.

A short time later, Dr. Vail, who had been visiting a mine in that locality, arrived on the scene of action and Frank Porter, who arrived at the same time, and, thinking that Dr. Vail was one of the robbers, opened fire on him. Dr. Vail, believing that Porter was one of the robbers, made a hurried retreat, going toward the northwest.

Dr. Vail soon overtook Grimes and Hawley, who were on foot. He spoke to them as he rode past and rode for some distance in front of them and they shot him four times in the back and left him for dead, then went on for about two miles and sat down to rest in a shallow arroya.

While they were sitting there, Andy Hall suddenly stepped out of a thicket a few yards from them and they both fired at him. He dropped behind a bunch of sacaton grass, but raised up immediately, with his revolver in his hand and called out,—"Hold on! I thought you fellows were Indians, there are some back there and they shot me in the leg; see, here's the bullet." As he walked toward them with the bullet in the palm of his hand, Grimes answered back,—"And we thought that you was an Indian too." Hall then said,—"Let's get away from here and get to town as quick as possible."

As they moved away, Grimes and Hawley kept Hall between them, "For," said Hawley, "when I saw him eyeing those saddle bags, that were on Grimes' shoulder, I knew damned well that he knew what they contained and was only waiting for a chance to kill us both."

They walked along in this manner for some time until

finally Hawley shoved the muzzle of his gun against Hall's back and fired. Hall dropped but, even though dying, he made a brave attempt at retaliation by firing five shots at his assailants, none of them taking effect. They shot him eight times. When he was found, he was dead, but facing the direction from whence came the leaden messengers of death, his right arm extended as though in the act of shooting, and his trigger finger crooked around the trigger of an empty six shooter, evidently expiring while firing his last shot.

It was evident that he had caught sight of the robbers as they passed over the hill in leaving the scene of the robbery and had, although wounded in one leg, followed them for four miles, unexpectedly discovering them as they were sitting down to rest in the arroya, but too late for him to get the drop on them. He had attempted to throw them off their guard by springing the Indian trick on them as his only chance of holding his own until he could have a chance of getting the proper drop on them. After the robbers had killed Hall, they buried their golden loot and went on into Globe. Grimes going on to Wheatfields where he was later apprehended.

When the officer returned from Globe, he was in possession of the necessary order to Gabriel and the prisoners were turned over to him and were taken back to Globe. At about ten o'clock that same morning, a mob of not less than 100 of Globe's best citizens took Grimes and Hawley out and hung them to a limb of a large sycamore tree which stood in front of J. H. Hill's store. Nearly all of the adult population of Globe assisted in the execution of these two men.

Just before Grimes and Hawley were hung they told where the $5,000 in gold coin was hid. Cicero Grimes was captured by the mob and had it not been for the intervention of Mrs. Vail, he would have shared the same fate as his older brother and Curt. Hawley.

Hawley was game to the last, but Grimes swooned just

as the rope was being adjusted. Previous to this, he had
requested permission to remove his boots and, as the "Florence Enterprise" stated, "he climbed the golden stairs in
his sock feet."

LYNCHING OF JOHN HEITH IN
TOMBSTONE IN 1884

LUKE SHORT

LUKE SHORT was a member of the Dodge City Shotgun Squad under Earp and came to Tombstone about the same time Wyatt did. Luke went to work as faro dealer in ·the Oriental Saloon and Gambling House and so far as is known, took no part with the wild bunch, but attended to his own business and insisted upon others attending to their own, insofar as he was concerned.

Charlie Storms was a bad man and wanted everybody to know it. He came into the Oriental one evening and bought into Luke's game and struck bad luck. He became angered and threw a handful of chips into Luke's face and proclaimed to all within the sound of his booze-laden voice,—"When I come in the morning, I'm coming a shooting."

When Luke saw Storms coming toward him from across the street, with his six shooter in his hand, he shot him through the heart.

Jim Courtright was an outlaw who operated around over Arizona and New Mexico. He went to Hatch, N. M., where he obtained a job as watchman at the mill. He put up a job with his partner to rob the mill office and then, knowing that he would get a reward, killed his partner when he came to rob the office.

Courtright then went to Fort Worth, where he met Luke Short, who had gone to that city soon after the shooting of Storms at Tombstone. Courtright became angered at Short and, pulling his gun, he pointed it straight at him, all of the time telling him what he was going to do to him. While he was talking, Luke pulled his own gun and shot Courtright dead.

Luke dropped out of sight and no one seems to know just what became of him.

KIV PHILLIPS AND FILEMENO ORANTE

FILEMENO ORANTE was considered a bad man and unusually so when drinking. On July 8, 1882, he entered the saloon of Moses & Wheeler, Tombstone, called for a drink and punctuated the request by flourishing a six shooter in the air and mouthing vile language to all within sound of his voice.

Jim Hennessey, the bar tender tried to get him to put his gun away, but Orante was not to be persuaded to do anything at all. Realizing that the Mexican was in a dangerous condition, he sent out for an officer and when Kiv Phillips responded Hennessey explained the situation to him.

Orante had gone out and Phillips followed with intention of arresting him. He located the Mexican and as he advanced toward him the Mexican backed up and stumbled, at the same time drawing his six shooter and firing one shot at Phillips, the bullet passing through Phillips' right shoulder and windpipe and lodging in the opposite side of his body, the bullet then striking a bone was deflected downward and cut through the aorta.

Phillips stood and completed his draw and fired one shot which struck the Mexican high up in one thigh and passed through into the pelvis and went out through the opposite side of his body.

Phillips, with remarkable tenacity of life, and although mortally wounded, turned and walked back into the saloon, blood gushing from his mouth. He walked on through and out of the back door, falling dead after having walked a distance of thirty steps.

Officer Harry Solon, hearing the shooting, hurried up and took charge of the situation, taking Orante to jail. There was much talk of lynching Orante but Sheriff Behan placed extra guards around the jail and this calamity was averted. Orante only lived a short time. He had four old bullet wounds on his body, all healed.

JAMES SHARP, ALIAS JIM McDONNELL
JESS HARRIS

JAMES SHARP, alias Jim McDonnell, and Jess Harris, two rustlers in good standing, decided the climatic conditions around Tombstone were entirely too torrid for the good of their constitutions, so they departed in great haste for eastern points and landed in Sierra County, New Mexico.

Shortly after their departure from Tombstone, the editor of the Tombstone Epitaph received a letter from a deputy sheriff at Lake Valley, New Mexico, which reads as follows:

"Lake Valley, N. M., Dec. 7th, 1881.

"Editor Epitaph:

"I wish you would give me some information, or put me in connection with some one who can, regarding James Sharp or 'Jim McDonnell.' I understand that he has been in jail in Tombstone and that there is a reward offered for him. Well, we have him pretty secure, and if there is a reward offered, want it as a fund for settlement with all such characters.

"This Sharp or McDonnell, last week stole some cattle from a man named Thompson, at Eureka. Thompson traced his cattle to a point near here, recovered and sold them. The men came here—this Sharp and his partner in the steal, Jess Harris. We now have them both safe. They served us a good purpose, for they started our cemetery.—* * * * *"

Sharp was shot while resisting arrest and Harris was lynched.

THE BOOTH BROTHERS

T HE two Booths played an important part in the Tonto Basin Cattlemen's War, and there were no less than twelve indictments out for them. In view of this latter fact, they counted themselves among the missing in the Tonto Basin and discovered themselves in Tombstone where, while they did not execute any rough stuff, they associated exclusively with the wild bunch.

Just as they were beginning to get acquainted with their environment and feeling as though they were at home, the sheriff from Globe located them and they were garnered in by the strong arm of the law and taken to Globe where they were filed away for future reference.

As both of these two men had always traveled together, it was not known which one had ever committed any particular murder and, had they been both arraigned jointly, a double hanging would have undoubtedly been the inevitable result. Realizing that one of them could be saved, they decided to flip a dollar to see which one would plead guilty to the crimes charged. One to hang and the other to live.

The dollar was flipped and the loser went to trial and pleaded guilty to all of the murders with which they were jointly charged, and, the winner, according to agreement, corroborated the statement of the other and the loser paid the penalty with his life. His brother became a law abiding citizen.

RED MIKE

RED MIKE became such a nuisance around Tombstone that he was invited to make a series of tracks with heel prints pointing Tombstoneward. The fact he was not wanted around Tombstone at last filtered through his booze-curdled brain and he departed without entering into any argument regarding his social status around that burg.

There was no specific evidence at hand to hang anything on Mike, such as a rope, but Tombstone decided that she could worry along without his presence, knowing full well that if he was needed they could send for him.

Mike was next heard from in Prescott and in due time, it is reported that he wore his welcome out there also and was very pointedly requested to make himself conspicuous from them by his absence.

Mike actually grasped the idea that he was not duly appreciated in the "mile high city" and departed, very much to the relief of all concerned. Further the deponent saith not.

HENRY M. HALL

HENRY M. HALL came to the conclusion Tombstone liquor had lost its flavor, and he migrated to Prescott, believing that the alcoholic circulation of his system might be benefitted. It seems as though the Prescott booze had a bad effect on Henry for he was not in Prescott very long until he had accumulated a "fighting, shooting jag," and shot a man named Bishop.

He was apprehended and tied for safe keeping. One end of the rope was tied around his neck and the other end to the limb of a large cottonwood tree. It is stated that during the night a heavy rain fell and shrunk the rope until Henry's feet could not touch the ground and he died of strangulation. To date this story has never been contradicted.

FRANK JACKSON

FRANK JACKSON was a member of the old Sam Bass Gang which flourished in Texas back in the '70's, but the Bass Gang met with a streak of bad luck at Round Rock on June 19, 1878, and Sam and Bebe Barnes were mortally wounded. Jackson took Bass up on his horse and carried him out of town for a distance of about two miles, to the place where he died.

Jackson, who at that time was only a mere boy, made his getaway and, who ever composed the well known Sam Bass song, evidently had some knowledge of Jackson's subsequent intention as the 17th verse of the song is rendered thus:

"Now Sam is a decaying corpse
Down in Round Rock clay,
While Jackson's on the border
A-trying to get away."

Jackson made his getaway and landed in Tombstone, but before he had much more than time to enjoy a good long breath, the Tombstone officers who had been notified that Jackson was worth $2,500, dead or alive, gathered him in alive and turned him over to officers from Texas. It is not just exactly known how, at this late date, he escaped, but he managed it in some mysterious manner, and went up into Indian territory. His presence there was discovered, but some of his good friends back in Texas slipped him the information and Jackson once more moved for the benefit of his health.

Eugene Manlove Rhodes, the well known writer of western fiction, is authority for the information that Jackson went down into Mexico, where he married, raised a large family and, for nearly fifty years, has been living the life of a model citizen, respected by all who have known him.

Now, after a lapse of almost half a century, Jackson is very desirous of having the old indictment against him annulled so that he can return to the home of his childhood and youth and spend the few remaining years of his life among his own people..

Jackson asserts that he was employed by Sam Bass to act in the capacity of a body guard and that when Bass fell, mortally wounded, he took him to the place where he died the next day and that he did not shoot any one in the fight at Round Rock.

An article by Hugh Nugent, appearing in the "Wichita Falls Record News" under date of July, 1927, and also in the July issue of "Frontier Times," conveys the information that while there were many witnesses to the killing of Constable A. W. Grimes, of Round Rock, Texas, on July 19th, 1878, upon the testimony of Morris Moore and Simon Juda, an indictment was found and a warrant issued for the apprehension of Frank Jackson, charging him with this crime.

Even admitting that Frank Jackson did not shoot, either fatally or otherwise, any one in that famous gun battle between Sam Bass and his supporters, in Round Rock on the 19th day of July, 1878, and the upholders of the law, he was one of their number, and amenable to the law as such.

It is believed that after nearly fifty years of self-banishment and atonement that the State of Texas could afford to be generous and award Jackson a full and unconditional pardon, to permit him to return to his native country.

JAKE GAUZE

JAKE GAUZE was considered a good fellow in the ranks of bad men and his favorite outdoor sport consisted in stealing horses. Jake became so proficient in the execution of this game that he was able to bat home runs with alarming frequency.

Jake threw in with the Clanton Gang between times, but usually played a lone hand, handling only one or two horses at a time, as he found them easier handled in small lots.

Jake's success as a horse rustler caused him to become careless and at last he stole a horse which was too slow to keep his pace at the head of a long procession which had formed in his honor, headed by the sheriff, and they overtook him at the head of Turkey Creek.

Jake was caught with the goods under him and he died suddenly of suspended animation, an act in which a rope and a conveniently placed limb of a juniper tree played a very prominent part.

SIX SHOOTER SMITH

SIX SHOOTER SMITH, a regularly ordained wrang-
ler of box cars for the Southern Pacific Railway Company, decided that he would garner in more easy money
by joining the wild bunch than by making forced collections
of two dollars per division, or what have you, off the hoboes,
so he transferred his scene of operations to the vicinity of
Tombstone and continued the shaking-down process.

In some manner or other, not stated herein or elsewhere,
it became necessary for Smith to indulge in a forced vacation as the result of some of his hilarious acts around Tombstone, so he went to Deming. He was accompanied by a
party of his friends also, who were among the missing from
Tombstone.

Upon arrival at Deming they proceeded to eat, drink
and be merry in every sense of the word. Smith entered
the most prominent eating emporium of Deming and, sitting down at a table, gave his order to the waitress, as follows,—"I want a humdinger of a porterhouse steak, a bottle
of whisky and a dog." The waitress departed and consulted
with the manager, who in turn approached Smith and said,—
"Stranger, I can furnish you the steak and the whisky, but
what do you want of a dog?" Smith replied,—"Oh hell,
got to have a dog to eat the steak."

While in Deming, Smith, in making some kind of drunken
display of his six shooter in a saloon, accidentally shot a
man through one of his feet. Smith's own gang gave him
a hearing on the spot and rendered the following verdict,—
"We find that Six Shooter Smith is too damned careless
with his gun and is liable to kill some one some day, so we
hereby sentence him to be banished from the gang and to go
back to work for the Southern Pacific Company." The sentence was duly carried out.

YUMA PENITENTIARY

THE Arizona State Penitentiary was established at Yuma during the '70's. Congress made provision for a state penitentiary in 1867 and left the location of same to the Legislature. A loan was authorized in 1875 for the erection of a territorial prison, and the following year Superintendent George Thurlow started to work with seven prisoners, brought down from Prescott.

The spot chosen was just below the junction of the Gila and Colorado Rivers, just north of Yuma. On the new site was located a low granite butte, covering about two acres. The top was leveled down to within perhaps twelve or fourteen feet of the yard level and a row of cells blasted in the solid granite. These cells were about 8x10 feet and 7 feet in height and there was approximately six feet of granite between cells.

With the temperature rambling from 100 to 120 in the shade for about eight months of the year, the territorial officials conceived the idea that this would be an ideal location for a penitentiary. All of this also inside of a thick adobe wall which was about 16 feet in height.

Many men, facing imprisonment in these sweltering dens in the solid rock, committed suicide, choosing to go to hell direct, rather than going via Yuma. The old cemetery behind the prison contains the bodies of many men who no doubt would have served their sentences and become good citizens had they have been confined in a humane establishment. The intense heat and poor sanitation probably was responsible for more deaths than from any other cause. Many men released from this institution, after having served their sentences, died of tuberculosis within a short time.

It is now but fair to state that a few years ago the Arizona State Penitentiary was moved to Florence, Arizona, and this institution is now considered to be one of the best in the southwest. The buildings are roomy and well ventilated and men who are unfortunate enough to be sent to this institution, are well cared for, and the all the year around climate of that locality, coupled with good treatment makes this an ideal institution of its kind.

OUTLAW OAK IN SKELETON CAÑON

Andy Darnell, one of the best known outlaws in Cochise County, was killed near Bisbee by a man named Johnson. The particulars of this event are not, at this late date, known.

———o———

William Lewis, alias Arizona Bill, shot and killed Charlie Collins over some fancied wrong. The Law and Order League heard his story and then took him out and hanged him.

SOME SCENES FROM

Tombstone

Arizona

in

1968

A Portfolio of Photos
which do not need captions

Robert B. McCoy
Photographer

ON THIS SPOT THE EARP
AND CLANTON FACTIONS
MET ON OCTOBER 26 1881.
TO SETTLE THE WEST'S MOST
FAMOUS FEUD. DOC HOLLIDAY
STOPPED ON FREMONT STREET
A FEW FEET FROM WHERE
INDICATED HERE. FRANK
AND TOM McLAURY FINALLY
DROPPED ON FREMONT
STREET. BILLY CLANTON
DIED WHERE HE STOOD.
VIRGIL AND MORGAN EARP
WERE WOUNDED.

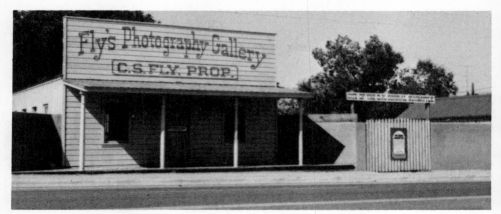

1878
WELCOME
TO
BOOTHILL
GRAVEYARD

BURIED HERE ARE THE REMAINS OF:
TOM McLAURY ⎫ KILLED IN EARP-
FRANK McLAURY ⎬ CLANTON BATTLE
BILLY CLANTON ⎭ OCT. 26, 1881.
DAN DOWD, RED SAMPLE, BILL DeLANEY, DAN
KELLY & TEX HOWARD HANGED LEGALLY BY J.E.
WARD, SHERIFF FOR BISBEE MASSACRE MAR. 8, 1884.
JOHN HEATH LYNCHED BY BISBEE MOB FEB. 22, 1884.
MR. PEEL MURDERED IN CHARLESTON MARCH 8, 1882.
GEO. JOHNSON HANGED BY MISTAKE.
DUTCH ANNIE, INDIAN BILL, QUONG KEE, CHARLEY STORMS,
LES MOORE, MARSHAL WHITE, 3-FINGERED JACK DUNLAP,
BRONCO CHARLEY, RED RIVER TOM SHOT BY ORMSBY.

DAN DOWD
RED SAMPLE
TEX HOWARD
BILL DeLANEY
DAN KELLY

LEGALLY
HANGED
MAR 8 1884

HERE
LIES
LESTER MOORE
FOUR SLUGS
FROM A 44
NO LES
NO MORE

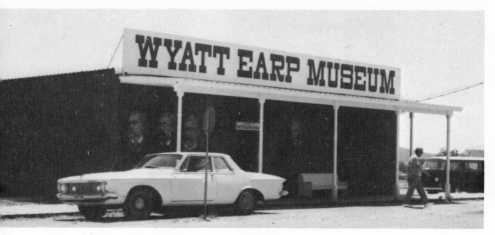

INDEX

Note: An index like this one is sheer murder to prepare. Apparently, nearly every man came to Arizona with his father, his son, his brother, or perhaps a cousin with the same name—either that, or the long arm of coincidence was practically wrenched from its socket. In any event, we suspect that the author recorded every name he ever came across in his research. It was not possible for us, and might not even be possible for anyone, to run down these hundreds of surnames to find the proper given name and identify to any extent the part that individual played in the Tombstone and/or Arizona story. For those contemporary readers who like to search for and find old and all-but-forgotten names of history, anyway, this index should be a veritable treasure. It will surely be useful.

—The Publishers

★ ★ ★

307

313

314

315

The Rio Grande Press Inc.,

Glorieta, New Mexico 87535

BASIC SOURCE DOCUMENTS OF AMERICAN HISTORY

64-20401
Amsden, Charles Avery
  Navaho Weaving, its Technic
  and History $12.00

62-20281
Bandelier, Adolph F. A.
  The Gilded Man $7.50

64-16598
Bandelier, Fanny
  Journey of Alvar Nunez
  Cabeza de Vaca $7.50

64-15127
Bartlett, John Russell
  A Personal Narrative of
  Explorations $32.50

62-21941
Bourke, John Gregory
  Snake Dance of the Moqui
  (Hopi) Indians $8.00

65-20151
Brooks, Nathan Covington
  A Complete History of the
  Mexican War $17.50

68-25389
DeFouri, James H.
  The Martyrs of
  New Mexico $5.00

62-17905
Dellenbaugh, Frederick S.
  The Romance of the
  Colorado River $7.50

63-21229
Falconer, Thomas
  Texan-Santa Fe
  Expedition $7.00

62-20282
Fewkes, Jesse Walter
  Hopi Katcinas Drawn by
  Native Artists $15.00

62-17906
Forrest, Earle R.
  Missions and Pueblos of
  the Old Southwest $7.50

63-21230
Grant, Blanche C.
  When Old Trails
  Were New $7.50

62-17907
Hodge, Hiram C.
  Arizona as it Was, 1877 $7.00

62-20279
Hughes, John T.
  Doniphan's Expedition
  1846-1848 $8.00

67-30871
Ide, William B.; Ide, Simeon
  Who Conquered
  California? $10.00

62-17904
James, General Thomas
  Three Years Among
  the Indians $7.50

68-31292
Jocknick, Sidney
  Early Days on the Western
  Slope of Colorado,
  1870-1883 $8.00

66-26008
Jones, Anson
Republic of Texas, its
History and Annexation $25.00

67-26680
Kluckhorn, Clyde
To the Foot of the
Rainbow $7.00

62-20277
Kubler, George
Religious Architecture of
New Mexico $12.00

63-21231
Lummis, Charles F.
The Spanish Pioneers $7.50

68-25390
Reichard, Gladys A.
Navajo Shepherd and
Weaver $8.00

68-25391
Reichard, Gladys A.
Spider Woman; Life Among
the Navajo $8.00

63-21232
Sedgwick, Mrs. W. T.
Acoma, the Sky City $7.50

64-15122
Shea, John Gilmary
The Expedition of Dionisio
de Penalosa $7.00

62-20280
Sitgreaves, Lorenzo
Report of an Expedition
down the Zuni $8.00

67-26678
Taylor, Bayard
Eldorado, or, Adventures in
the Path of Empire $12.00

63-21233
Twitchell, Ralph Emerson
The Military Occupation of
New Mexico $8.50

63-21234
Twitchell, Ralph Emerson
Old Santa Fe $12.00

62-17908
Villagra, Gaspar de
A History of New Mexico $7.50

68-25392
Walters, Lorenzo D.
Tombstone's Yesterday:
Bad Men of Arizona $7.50

68-25393
Wharton, Clarence Ray
Remember Goliad: A
Rollcall of Texas Heroes $5.00

64-15130
Winship, George Parker
The Coronado Expedition,
1540-1542 $15.00

The Beautiful Rio Grande Classics

If your favorite bookstore does not carry our books, write us for
A FREE CATALOG